D1307971

Poor Richard's E-mail Publishing

Creating Newsletters, Bulletins, Discussion Groups, and Other Powerful Communications Tools

by
Chris Pirillo
chris@lockergnome.com

TOP FLOOR PUBLISHING

Poor Richard's E-mail Publishing:
Creating Newsletters, Bulletins, Discussion Groups, and Other Powerful
Communications Tools

SAN#: 299-4550
Top Floor Publishing
P.O. Box 260072
Lakewood, CO 80226

Feedback to the author: feedback@topfloor.com
Sales information: sales@topfloor.com
The Top Floor Publishing Web Site: http://www.topfloor.com/

Library of Congress Catalog Card Number: 98-96891

ISBN: 0-9661032-5-4

01   00   99   6 5 4 3 2 1

To All My Lockergnomies: Past, Present, & Future

About the Author

From the heart of the Silicorn Valley, Chris Pirillo has been electronically publishing Lockergnome via e-mail since late 1996. Upon graduating magna cum laude from the University of Northern Iowa with a bachelor's degree in English Education, he began to work on this free newsletter covering Microsoft's mainstream operating systems, Internet, and noteworthy technology tidbits. Since then, Chris has grown into a leader of the e-mail publishing industry.

The daily HTML and weekly text versions of this newsletter have won numerous awards. His writing style conveys even the most technical knowledge in such a way that the novice can understand and learn from it. He credits both his English studies in college and Iowan upbringing for the user friendliness his newsletter is noted for. The quality of his writing coupled with his astute understanding of computers has allowed Lockergnome's subscriber base to grow to over 160,000 individuals. To reach Chris, e-mail chris@lockergnome.com.

Acknowledgements

Gretchen Hundling: for putting up with my constant shenanigans, being honest, and not forcing me to get a *real* job. You're a supermodel in my eyes.

Joe and Judy Pirillo: for allowing me to make my own mistakes and sending me outside every once in a while. I just have one question: how many grandkids do you want?

Ben and Adam Pirillo: for still talking to me after all those years of childhood "brotherly" abuse. I was always "the boss of you" when I should have been a co-worker.

David, Shelley, and Brice Hundling: for your enduring patience.

Bill and Pam Gerrard: for seeing my vision and wanting to be a part of it, and for keeping Digitaldaze.com running smoothly.

Michael Robertson: for providing space when I needed it, and for helping turn the industry on its ear.

Tom Heightcamp: for giving me a speed boost when I needed it most.

Shaun Shulba: for listening to my endless rants and putting out fires.

The University of Northern Iowa's College of Social and Behavioral Sciences: for giving me a job when I really needed one. Dr. Aaron Podolefsky, Dr. James Chadney, "Bob" Kramer, and Tom Turner—you fostered what others failed to understand.

"Graz": for being the first to call me *Gnome* and inspiring me to become an English teacher (only to slap me around later for not doing something in the computer industry).

The people who were there for me in the beginning: Jason Best, Evan Marshall, Steve Duever, Matt Mick, David Gabel, Neil Christiansen, Adrienne Lamberti, and Jon Palmer—your support was appreciated more than you realize.

My Tau Kappa Epsilon YITB brothers: for actually respecting my abilities and not touching my computer.

"Commander" Cory Smith: for giving me extra cheese when I didn't ask for it.

Peter Kent: for approaching me to compose and collect resources for this book.

The 1993-95 UNI Towers Dining Center staff: for letting me get creative with the deli sign and laughing at my 'Beef Olé' jokes.

All my college roommates: Pat Carr, Dan Olson, Thomas Nordlander, Steve Wibe, Craig McClure, Bill Lemons, Brad Bergeson, Erik Egeberg, and Eric Myszka—thanks for supporting (and not challenging) my geekiness.

All the people who never believed in me: for telling me that I was a loser; that I was too weird for my own good; and that I couldn't do it. For those of you who mocked me, who hated me for the sake of hating me . . . you were wrong, and I'm extremely thankful for that.

Contents at a Glance

Table of Contents

Appendices

Step with me for a moment behind the veil of *!*!*HYPE*!*!* that is the Internet as we know it. Avert your eyes; look with your mind and heart. You're on the threshold of the Real Internet, and holding the key to the part people actually read and respond to.

Ask the experts what people miss when they don't have online access for a day or two. It's not the Web that haunts them. It's not Yahoo! or Amazon that people check at 3 a.m. "just to see if anything's new." It's e-mail—homely, unglamorous, ubiquitous, and maybe the last best hope for the survival of the 'Net.

So how come you don't hear tons of hype about the e-mail revolution? Why aren't e-mail newsletters doing those hot "dot-com" IPOs and getting big press? Because, fearless reader, e-mail newsletters are a hard commodity to pin down. They can be about anything or nothing. They're advertised not by splashy TV commercials but by great word-of-mouth. In many cases, they're an uncut dosage of someone else's personality, and selling that kind of thing on the stock market would bring the DEA down on you like white on rice. No, doing an e-mail newsletter or mailing list isn't likely to make your fortune, or even your reputation. It'll just save the 'Net and change your life, that's all.

Why do a newsletter? Some folks use them to guide readers to other parts of the 'Net, such as to a Web site. If that's your objective, it is both respectable and reasonable. Build a Web site and, no matter how great your content is, you'll spend your days fretting over your hit counter and wondering how to get readers to come back. Undertake a newsletter and the initiative is yours; instead of hanging around like a wallflower in your readers' ever-expanding bookmark lists, you rule the dance floor. (And the overwhelmed Web surfers of the world, turning and turning in the widening gyre of 4000-plus new Web pages each day, thank you for tapping them on the shoulder like that. They meant to come back, really they did. They just need a little reminder sometimes.)

More than this, though, publishing an e-mail newsletter puts you in touch with people who need to hear what you're saying, whether you choose to say it on a Web page or in the newsletter itself. A good e-mail is as immediate and effective as jumping out of the monitor and grabbing each recipient by the nose. Web pages, no matter how clever, are like Stonehenge or the Pyramids: impressive edifices, certainly quite interesting, but nothing that requires immediate action. They endure. A piece of e-mail, on the other hand, lives entirely at the whim of the sender, the recipient, and her Delete key. And e-mail is utterly of the moment—*today's* discovery, *this week's* outrage, *this month's* celebration, my thoughts *right now*.

What *you're* thinking of doing right now, by the way, is practically criminal. (And the thought of e-mail publishing surely has crossed your mind, or why are you holding this book?) Listen to me: E-mail is dangerous to people and entities that don't take kindly to being threatened by free speech and free thought. Here again, the Web promises but e-mail delivers. E-mail can get to places Web pages cannot. E-mail is far more accessible than the Web to users on slow modems and bad connections. For those people with limited Internet access, e-mail is great because it can be downloaded and read offline—or even printed out and passed along to those unwired. If your goal is the free flow of ideas, e-mail is far more liquid than any other means of communication, online or off.

This is not to say that newsletters are strictly the realm of wild-eyed radicals, freedom fighters, cranks, dreamers, visionaries, and the irrepressibly and compulsively communicative. Newsletters are also the province of car dealerships, cat-fanciers' clubs, mayor's offices, beauty consultants, corporate PR machines, teachers, and all manner of folk who have a message and want to get it to people who can benefit from it—not (directly) for profit, but for the sake of that basic human urge to communicate that drove us to create the 'Net in the first place.

There are other, less tangible benefits. One of the most compelling reasons for doing a newsletter is the same reason many folk go into other forms of publishing and broadcasting: an addiction to cheap notoriety. The vanity of the average newsletterist is a powerful thing. I don't know any newsletterist who doesn't get a little bit of joy in watching the "subscribe me" messages roll in, nor one that doesn't wonder why the unsubscribers are leaving. Was it something I said? Well, what else could it be?

That works both ways. Readers sense the human behind a well-written newsletter, and they respond as if that human is speaking directly to them. (For instance, I felt I'd met Chris Pirillo, your gracious host, long before I actually had, simply because his newsletter is such an irresistible and useful read.) On the 'Net as in life, we're already awash in stupid and impersonal junk mail and pseudo-info. Your publication won't be that kind—at least, it had better not be.

And by the way, newsletters, properly done, are not junk mail, a.k.a. spam. If you're buying this book to become a make-money-fa$t spammer guy, do me and Pirillo and the rest of these fine writers a favor—put down the book, walk outside, and throw yourself into a wood-chipper. (The 'Net thanks you.) Your newsletter should be in no way confused with spam. If it is on a regular basis, you need to get right with the newsletter vibe, which is why we're here.

To that end, I've got some practical advice for you to keep in mind as you read through this book. I've also got a little *im*practical advice—which, like all impractical advice, should be kept even closer to your heart than the other kind.

Three practical things to worry about with your newsletter:

- *Functionality*. Make it worth the readers' while to open your message. Get to the point. If you include Web links, see that they work. Make sure your software doesn't insert a lot of junk and garbage into your e-mail. Don't think that just checking it out in your own favorite package will do the job; make the effort to view it in AOL, YahooMail, and whatever else your readership uses. And whatever you do, give the nice people a way to subscribe and unsubscribe easily. All this will be covered in this book, of course, but these basic rules ought to be branded on the inside of your skull. Might as well start now.

- *Relevance*. The best newsletters have a target reader in mind and write specifically to that target. I may not be able to make any sense of the mountain-biking newsletter you adore, and you may think my weekly makeup-tips update silly and dull. And that's fine. The best newsletters find their own level by writing for their audience—and *only* for their audience—and to hell with the rest of the world. Not only is this not prose for the ages, but it's not prose for *everyone* in this age. (Or even everyone in this room.) If your newsletter stays on focus, whatever that focus may be, it'll be valuable to its audience.

- *Not being Hemingway*. Get to the point. Save the cute stuff for your Web site. The best newsletters are well into the gist of their message by the bottom of the first screen. You may have been told by marketing folk that teaser copy excites the reader's interest, but *this* reader is telling you that I read my mail with the mouse cursor poised over the Delete button. You have five seconds to tell me why I shouldn't move to the next of the 150 messages in my Inbox this morning. On your mark, get set, *go*.

And here are three practical things *not* to worry about:

- *Looks*. Many designers dislike e-mail because it's ugly. Then again, many designers dislike words because they get in the way of the pictures. Overeager designers have turned the Web from a vehicle of nonlinear thought into the world's biggest television. I have nothing against TV, and I like bright shiny multimedia as much as the next entertainment-addled American, but let's leave all those overeager designers out of the newsletter business. Readability is the highest good. Do not deviate from this core truth.

- *Hate mail.* Obviously you've done something right if people are pissed off enough to hit "Reply." The only kind of hate mail you should pay attention to is hate mail about not letting someone off your subscription list (or about crashing their machine with your newsletter). In those cases you should apologize, fix it if you can, and move on. Strong opinions get you read—even if it's people forwarding the newsletter to friends with a "can you believe this crap?!" note attached.

- *Not being Faulkner.* William Faulkner was a brilliant writer. He was also long-winded and occasionally obscure. Focus on being clear, concise, and honest in your writing. Deathless prose is not your primary goal. (Trust me, over time you *will* get better; writing is one of those skills that sharpens with use.) If you're providing good information clearly, your readers will stick with you.

The most *im*practical advice I can give you is to read, read, read other newsletters. The overwhelming majority of e-mail newsletters are free; that means that you can dip your toes in pretty much anything. And newsletter subscriptions are like tattoos or orchids or chess sets—once you get your first, some part of your mind will ceaselessly seek to add to your collection. Sample other writers' strategies of attack on this uncharted terrain, looking for a variety of writing styles, techniques, and above all, personalities. It's going to be a wicked time sink; deal with it. You might not stick with any particular newsletter for any great length of time, but definitely do check out the world from other people's point of view.

Which brings me to the promised bit about the Last Best Hope for the Internet, which is *you*—your ability to make people care enough to get online and stay there, reading what you have to say. The 'Net's hype machine is an unholy creature made up of soulless electronic billboards and silicon shopping malls, and it sucks up more valuable bandwidth each day. Break through it! All you need is something to say—and, to help you say it, this book. Welcome.

Angela Gunn is a columnist for the Seattle Weekly *and* Sam Whitmore's Media Survey. *She has written regularly for publications ranging from* Yahoo! Internet Life *to* PC Magazine *to* New Directions for Women, *but says that doing her own newsletter* (Another Precinct Heard From) *has been the most consistently rewarding (and harrowing) writing experience she's ever had. See for yourself at* http://www.agunn.com/. *Subscribe to* Another Precinct Heard From *with an e-mail to* newsletter@agunn.com.

Chapter One

Are You Ready?

You're obviously interested in learning more about how to publish information via e-mail—you're in good company. Thousands of individuals like yourself (and, quite possibly, *not* like yourself) are circulating electronic newsletters and discussion lists on the Internet right now. It's a very powerful communications medium, and just about anyone can harness that power. The great thing about online publishing is that it really doesn't have to cost you anything to get the ball rolling.

Start Thinking

What do you find to be fun and/or interesting? That is to say, what topic or topics do you want your e-zine to cover? The world is your oyster, and if you want to publish a newsletter on oysters of the world, be my guest. If you have a fascination with paper airplanes, then why not write about them? Nobody's stopping you, and nobody should stop you. Here are a few things you should keep in mind when choosing your subject matter:

- Am I excited about my topic?
- Do other e-zines cover my topic? How many?
- Are those other e-zines doing a good job at covering my topic? Can I do better?
- How much information is out there (online) on my topic? Can I create new content?
- How many Web sites relate to my topic?
- How big an audience could I potentially attract with this topic?
- Is the information on my topic easily accessible?
- Do I know enough about my topic?
- How often do I want to publish?

- Who is my target audience?
- What are my short-term goals for this e-publication? Long-term goals?

These questions should help you focus in on what you really want to accomplish through publishing via e-mail. I'm positive that working on the Internet is the "job of the future." I can think of no better way to start your career than with an electronic publication.

You Say Tomato

It's easy to call a sweater a sweater, but there are different kinds of sweaters (cardigan, pullover, and so on). In the same respect, there are many kinds of e-mail broadcasts. The general umbrella term for an independently published document is *zine*. This word's concept predates computer distribution; people have been circulating various works using "unconventional" methods for decades. When the Internet started gaining popularity, e-zines (electronic zines) began to pop up. An e-zine can be delivered via e-mail or simply put up on the Web (thus becoming a *webzine*). It's distributed in an electronic fashion, and that's all it needs to be in order to have that little *e* affixed to it.

So, we've got this blanket term—now how many applications can we find for it? I'd like to believe the world will never run out of new ideas for electronic communications. However, for the sake of argument, let's look at the five major types of e-mail publications around today: e-mail newsletters, announcement lists, bulletins/action alerts, moderated discussion lists, and unmoderated discussion lists.

> **NOTE**
>
> *Some people choose to write the words e-mail, e-zine, and e-publication without the dash, but (in my opinion) it looks a lot cleaner when you insert that small divider. We've got a relatively new medium at our doorstep, so the rules haven't been completely written yet (which, for the most part, is a good thing for all). Whatever you decide to do, please be consistent.*
>
> *What's the correct pronunciation for e-zine? I believe zine should rhyme with mean or teen, but too many people are rhyming it with wine or mine. My logic is this: Do you read magaZEENs or magaZYNEs? No matter what you choose to call your publication, you're correct. After all, it's yours. Isn't it nice to be in charge?*

E-mail Newsletters

Pick a topic, any topic—you can make an e-mail newsletter for it. Just as a regular off-the-street newsletter isn't incredibly large, neither is one sent through e-mail. Each one is content driven; it is usually the publisher's job to come up with all the "stuff." For the most part, e-mail newsletters tend to revolve around a particular topic. You might see an "eyeglass cleaner" newsletter here and a "dinosaur" newsletter there. Inside each issue, the reader might expect to see any new bit of information or insight regarding the given subject matter. An e-mail newsletter may contain one article, a series of articles by the publisher and/or independent writers, links to other related Web sites or newsletters, etc. It's just a simple venue that may be used for nearly anything the publisher desires. You're keeping people informed—that's the whole idea.

E-mail newsletters can be distributed in plain text, RTF (Rich Text Format), or HTML. HTML mail is essentially a Web page that is sent through e-mail; not all HTML conventions are supported in every HTML-capable e-mail client, but for the most part, you'll be able to use images, hyperlinks, tables, and colors. RTF mail is somewhere in between HTML mail and text, supporting formatting features such as underlining, italicizing, and bold. A majority of today's e-publications are text-based, but you're probably going to see a major shift to HTML within the next five years. The content will hopefully remain top-quality, but users will have their text enhanced with pictures, sounds, colors, etc. As with anything, however, publishers will need to give their readers valid reasons to want an HTML newsletter over a text-based one.

Announcement Lists

Say you already have an existing product or service, either online or offline. What better way to inform your installed user base about a price special or new development than through an announcement list? These lists aren't as long or as content-driven as e-mail newsletters are, but they're just as valid. If you're trying to drive traffic back to your Web site, this is most likely the medium you're going to want to use.

This is not to say that you couldn't infuse a little content into your announcement list. Remember that your goal is not only to distribute the message, but also to have the end user *read* it. This has been a challenge for many electronic publishers.

At one point, someone got the bright idea that junk e-mail would be an awesome idea. Well, it wound up hurting e-publications more than helping them. Junk e-mail might disguise itself as a personal message or as some sort of announcement list. The idea is to trick the readers into believing that they subscribed to such a service. Of course, not everyone is that stupid. Most people don't want to read a message that looks like one big advertisement—do you? Nine times out of ten, the users delete the message without even looking at it. This could be a potential problem for you and/or your company's announcement list.

If your customer is accustomed to not seeing anything valuable in your e-publication, he'll delete it without even thinking about it. You might have that customer listed in your subscriber database, but that doesn't mean anything. I could be sitting here with 400,000 subscribers. That's an impressive number, but if only 25 percent of them are reading what I'm sending out, then I've got a major problem. For the most part, once you've lost a customer's interest, you've lost him for life.

If you're going to be pushing people back to your site for products, be sure you keep your content fresh; give them solid reasons to open your message every time they receive it.

Bulletins/Action Alerts

Bulletins and action alerts run along the same vein as announcement lists. However, they're typically geared less toward product announcements and more toward "this is what's new on my site this week" informative tidbits. The idea is to grab the reader's attention and get him to come back to your site. If you've created content on your Web site and want subscribers to visit, a small bulletin will keep subscribers "in the know." Give them a byte or two in the mailing, and then point them to a URL for details.

Putting together a bulletin doesn't take much work, assuming that you already have content elsewhere on the Internet (Web site, newsgroups, etc.). If your advertising model is Web-based, a bulletin might be your best bet for e-publishing. Push people back to your site to keep your advertisers and/or sponsors happy. If you have a Web site with original content, you should definitely send out something to your user base via e-mail on a regular basis. Don't ever count on them to visit you more than once without prompting.

Moderated Discussion Lists

Imagine having a Usenet newsgroup come directly to your Inbox. That's pretty much what a discussion list (and/or group) is. When you hear people talk about a LISTSERV, they're most likely referring to a discussion list. The two kinds of discussion lists are moderated and unmoderated.

Moderated means "supervised." Most Usenet newsgroups are unpoliced; anybody can post to them without fear of deletion (censorship). Some, however, are looked after by a designated individual (or autonomous individuals) who are authorized to remove unsuitable posts. Whether in newsgroups or on a list, moderation is great . . . in moderation. As the moderator, you have control over which posts are viewed by your members, but you don't want to take that control to the extreme.

The other key component is *discussion*. Since 99 percent of the list's content is going to be created and transmitted by members of the list, you need to keep them from being silent. If things are slowing down, give everybody a kick in the pants; don't be afraid to stir up controversy once in a while. For a list to be successful, you need participants who love to share their opinions.

Typically, discussion list messages can be mailed out to members either "as they are approved" or in a compiled digest format at regular intervals. Many choose to receive the latter (which is easier on their Inbox). It's the same stuff no matter how you slice it; the different formats suit different users' needs.

If you get accused of being a fascist censor, press on. You are always going to find people who believe that they're right and you're dead wrong. You have the right to ban anyone from your discussion group—it's *yours*. My favorite thing to say to those who do nothing but complain about my publication is: "Make your own list." They seldom do.

Unmoderated Discussion Lists

An *unmoderated* list can be wildly unattractive to an electronic publisher; there is no censorship involved in regard to messages broadcast to the list. Imagine spilling a barrel full of candy bars into a room of preschoolers. The exact same thing could easily happen with an unmoderated discussion group (in one way or another). Your teeth won't rot, but you might not get anything accomplished; most people could be "bouncing off the walls."

Why would you want to start an unmoderated group? There are several reasons. Perhaps you want information to flow freely, and the members are people whom you know and trust. An unmoderated list works well when there is a small group of users that will continue to stay small, and when the list's focus isn't too broad. It can also (obviously) save you a lot of time because you don't have to scrutinize and approve every message.

I would strongly advise against starting with an unmoderated list if you have never published through e-mail before. Situations can get out of hand relatively quickly; without some form of control, you could be inviting disaster. Only if it is a small, closed group of individuals would I suggest operating an unmoderated list.

You da Man (or Woman)

That's the best thing about writing (or editing or publishing) your own e-zine. If you don't want something to be in there, it doesn't have to be. Of course, you have to be sure that your audience is receptive to the choices you make, but as long as you keep a level head, you shouldn't run into any major problems. One of your first official decisions should be: "I want to do something through e-mail." By picking up this book and reading this far, you've pretty much made that leap. If friends laugh at you and peers criticize you, simply ignore them. If *you* want to do it, then just do it. Deciding to actually do *something* is a big hurdle in itself.

You may already be an electronic publisher—already in the middle of the "battle zone." But no matter who you are or what you want to do, this book will help you gain a new perspective on how to make *your* electronic publication the best it can possibly be. While you could shoot for the stars and attempt to have the best e-zine in the entire universe, I'd suggest aiming to be one of the better (or more memorable) high-quality e-publications. You'll stand a better chance of succeeding. And yes, there's more than one way to skin a zine. Every e-author is entitled to have his own e-opinion.

It's great to have long-term goals for your e-mail publication, such as a certain number of subscribers by a certain date. However, don't get too far ahead of yourself. When I started Lockergnome a couple of years ago, I brought a few of my friends into it before the first issue was even distributed, thinking it would be too much work for one person. But ultimately I found out that I didn't need to have more than one or two more people involved. Heck, I've been able to manage a lot of it on my own thus far. You'll probably find yourself in the same boat, too.

One Step at a Time

If you're looking for the end-all, be-all "make money with your zine" book, then you're probably barking up the wrong tree. Sure, this book is going to cover marketing, advertising, and so on, but I'm not going to throw these gigantic claims at you. Most people think that they'll be making money hand over fist when they independently publish information over the Internet. It can happen, but the likelihood of you becoming an instant millionaire is . . . extremely unlikely. Over time, an electronic publication can pull in a steady stream of income, but you need to have a solid foundation underneath you before that can happen.

When I started doing my first e-zine (Lockergnome), few e-publication resources were available. There were no books or rules . . . just people trying to make things happen. Some have succeeded, some still don't have a clue, and others have moved on to other ventures after realizing that it's tougher than it looks.

E-zine publishing isn't difficult to do, but if you want to be successful, plan on pulling a few all-nighters. It could easily become a full-time job without any of the benefits. I don't suggest quitting your day (or night) job immediately after committing yourself to publishing something via e-mail. That may sound logical, but I really don't want anybody to go overboard. Take things one step at a time. You'll encounter frustrations along the way (everybody does), but it will be just as important for you to take a step back and realize why you're frustrated. Identify the problems and take steps to solve them. Nobody else will do it for you, so don't put it off. All of this responsibility comes with being an independent e-publisher. You're on your own . . . for the most part.

Show Me the Money

I took an informal poll of other respected (and experienced) e-zine publishers a few months ago. The common belief among them was that that 80 percent of all currently published e-zines deal with marketing on the Internet and/or making money online. Those types of e-publications are everywhere. So, if you plan on covering a similar topic, you're going to have very stiff competition. Remember, too, that not all e-zines that promise to show you how to make tons of money are actually making any money themselves. A majority of these "marketing" e-mail newsletters are filled with fluff and are designed to make money from people who want to make money from people who want to make money. Very few business, marketing, or advertising e-zines are content-rich, original, and worth reading.

When Peter Kent asked me to write this book, I was ecstatic. After all, this is my first book. I have a wealth of e-publishing information swimming around in my head, so why not share it with the known universe? I'm a strong proponent for keeping information flowing free, and other e-publishers agree with this philosophy. That's one of the reasons most electronic publications don't cost the reader one red cent. So how do e-zines make money? I'll cover that topic in another chapter. An e-zine needs to be financially viable in order to survive, and I plan on arming you with the resources necessary to make a killer e-publication on your own.

Understand, too, that the average e-zine might have between 5,000 and 15,000 subscribers. Don't feel bad if yours is below that number, and don't feel great if you're way above it. There's always room for improvement. Also keep in mind the kind of audience you're attracting; the readership for humorous messages is going to be larger than the one for eighteenth century horseshoes.

If your readers love what you send to them, you've won half the battle. I don't have exact statistics or fancy charts to show you, but I've got one thing that very few "computer book" authors have: practical experience.

Getting Comfy

Don't get me wrong; statistics and charts are great indicators to use while you're building and developing your e-publication. But I believe you'll understand a lot more about the process after you've been through it yourself. Numbers tell only half the story, and everything looks great on paper. Of course, that's just my point of view—you're entitled to your own.

This book is based on my own experiences. I'm not a "marketer" per se, but a real-world user who has been able to develop his own newsletter in a successful approach. By the time you finish this book, you should be able to do the same thing. I'm not sitting behind stacks of journals while I'm writing this paragraph. In fact, right now I'm in an old T-shirt and blue jeans and surrounded by a few empty cans of carbonated water and string cheese wrappers. But I'm very comfortable. That's something to keep in mind when you enter "writing mode."

Think back to your college or high-school days. Can you remember how you wrote best? Did you like waiting until the last minute before typing the first sentence? Did you like planning everything in your mind before you even picked up a pencil? Did you wear a "lucky" hat? Well, I doubt that much has changed since then. There's no correct angle to hold your pen, no certain type of computer you need to use to publish electronically, and no particular subject matter your zine needs to address. If it isn't fun or interesting for you, then why bother doing it in the first place?

Powerful Stuff

The true power of e-mail has not been seen or realized to this day; very few individuals understand its potential strength. E-mail is a very important online element. It has been around from the very beginning (as far as the mainstream, global Internet is concerned). The average person believes that the World Wide Web is the Internet, but in fact, the Web is merely a subset of the Internet. E-mail, by far, is the killer application that everybody uses. Think about it for a second. When you first log on, what's the first thing you consciously do? I'll bet you check your e-mail before anything else, before you call up a Web page, and before you call up your instant messenger program to see who else is online. Keeping this in mind, can you see how it's wise to pursue an e-mail publication model rather than (or on top of) a Web-site one? I knew that when I started doing something online (even before I had the specific idea for Lockergnome) it would be best accomplished via e-mail.

But Why?

But why distribute an e-mail publication instead of (or alongside) putting up a Web site? Think about your own Web-surfing habits. Do you visit new sites every day? Do you visit sites frequently? Which sites do you frequent most often? Which sites are most interesting to you? What do those sites provide to you that is of value? These are the things to keep in mind when you get ready to design your own page and/or your own e-mail publication.

When individuals visit any given Web page, they might stay there for 10 to 20 seconds before their attention fades. Either something else draws their attention, they click on a link that leads them away from your site, or they simply get bored. Therefore, your first (main) page needs to have enough information to entice users to read on. Unless you have something worth returning for, most users are probably never going to return. Sure, they might bookmark it, and they may even put a link to your site on their own Web pages, but the chances are slim that they're going to keep coming back to you regularly.

However, if you can show visitors what you have to offer up front and get them to subscribe to your e-mail publication, then they'll be captive audience members until they decide to unsubscribe. You don't have to count on them to revisit your Web site at all; they're going to receive your e-zine whether or not they're online when it arrives in their e-mailbox. Entice them to join, and then send them on their merry way.

Look around You

Keeping one eye on your competition is always wise. If you don't have competition yet, just wait a few months. Once you start building something successful, everybody will start to emulate you in every aspect (all the way down to your writing style, which is very difficult to copy). Whether or not they're related to your subject matter, take a look at other e-mail publications and their Web sites. You're going to see things you like and things that you don't. Keep notes as you do your research. Have those notes somewhere close—look at them when you start to put your publication together. Do the stuff that you liked, and don't do the stuff you didn't like. Simple enough?

But don't try to rewrite the book on your first day. Many people and companies have failed in their online ventures because they took shortcuts and didn't immerse themselves in the Internet's culture. Yes, for a wise man to achieve brilliance, he must first look foolish to the crowd. But you need to get a little experience under your belt, understand the industry, and understand the users. *Then* you can push the envelope. If a tried-and-true method works, follow it. Once you've accumulated a strong knowledge base and have worked online for a period of time, then try a unique angle. This isn't to say you shouldn't try something new, but existing e-mail publications have already proven (and continue to prove) themselves to be valuable. By initially following in the footsteps of others who have already succeeded, you'll have a better chance for success yourself.

Jumping on the Bandwagon

Several hundred thousand independently owned and operated e-mail publications were distributed today. I'm positive that larger corporations will start to realize their genuine value tomorrow (if they're not "onto us" already). This fact shouldn't concern you, though. An e-zine run by one person can make just as much of an impact (if not more) than one distributed by a well-known, established corporation. That's how powerful words can be.

Visitors may see your Web site once or twice in their lifetime; millions and millions of pages are available out there. That's great to hear because there is so much information, but not-so-great because, well . . . there is *so much* information. Everyone and his dog has a Web page, but not everybody has an e-mail publication worth subscribing to. There's no worrying about cookies, no worrying about browser compatibility issues, no worrying about how you're going to get that user back to your site at some point in the future. If you can get a visitor to subscribe, you can make a friend for life.

Once you publish your first issue, you automatically become an "official" electronic publisher. Unfortunately, no glorious sounds will be coming down from the heavens when you do this. But there are also no clubs to join and no membership dues to pay. People will start paying attention to you—but only if you continue to distribute "good stuff."

Writer's Block

You need to ask yourself: "Am I a good writer?" Then, after you've given them an example of what you plan on doing, you should ask your friends and/or relatives the same question—especially if they're familiar with your subject matter. While some would say that you are your worst critic, I believe that other people can (and often will) be infinitely more brutal. They'll catch more of your mistakes and be a bit more candid with their opinions. Cross your fingers and hope that they're being completely honest. You don't have to follow through with their suggestions or corrections, but at least listen to what they have to say.

If you can't write, don't expect your readers to understand. Find someone who comprehends language and has strong communications skills, or simply consider moderating a discussion list and not doing much writing at all. Similarly, if you know you can't design something, then by all means, *don't*. Find someone else to do it for you.

Don't rely on the fancy, high-end HTML or text editors to design your publication, either. While having the latest tools is a plus, tools usually don't foster creativity, originality, or professionalism. A good designer could do more with an old PC and a simple word processor than a novice could do with a brand-new one loaded up with all the latest tools. You have to understand the technology before you can hope to use it efficiently. Far too many *potentially* killer e-zines and Web sites out there are plagued by poor design, lack of information, typos, too-large graphics, and other problems.

I've tricked many people (unwittingly) into believing that Lockergnome is a publication run by several individuals; both my Web site and newsletter are presented in a very professional, straightforward manner. Having true legitimacy and looking good are important, especially in the potential subscriber's eyes.

> **NOTE**
>
> *Understand that your friends and family might not completely understand what you're trying to accomplish online. People may even try to convince you to do a Web site instead of an e-mail publication. At that point, you should turn around and run the other way. Oh great—this is starting to sound like some sort of cult. No, really . . . this is all legitimate. I just ask that you wear this armadillo shell while you're distributing stuff electronically.*

Chapter Two

E-mail Primer—How It All Works

Sending an e-mail message is easy to do, but there are certain conventions to keep in mind before you start broadcasting electronically. You'll discover traditional communication methods falling to the wayside as e-mail becomes a larger part of your life. Business relationships will become easier to establish and (more importantly) maintain as you master the e-mail basics. Pretend that you're entering a foreign country that has new customs, procedures, and unspoken rules. Anybody can send an electronic message, but not everyone will do so effectively. It's time to leave the analog world of envelopes behind you. . . .

Split-Second Timing

My lawyer is a decent human being (no, really). But the other day he mailed me an invoice for a service that had already been paid for in full. I had a few options at that point. I could (a) pay him again, (b) return the invoice along with the cashed check and an explanation through the mail, or (c) scan the offending invoice and the deposited check into graphics, and then e-mail them to him immediately. Guess which option I went with?

In a matter of minutes, my lawyer responded to my message with a strong mea culpa.

There are huge differences between traditional (snail mail) and electronic (e-mail) delivery. My lawyer had his secretary type up an invoice, stick it in an envelope, affix a stamp to it, drop it in the outbox, and wait for the mail carrier to pick it up. The mail carrier then drove back to the local post office, where it was sorted (probably by a machine) and then stuffed into a bag heading to my city. That bag was then picked up by a larger mail transport and taken to a postal dispatcher, who then sorted through the bag and pulled out the envelope with the invoice inside and gave it to my local postal carrier, who then drove to my house and placed the mailing into my mailbox. There it sat until I retrieved it. Then I opened it, reacted, and responded electronically.

The process probably took a couple of days, even though my lawyer lives in the same state as I do. Had he delivered the invoice through e-mail, not only would he have saved postage, but the turnaround time would have been a fraction of what it was.

Different Verse, Same as the First

While e-mail is a totally different venue, its delivery process still operates much in the same way as that of traditional mail. The only major differences: time and the human factor. Just as you need to have a physical address in order to mail a letter to a friend, you'll need to have an e-mail address in order to e-mail a message.[1]

When you send an e-mail message, it goes to your mail server and from there is routed to its destination server in a matter of minutes (sometimes longer, sometimes shorter). At that point, your message waits in the receiver's e-mail Inbox until he logs on and retrieves it. As you can see, it's a similar process to the one for snail mail; the process is just more automated.

Bouncey Bouncey

If my lawyer had snail-mailed the invoice to an incorrect physical address, the post office would have returned the envelope to him. This would have taken days (or weeks). On the other hand, if he had e-mailed my invoice to an incorrect e-mail address, he would have received a "bounce" notification almost immediately. The postmaster of the mail server his message reached would have informed him (either through an automatic mailing or through a regular e-mail message) that the user he was trying to send mail to didn't exist on the server.

Bounces are the scourge of e-mail broadcasting; if you haven't seen enough of them by now, don't worry—you'll get sick of them within a couple of days of your first e-publishing event. You're going to be distributing hundreds (possibly thousands) of e-mails to addresses all over the world. You can expect there to be people who closed their accounts and forgot to tell you, or changed addresses, or lost their accounts without warning, and so on.

Your Client

To send or receive e-mail, you need some type of e-mail program (a.k.a. an *application* or *client*). It doesn't matter what operating system you're running on,

---

[1] We're not going to get into all the complicated technical details related to exactly how e-mail systems work, or how to use a specific e-mail program—if you'd like more information on these subjects, see *Internet Messaging* by David Strom and Marshall T. Rose (Prentice Hall), ISBN 0139786104.

either. BeOS; Windows 3.11, 95, 98, or NT; MacOS; any flavor of UNIX—even MS-, PC-, or DR-DOS will do! E-mail programs are available for all those operating systems. You will use your e-mail program to help manage your recipient list, as well as take care of day-to-day matters that will arise.

Some service providers require you to use their e-mail program. (AOL is one such service.) Other service providers allow you to use any e-mail program you choose. Even if your system came preinstalled with an e-mail program, you might consider upgrading to a newer, more feature-packed one if possible. E-mail is going to become your livelihood, and it's always good to have the right tool for the job. For a partial listing of potentially usable e-mail clients for mainstream operating systems, please refer to Appendix E.

Carbon Copying

You just got back from France; the first thing you want to do is tell your friends about the trip. Let's say you have 15 friends with e-mail addresses. You could either write the same message to each one of them in 15 separate e-mail messages, or save time and let them all know how much you liked the Eiffel Tower by using the "carbon copy" feature found in most e-mail clients. The message will be sent out in 15 different directions, but you will have to write it only once. You simply enter one person's e-mail address in the "To" field, and the other 14 addresses in the "CC" field.

While adding any number of e-mail addresses in the To field is perfectly acceptable, that's generally reserved for the main recipient of your message; the CC field should be used (out of courtesy and clarity). Be careful, though. If your friends don't all know each other, they might get very upset with you for broadcasting their e-mail address to 14 strangers. My suggestion is that you use the CC feature in moderation; use it only with people who know each other, and never CC too many people at one time.

In the average e-mail client, you will have two response options: "reply to author" and "reply to all." Generally, "reply to author" is sufficient. Be careful when you're replying to messages that have been openly CCed to other individuals; if you invoke the "reply to all" function, you could be upsetting other users. Some might not care about what you have to say in response to the original message.

NOTE

"Too many" would probably be any number over 20. Use your own discretion with this—it's just a guideline to keep in mind.

Using the CC feature to distribute your publication is like a "Poor Man's Mailing List." You don't need any fancy software to do it, but you may be limited by your e-mail program in the number of subscribers you can put into a CC field. It also is considered bad e-mail manners to include people's e-mail addresses where other recipients can see them without first asking permission. There's a solution, however, in some e-mail programs: blind carbon copying, or BCC.

Blind Carbon Copying

What if, instead of showing all the recipients who else is receiving the message, you were able to hide the list from each recipient? That's the idea behind the blind carbon copy (BCC) feature, available in some e-mail programs. Blind carbon copying is another "Poor Man's Mailing List" alternative (although a lot more private than the normal CC).

If you're not ready to venture into the waters of e-mail publishing on a professional level, consider using the BCC option in your e-mail program to distribute your first few issues. Keep in mind, however, that this is neither the best nor the easiest way to run a mailing list with many subscribers. You'll be managing the bounces and subscribe/unsubscribe requests by hand, and there may be a wait while the BCCed messages leave your Outbox if you're on a dial-up modem connection to the Internet.

E-mail Etiquette (Netiquette)

This part of the chapter is not just for newbies; even if you've written e-mail for years, review this section carefully. Certain unspoken conventions are very important to keep in mind when you're composing e-mail messages. If you were a novice before, you need to be a professional now.

- ONE OF THE BIGGEST MISTAKES PEOPLE MAKE IS TO TYPE WITH THEIR CAPS LOCK ON. All-caps might look cool to you, but experienced users will write you off as an idiot. It's okay to use all-caps for headings and/or titles in your messages, or even to EMPHASIZE certain words, but anything beyond that is equivalent to screaming at someone. Do you like being yelled at?

- When you're upset with someone, the last thing you should do is write him an e-mail message. Yes, I've broken this rule quite a few times (and everybody probably has or will at some point). I've regretted blasting "nasty" e-mails to friends before chilling out first, but it's even worse to send angry e-mail in a business context.

- If you can say it in three words, please . . . say it in three words. The last thing anybody needs is a 30-paragraph document explaining how to open a door. If a user sees a message that contains several paragraphs, he'll be less likely to read everything in it. Keep that in mind when you're trying to determine how much content you want to include in an e-mailing. Don't try to send out the entire text from a Web page if it isn't necessary. All Web pages (online) have URLs—refer the readers to the actual Web page instead.

- While discussion lists are great for promoting and sharing ideas, be sure you're adding something valuable to the "conversation" if you want to toot your own horn. Offer help or advice, and then mention what your product or service is. Randomly interjecting your URL is simply rude.

- Keep signature files down to 4-6 lines; this part of your message is the last thing the receiver will read. A signature typically includes your name, title, contact information, URL, and sometimes a little ASCII graphic or two. Many e-mail clients can be set up to automatically attach a default signature file to the end of all your outgoing messages (including replies). They're perfect for conveying important information, but should remain short and sweet.

- If you're going to forward a message to someone else, strip all the extraneous information and characters from it beforehand. It cuts down on the size of the message and makes it easier to read. This is just another form of common e-courtesy that too many people have forgotten (or don't think about).

- When replying to a person, be sure to include a quotation from the original e-mail that can provide context for your response. Most e-mail clients will insert a character before the original text of the sender's message in your reply. (The most common is the greater-than symbol.) Whatever you do, make sure your responses are clearly separated from their original text, to avoid confusion.

- You may think you're being funny (or serious) in your writing, but it may come across differently to the reader. If you want to ensure their understanding, use an emoticon or two. They are also known as smileys . . . and there are thousands of possible combinations. The two major ones are :) and :(— do you see anything there? Turn this book sideways and look at them again. The colon and parenthesis (when placed next to each other) form a "face." If you're trying to be funny, inserting a smiley face can convey your intent, preventing misunderstandings or hurt feelings. Likewise, if your writing isn't indicative of your foul mood, perhaps a frowning emoticon should be dropped in at the end of a sentence.

- If you use abbreviations or acronyms, be sure your audience already knows what they stand for. You want to make your readers feel welcome. If you're unsure, use the abbreviation with an explanation immediately behind it. You might even design an FAQ (Frequently Asked Questions) document that they can retrieve via a Web page, an FTP download, or e-mail message.

- Check with sources before distributing information. If something sounds too good to be true, it just might be. The last thing you want to do is broadcast to the world that the next 100 people to visit flyingteddybearaglets.com will get a free pair of shoes . . . only to find out later that it was a hoax.

- Personal computers are like fingerprints—no two are exactly alike. Everyone has different hardware and software installed, resulting in different system capabilities. Even if you have a fancy e-mail program that can generate beautifully formatted messages with HTML, you should not rely on your recipients having the capability of reading such messages. A fancy HTML-formatted message might come across like gobbledygook to people with noncompatible e-mail programs. I strongly suggest using text (ASCII) as your default message format— that way, you're pretty much guaranteed compatibility with everyone else's mail reader.

- Nobody likes reading run-on sentences because they're not very easy to read, and besides, readers' brains might get tired of thinking about the words by the time their eyes finish with the sentence a few minutes later before having to move on to the next sentence, which might be part of a bigger paragraph that seems to be lumped together without any signs of visible separation.

- Use blank lines (hard carriage returns) to separate your paragraphs. Steer clear of tabs, because different e-mail programs can show tab stops differently onscreen. Use spaces if you need to indent something, but indenting the first line of each paragraph is largely unnecessary and should be avoided if possible.

- In multiline paragraphs, keep the line length under 76 characters. The reason: not all e-mail clients will format your message correctly if you go beyond that number. In the recipient's Inbox, your paragraphs might appear choppier than you intended them to be. To ensure no problems with formatting on the other end, set the character wrap between 60 and 65. (Most e-mail programs allow you to set this option.)

- You can attach items (documents, pictures, compressed archives, etc.) to an e-mail message. This feature is great . . . but don't abuse it. Mailing a simple 30K attachment is harmless enough, but when you need to send files much larger than that, ask the receiver's permission first. I was once locked out of my mailbox because a user mailed me a 7.2M attachment! I was livid because he wasted my time, stopped productivity, and sent something that large without my consent. If you're unsure of the file's size, don't send it.

- It's also important to understand that users in your discussion lists probably don't want anything more than text-based messages. Don't use attachments or post messages in HTML format to a discussion list.

- Your writing style says more about you than you realize. While e-mail might be viewed as an informal means of communication, your e-composition skills are still quite reflective of your knowledge and abilities. Yes, everybody is allowed to make a few typos, but if you're consistently not capitalizing words that should be capitalized, using unconventional punctuation (i.e., putting 15 periods in a row instead of just three), spelling words incorrectly, and so on, you will not come across as a person who knows what he's doing. Neatness counts.

- Use a relatively descriptive subject line. I find it really annoying when someone sends me a message with just the word "Hi" in it. That tells me absolutely nothing about the message's content. I'm not suggesting that you sum up your life's story in one sentence, but I do recommend that you use words that will describe the general purpose of your e-mail.

> **NOTE**
>
> *An e-mail provider may place restrictions on the size of messages a user is able to receive. When someone sends a "large" attachment, the receiver may be locked out of his mailbox.*

- When you interact with others on an unmoderated mailing list, don't post small, vague messages. Messages such as "Me too!" or "Can someone help me?", without any further description or qualification, do nothing to contribute to the conversation. Posting such trivial messages is considered very rude (and is a major waste of resources).

- In a similar vein, don't reply to e-mails with one-word answers or questions. "What?" "What what?" "What?" It's another fantastic time waster.

- When you have an e-mail address link set up on your Web site, that means you're ready for people to contact you via e-mail. Try to get back to people who write to you within a couple of days (and if you can't offer an extended reply, at least inform them of your situation). I've turned down several potentially good deals because people were extremely tardy in their e-mail responses. Big businesses are the worst offenders—don't be like them in this respect, please.

- Don't forward forwarded messages on to your friends and co-workers. Yes, I realize that someone else forwarded them to you, but that doesn't mean you have to pass them along to even more people. I don't care if you thought it was funny. When I want to laugh, I'll find something funny to read on my own. I'm not the only one who's sick and tired of receiving chain letters on a daily basis. E-mail can be fun, but don't take it to the extreme.

Don't Rewrite the Rules

You may be new to the electronic publishing game, and a fresh perspective is typically a positive trait. But don't get too far ahead of yourself—e-mail has been around for decades. Chances are, you're not going to rewrite the book on effective communication tactics. Just because a method may seem smart to you doesn't mean that it's electronically savvy. There's a reason this chapter was written: to stop you from making a potentially damaging or offending mistake. "When in doubt, take the safer route."

Now you'll be minding your Ps and Qs, but do you understand why e-mail is a better means for your service or product? It isn't just for keeping in touch with your folks. . . .

Chapter Three

Why E-mail? Little Glamour, Plenty of Results

People like e-mail—they just do. They love sending e-mail; they love receiving e-mail. When people first log on to the Internet, the first thing they want to do is send an e-mail message off to a friend, relative, or mortal enemy. Sending messages back and forth with others is an absolute thrill when you first get online. I remember the first time I used e-mail—do you? A friend was sitting across the computer lab from me, but it was still thrilling to be able to type something on my terminal and have the message sent immediately over to his terminal. In a matter of seconds, he was able to read that message.

That's probably the way e-mail got started—in some computer lab a few decades back. It doesn't take much; simple text is all you need. If you've got something to say to anyone, e-mail is an excellent venue. Can you let a day go by without checking yours? If you answered No to this question, you're in good company. If you answered Yes, then you might reconsider pursuing such an Internet-centric occupation as electronic publishing.

Nowadays, various software packages are available for most platforms, and they enable users to spice up e-mail messages. HTML mail is a relative newcomer to the e-mail scene. Essentially, sending an HTML message is like transmitting a Web page in your e-mail client . . . replete with sounds, graphics, different fonts, colors, etc. Of course, the worst parts about HTML mail are that not every mail program can accept it and not everybody likes to receive it. Always keep this maxim in mind when it comes to interesting technological toys: Just because it *can* be done, doesn't mean it *should* be done. Have a solid reason for everything you do—e-publishing included.

Everybody Does It

Even the newest Internet users (newbies) send and receive e-mail. Countless studies show that while a lot of people are "online," not every user surfs the

Web. Some individuals only have shell access (which means they're stuck working on a text-based system). That's not bad, though . . . at least, as far as we e-publishers are concerned. Those people can still send and receive text-based e-mail messages!

But what about the people who *do* have Web access? Again, one of the first things people do is check for new mail. How many times have you logged on just to check your messages and then logged out again? A million and one Web pages are available out there, but users (typically) have only one Inbox. They might not have time to surf the Web, but rest assured, they'll find time to read incoming e-mail.

Well, they'll read it as long as it's worth reading. You can talk about disturbing trends . . . like the rising price of pork rinds. You can brag about how you got backstage passes to your favorite rock band the other day. You can write the coolest sonnets in the world. But if no one is reading what you're writing, what good is it is doing anybody? Make your content so incredibly exciting that nobody (in their right mind) would dare miss an issue. That way, when you send something out, you'll be confident that your subscribers will take the time to read it.

This is another way in which Web pages fail and e-mail newsletters and discussion lists succeed: Web pages rely on people to visit and revisit them; e-mail messages will sit in your mail account and wait for you to retrieve them . . . which you'll probably do eventually.

One Step Further

You're well on your way to creating the Internet's latest fantastic resource . . . whether you knew it or not.

If you can send e-mail, you can be an e-mail newsletter publisher or discussion list moderator. There's no big trick to it—honest. If you want to boil things down to their barest essentials, each e-mail message you send could be an e-zine of sorts. Instead of writing to your Uncle Max to tell him about your latest trip to Missouri, you could be telling everyone else in your family the same story at the same time—including your Aunt Grizelda (who admittedly looks a lot like your Uncle Max).

Just because you can pull up a Web page doesn't mean you can create one. But with e-mail, it's all the same skill set—if you can read and write regular e-mail, you can create a newsletter or discussion list. This is just another way in which e-mail has the Web beat by a long shot. And the application everybody seems to have skipped over.

Your subscribers will grow to love you (let's hope). You'll have them eating out of the palm of your hand eventually (and you best not abuse that power). If you post information on a Web site, they might miss it while they are out of town for a month. But if you send the same information in an e-mail publication, they will have it sitting in their message queue when they get back home.

Pick a topic, find an audience, send an e-mail message, publish an e-zine.

The Original Push

You hear all this talk about how you have to be at the top of all the search engine rankings to be the best Web site in the world. Who told you that? Slap those guys around for me next time you see them, will you? While search engines are great for people who are looking for things, their results are far from accurate. You may be ranked in the #1 spot for "mouse pads," but unless someone is doing a search with those keywords, that placement isn't doing you any good. The "best" Web site in the world would have users visiting it day after day without thinking, without fail, regardless of its search engine rankings.

Every time an e-mail newsletter or discussion list is distributed, subscribers will receive it. Period. You're pushing content to them, just as they requested. Your Web site may be getting 100,000 unique impressions (visitors) per day, but out of that many impressions, how many are returning users? How many of those visitors already knew about you and are coming back for some more great stuff?

Returning visitors are "better" visitors; they know about your services, products, or information; know what they are looking for; and will be much more likely to give you feedback when you ask for it. Trying to develop a dedicated following by simply putting up a Web site is like trying to make a million dollars by setting up a lemonade stand on a cul-de-sac. Sure, some rich guy might be thirsty one afternoon, but your chances of attaining any level of success are slim to none.

And the search engine rankings probably aren't going to help you one bit (for your site, not the lemonade stand). You need name and brand awareness, you need to have something users want, and you need to build up a base of users who rely on you to provide them with the services/products/information that only you can offer. The average Web surfer may view a site for about 10 to 20 seconds and then move on to the next one. If you can impress someone enough to sign up for your newsletter, bulletin, discussion list, etc., then that person will receive your "stuff" the next time you distribute something.

You're wasting a colossal opportunity if you don't get a user to return to your site. "Push" software was created to keep the user informed of all the latest happenings on the Internet (and to help drive traffic back to certain ones). The end user was required to install proprietary software to receive the latest news, weather reports, and so on. Well, I hate to tell companies who invested in this stuff, but they could have used e-mail for a lot less, and their mission would have been a million times more effective.

Community Service

A big buzzword nowadays is "community." I see everybody scrambling to create communities online. What the e-commerce fanatics don't realize is that Usenet newsgroups and e-mail discussion lists have beat them to the punch. And I'd wager to say that they're a heckuva lot cheaper.

Discussion lists are awesome places for people to share their experiences with one another. Friendships can be formed in no time at all. (You'd be surprised at how quickly some people can "open up" online.) They'll be talking to each other, they'll be laughing and crying with each other—they'll be a family. And you could be the head of the household.

E-mail newsletters (unless combined with other services) will not have such a strong community; subscribers are going to receive only the information that you send to them through e-mail. Unless you offer them the option of posting their opinions on your Web site, in your newsgroups, in a chat room, or in some other venue, subscribers are not going to become acquainted with any other subscribers.

Through e-mail publishing, you can *push* your users content that they want to read . . . and develop a *community* within a matter of hours. Let's see, have I left out any other buzzwords? I suppose we could say that you're potentially creating a *microtargeted audience* that will be receptive to any future *e-commerce* you might pass their way.

I think you're starting to get the picture.

> **TIP**
>
> *Try giving subscribers a nickname to help evoke a sense of belonging to something more than just an electronic missive. It may sound dorky, but I've got thousands upon thousands of Lockergnomies sitting in front of computer screens all over the world. And they'll happily call themselves that before I ever would.*

Game Over?

E-mail publications aren't the status quo at this time. These days everybody has a Web site that he believes is "killer." Seventy percent of today's Web sites, however, should probably be killed. The same "everybody" is completely missing the boat. Internet businesses are searching for answers, but few dare to ask the right questions of the right people. A Web site is fine and dandy; I'm not suggesting that you forget about putting one up. But the real game has not yet begun. Businesses and individuals will eventually warm up to the fact that e-mail is a far better avenue for distributing and collecting information than the Web ever was.

Isn't it nice to know that you're going to be ahead of the pack? When others are struggling to create user bases in the present and the future, you'll be sitting on top of one you've been developing for years. Just hope they're not reading this book, too.

International Appeal

What country a user is from shouldn't matter; a subscriber is a subscriber. In fact, you may find that users in other countries are your most enthusiastic fans. Most Americans take their flat-fee Internet connection for granted. ISPs are a dime a dozen in the States, whereas citizens of other countries are often charged by the minute! This means that many of them must maximize their efficiency online; random clicking isn't an option. For this reason, you'll find a lot of international interest in your e-mailed publication. International users are just as in love with the Internet as the average cyber-surfer, but they can't afford to waste time downloading information from Web sites filled with bloated code, graphics, etc.

The Most Sacred Place in the World

As a kid, I was always told to "never talk to strangers." I wasn't supposed to let anybody I didn't know into my house. Now that I'm grown up and married, the same rule still applies: If I don't know you, I ain't lettin' you in. But if I know who you are because of a mutual friend, or I think I know you well enough to let you see my carpet stains, I'm probably going to invite you inside. Over time, we're going to develop a relationship of sorts, and I'm going to let you come into my home more often without concern.

You can publish a Web page within seconds and wait for users to stop by. With any luck, a few of them eventually will. But they're not inviting you into their homes. Sure, they're grabbing information from your page, but they're doing all the work. Remember, they had to come to *you*. So, why not turn the tables? You go to *them*. The easiest way to do that is by getting them to subscribe to your e-mail publication.

Getting inside a user's Inbox on a regular basis is like taking first prize in every beauty pageant you enter (as long as Aunt Grizelda isn't running). People will protect that place like no other. You can easily send one message to anyone, but if he doesn't know who you are, he's probably not going to let you do that again. The Inbox is a user's personal space. Invade it without warning, and you'll create an instant enemy. But if you let users make up their own minds, they'll be more likely to accept you.

Nonerasable Pen

Since your subscribers will be inviting you into their Inboxes, they're going to take the things you say a little more personally. And there's nothing wrong with that. In fact, I'd encourage any sort of style that evokes any emotion in readers. However, keep in mind that if you say or do something wrong in one of your issues, there's no way of taking it back. While any Web page can easily be edited without anybody ever knowing, an e-mail message will remain "the same way" forever. So be careful in what you say or do with your e-mail messages.

You don't want to take that point to the extreme, however. Don't be afraid to push the envelope at times. There will always be someone who doesn't agree with you—but try not to take it personally.

A few months into first distributing Lockergnome, I received a rather rude e-mail message from a newly unsubscribed reader. He was irate about a comment I made in some recent issue. Well, this kinda put me in a bad mood—I felt personally responsible for losing any particular subscriber. After seeing me moping in front of my monitor, my roommate asked me why I looked so glum. I explained the situation to him and he nodded his head.

"How many subscribers you got?" he asked.

"About 30,000," I answered.

"And how many people complained?" he asked.

"One," I answered.

"Then get over it. Now!" he shouted. That's darn good advice he gave me, and now I'm passing it along to you. Thanks, Eric!

Click-Thru the Roof

Let's go back to the issue of trust. (Can you see how trust plays an important role in the success of your e-publication?) If you were looking for a brand of toothpaste, and your friend told you to get X and not Y, which one would you consider purchasing? I'll assume you would have picked X over Y based on that friend's recommendation. If you trust people, you'll listen to them.

A Web page is user-unfriendly in terms of interaction. Oh sure, an applet here and there can really make the site shine, but is any personal connection going on between the site owner and the site surfer? Highly unlikely. The user is just pointing and clicking his way across the Internet, looking for the latest pictures of a favorite supermodel, listening to MP3s, etc. "Interesting site . . . I'll have to bookmark it and check it out later." Much later, apparently; some users never return.

But your subscribers, in contrast, trust you. They know you (or they think they do, anyway). If you tell subscribers to "click here" for more information on a dynamite book covering e-mail newsletters, they're going to think, "Gee, he hasn't steered me wrong yet." And a click-thru will occur.

Try telling ordinary Web surfers to "click here." Unless they know you, they're probably not going to do it . . . even if you try to use ALL CAPS. Too many Web sites throw up hundreds of links on a page; they're lucky if a user clicks on more than two of them. But if you can break down those links into separate e-mail messages sent to the user (in the form of e-mail newsletters, bulletins, discussion lists, etc.), your click-thru rates will be much better. And they'll be better still when you have more users trusting your recommendations.

Your ultimate goal is to have all your subscribers sitting in front of their computers anticipating the moment when your regularly scheduled e-zine arrives in their Inboxes. You'll want to make them wait for it (I suppose this is the Internet's version of foreplay); when your issue finally arrives, they'll take their time with it, knowing that your next mailing won't be for a little while. Once they get hooked, you can hope they'll be hooked for life.

At that point, you're really going to start seeing results. More new users will subscribe based on their friends' recommendations, click-thru rates will be phenomenally better, and your name will (you hope) start to be known in industry circles. Your success won't happen overnight, but once your readers have confidence in your publication, they are going to read just about every word you write. Of course, part of that magic depends on how well you write (or compile) your issues.

Now, if you don't know what a click-thru is, or why getting good click-thru rates is a good thing, keep reading. I'll be covering applications for this invaluable phenomenon in Chapter 15.

Banners Don't Work

I've heard it said that there are more advertising banners online than stars in the sky. And ya know what? I believe it. Nearly every page you visit has at least one banner ad; some have dozens.

Banner ads take a few seconds each to load, and collectively they can slow down the loading of a Web page, resulting in frustrating delays. This situation has resulted in the creation of programs (in the form of downloadable software) for all platforms that will automatically "kill" (that is, block the display of) advertisements that would normally load up in any given Web page. Now, just to illustrate for you how some site owners "don't get it," I've seen ad-killing programs listed, described, and linked to on sites relying on banner advertisements for income. Ironic? No, plain stupidity. Banner advertising is good—it's a way to keep services for end users *free*. (Of course, sites that post 18 different banners all in a row aren't helping matters any.) That's why I don't support banner-killing programs.

Advertisements are necessary evils for "free" Web sites trying to turn a profit. But they don't work as well as they should. A "text" advertisement will typically yield better click-thru results than will a banner advertisement.

What!? How could that possibly be? What about all those great graphics editors and ad gizmos that will make animated images more attractive to the clickers? *But people don't read graphics. People read text.*

CAUTION

Please...if you're going to use banners on a Web page, separate them visually...and I suggest not using more than five on a page. If you've broken this unwritten rule of ad banner etiquette, perhaps starting a text-based e-mail newsletter will bust you of that habit.

And the "advertising world" has not yet caught on to this little factoid. Everybody is caught up in placing and selling banner ads. There's nothing wrong with that, except they're not incredibly effective.

I believe an advertiser would be much happier with a five-line text ad that fully describes the product or service than it would be with a 16k animated banner showing a flying teddy bear with the words: "CLICK HERE FOR FLYING TEDDY BEAR AGLETS." You have the opportunity to describe what Flying Teddy Bear Aglets are in detail with a text ad, as well as how they could benefit the average aglet purchaser. The banner may be cute, but which type of advertisement would you click on (assuming you needed aglets)? Would you fall for the fluff, or for the who, what, why, and where?

What Are You Saying?

So I'm saying that you can send one message to 1,000 people and get better results from a text ad than if you had 50,000 people view a banner ad on a Web page. Allow me to further defend my claim.

People who rely on banner ads are assuming a few things about Web surfers: They're using a graphical browser, they're not running any ad-killing software, they're surfing with graphics "turned on," they haven't scrolled past the image area before the graphic had a chance to completely load, and they're actually looking at or for banner advertisements. All these possibilities are just that . . . possibilities. How about some absolutes?

I *know* a few things about people who read text-based e-mail publications: They don't have to wait for a text ad to completely load—it's already there. They're reading your publication anyway—they're also going to read the advertisement. There's no way to kill a text-based advertisement (yet), and—if you've built up a trust with your subscriber base—they'll be more apt to check out your sponsors. But don't take my word for it—talk to other e-mail publishers. They'll tell you the same thing. Better results come from text-based advertisements than from banner ads.

Laziness Not an Option

When you publish something by e-mail, you're sending out a complete message. That is to say, you can't take shortcuts by inserting an "under construction" banner under one of your sections. If you do, that's just silly. Why bother e-mailing something if it isn't done yet?

If you don't publish your issues on a regular basis, you're going to disappoint your readers (and potentially lose them). If you start out with a daily publishing schedule and find that it creates more of a workload than you can handle, by all means change! You don't have to remind your users on a daily basis that you're alive. Try going to twice a week, or once a week, two times a month, or once a month. I wouldn't suggest going much past that time frame, however. If you're out of your subscribers' thoughts for too long, when you finally do get around to sending something new, people will have forgotten about you. Find the "frame" that works best for you and your e-publication.

It's publish or perish. Period.

Branded for Life

I still remember when Yahoo!'s URL had a tilde (~) in it. Then there was Scott Yanoff, who was still compiling and distributing his famous *Internet Services* list through e-mail, newsgroups, FTP servers, and so on. Wait . . . have you ever heard of Scott Yanoff? What about Yahoo!? Well, of course, you've heard of Yahoo!—even if you've never been online before. Yahoo!'s URL is on everything nowadays . . . but that's a good thing, from a business and marketing point of view.

If I said "Yahoo!" 10 years ago, it would have been heard as a joyous exclamation. But, if I say "Yahoo!" today, most people automatically think of the Yahoo! Web site. This name is indelibly etched into our brains—that's the power of name branding. Name branding is extremely important, especially in a world filled with companies vying for users' attention. "Look at my Web site. No, look at *my* Web site." No, look into creating a tool that will help create brand awareness. Something like an e-mail publication.

The word *lockergnome* has no inherent meaning. Or, at least, it didn't when I first started using it as a nickname in high school or as an online BBS handle. When I eventually decided to publish information online, I had difficulty coming up with a good title. I didn't want to choose a word (or part of a word) that had been overused. When a friend suggested that I use Lockergnome, I knew immediately that it would work. Uniqueness counts, especially online.

I don't have the biggest e-mail newsletter in the world, but by the time all is said and done, the word *Lockergnome* will mean something. Heck, I suppose it already means something for tens of thousands of people. I can only imagine what it'll be like a few short years from now. No matter what name *you* choose, your goal is to brand your title/name in the minds of Internet users if you're using it in an e-mail publication. The more they see it, the more they'll trust you.

What's in a name? What can name branding do for you? Ask the folks at Yahoo!. You can't turn anywhere nowadays without seeing the word *Yahoo!* on an object, magazine, or television commercial. You could use it in conjunction with just about anything and it would attract attention.

Such a Tool

The printing press was one awesome invention. Of course, it's also to blame for all those silly textbooks I had to read in high school. The telephone was another pretty sweet creation. But then again, telemarketers have been trying to sell me a subscription to *Doorknobs Monthly* for years. The world is filled with powerful communications tools, and rest assured, each one of them is used (and, unfortunately, abused).

E-mail is the world's latest (but I'm not going to say greatest) broadcasting instrument. It has been in the mainstream for only a few years now, but it has been extremely effective in changing the way people interact with others on a global scale. It's easy, somewhat fun, and most important, affordable. I just hope e-mail stays that way . . . at least for the next 50 years or so. While it's true that not everybody has an e-mail address today, in a few years, when the Internet is even more tightly woven into our daily tasks, people won't be able to live without one.

No wasted paper, no busy signals, no international boundaries. E-mail is an incredible tool, but its importance has been sadly overlooked. I have found no better (or easier) way to get my ideas across to people from around the world.

When the world starts accepting electronic publishing as a profitable, legitimate, and respectable venue, you'll see smaller e-zine publishers leading the way in terms of innovation, creativity, and popularity. They've been doing it for years and will continue to do so for years to come. Good news: It's never too late to join the ranks!

Chapter Four

How to Communicate without Spamming

I've seen sworn pacifists turn into bloodthirsty beasts right before my very eyes. There's no better way to upset a person than by sending him an unsolicited e-mail message. This is also known as junk e-mail . . . or spam. Obviously, it's impossible to distribute processed lunchmeat electronically at this time (and hopefully it'll never happen). Junk e-mail gained this label in the newsgroups a few years ago, when advertisements started to be posted to unrelated newsgroups. It was all junk . . . and unfortunately, individuals are still doing it. My question is: *Why?*

Spam is annoying, everybody hates it, and nobody reads it. So why do start-up Internet businesses (and even experienced ones) think that it's okay to broadcast unsolicited advertisements in the newsgroups or in people's Inboxes? Think of the dumbest person you personally know and take his stupidity times 27. That's about how smart spammers are. If that's not a fact, I dare you to find out how quickly your reputation will become tarnished if you venture down this dark path.

Everybody knows that sinking feeling—when you see that you're receiving 10 new e-mail messages and then you discover that 9 of those messages are spam. If you've never received junk e-mail, you've apparently never been online; I've yet to meet a user who hasn't received at least one piece of unsolicited e-mail. Spammers have found a variety of ways to get e-mail addresses illegally and/or unethically. If you have ever posted your address somewhere public, forget about having a spam-free life.

I can't think of one good reason why anybody would want to purchase a list of "five million and one" addresses that had been extracted from the newsgroups, Web pages, and so on. They're largely unqualified, uninterested users who would gladly give their right leg just to beat you into a bloody pulp.

And I'm not exaggerating; people get very passionate about this topic—for good reason.

Don't Stay Silent

The very first thing on your list should be to get in touch with all your service providers to let them know what you plan on doing. This list includes (but is not limited to) your local ISP, on whom you rely for your Internet connection; your Web-site host, who is most likely running your mail (POP3) server; and your list host, which will be the company that enables you to distribute your e-publication (as well as provides subscription database storage).

If any one of those contacts doesn't agree with what you're doing, find a new one for that particular service. You need all three of those providers supporting you 100 percent of the way. If there's any doubt, throw them out. In the long run, you'll be much safer from false accusations and repercussions if you inform and actually demonstrate (to your service providers) what you're doing online. Invite these contacts to ask questions and subscribe to your list, show to them how you're taking steps to ensure legitimacy, notify them of any major changes in your subscription policies, and so on. To make a long story short: You *must* keep them in the loop.

Just about every legitimate e-mail publisher has been wrongly accused of distributing junk e-mail messages. Instead of contacting you directly, offended users will probably get in touch with any or all of your service providers. If your service providers know you and trust that you're not doing anything on the sly, they're going to defend your position and inform the whistle-blowers that they are incorrect in their assumption. My providers have gone to bat for me more than once, and that kind of support is priceless.

Failure to communicate with any provider directly or indirectly involved with your e-publication could result in an abrupt termination of service without notification. I've known certain lists to be shut down for months because someone on the other end didn't realize what was going on. That's obviously not a good thing for you or your satisfied subscribers. You can get your free "nonspammer insurance" by simply opening up the lines of communication. Pardon my bluntness, but you're a fool if you don't. I take incorrect accusations to heart; I don't want any of you to get blamed for something that you didn't do.

Don't Impose

Obviously, one of the primary things you can do to protect yourself from being incorrectly labeled as a junk e-mailer is to wait for people to subscribe to your service.

Don't force yourself into users' Inboxes unless they invite you first. Remember, the Inbox is a very sacred place to them. Wait for them to sign up for your e-publication. The easiest (and best) way to get subscribers is to publicize the offer on your Web site, and let related Web-site and list owners know what you're doing.

When I'm talking to people "on the street" about Lockergnome, oftentimes they'll ask me to add them to the list. I won't do it—never have, never will. I can never be accused of directly signing up anyone for my service. I wait for people to come to me. It may take a while, but I want to be 100 percent positive when I tell people that I don't personally add people to my databases. Now, a friend or enemy may sign up someone for my newsletter, but that's not my fault—you can't blame me for someone else's improper actions.

Don't Buy

A database of qualified subscribers cannot be purchased—that's a fact. If anybody tells you otherwise, he doesn't know his lips from his belly button. Your money will be better spent on other things (like advertising, marketing, and/or candy bars). People who sell e-mail address databases are often referred to as *list brokers*. Believe it or not, this business is very lucrative (and legitimate).

Have you ever filled out a warranty card and been asked whether you wanted to receive "more stuff" through e-mail and/or snail mail? Legally, a company can turn your contact information over to a list broker—and who knows what the broker will use it for. You've indicated to "the world" (knowingly or not) that you're interested in getting more stuff . . . so you're inadvertently giving companies the go-ahead to send you stuff that you'll (most likely) see as junk e-mail. You asked for it without actually asking for it. Scary, huh?

Then you have people on the other end of the spectrum who believe that it's totally okay to use any given e-mail address for any given reason at any given time—with or without your permission. If they see your e-mail address somewhere on the Web, in a chat room, on a mailing list, or in the newsgroups, your Inbox will never be the same. They might use your information for their own needs, but most likely, they're collecting these addresses for spammers to use.

You may hear the term *opt-in* often used; when someone requests to join a list, he is opting in. However, *opt-in lists* are a different story altogether. Companies set up Web sites that appear to offer you a ton of newsletters covering a variety of topics. This business is completely legitimate and straightforward, but the average user doesn't have a clue. The only reason that opt-in lists exist is so that the companies who collect addresses for those opt-in lists can turn around and sell them to advertisers. But that's not the worst of it.

My suggestion is to avoid the purchasing of e-mail databases altogether—especially if you're a start-up company. Consumers are more likely to think of smaller companies as spammers, so unless you have a name for yourself, don't give people a reason to place the blame on you. Once you've done something questionable, it's on your permanent record.

Don't Use Certain Words

In the subject line of a message, a few words, characters, and conventions tip me off to the message being spam: *Money, sex, girls, free, opportunity, sale, power, powerful, new, invest, investment, maximize, profit, buy,* and *special* are the words (in no particular order); dollar signs and exclamation marks are the symbols; and if the subject line is written in ALL CAPS, I delete it without thinking twice. This is by no means a comprehensive list. And, of course, I'm not suggesting that having any of those words or symbols in the subject line means a message is junk e-mail. But I've seen them far too many times not to recognize the pattern. Some spammers will go as far as to use a more "personal" subject line: "I saw you the other day," "This weekend," "Was that you?" and so on. They're hoping I'll open their message and consequently call their number and order their products. Silly, silly people.

Your workaround when sending your own messages is simply to avoid using those words, symbols, and tactics. As an added measure for optimal recognition, I strongly suggest inserting the name of your company and/or publication in the subject line of a message before writing anything else. For instance, I used to have three random (but interesting) words in my subject line—all of which could be found somewhere in that particular issue. But before I listed those words in the subject line, I inserted "Lockergnome" surrounded by brackets. The subject line would appear as such: [**Lockergnome**] **Cartoons, Clocks, & Chocolate Cokes.** You can use just about any regular keyboard symbol to offset your own publication title (again, except for exclamation marks or dollar signs, which have been overused by spammers). You're limited only by your own creativity.

Don't Hide

Who are you? Why are you trying to sell me something? Where are you from? Why is this happening to me? We all ask these questions as unwilling recipients of junk e-mail, but the answers are never to be found.

In your own e-mailings, use your real name, if possible. Not only will it show your subscribers that you're easily accessible, but it will also make them aware that you're a "human being" and not just another employee in the cold, corporate world. If using your real name is too much to ask, then make one up. There's nothing wrong with a pseudonym, as long as you use it consistently in conjunction with your e-publication.

Spam messages usually include "traditional" contact information, including phone numbers, FAX numbers, and P.O. boxes. Very seldom will you see a spammer posting a Web or e-mail address in a mailing. That could be a fatal mistake for them; their online presence would be easily identified, and they could be kicked offline by their Web host or connection provider. So, if you post your Internet contact information (Web site and/or e-mail address) close to the top of your mailing, you're at least showing who you are and where you're coming from.

But be careful. . . .

Don't Invite Removals

There has been a great debate among e-zine publishers as to where unsubscribe directions should be placed within a mailing. Most put directions toward the end of the message, a few place them in the upper-middle, and a handful actually put the instructions at the beginning. People have tried putting the directions in different places and found, by and large, that there was no difference in the number of unsubscribe requests. Besides, you could make an entire newsletter about unsubscribing directions, and you'd still get users asking you how to do it.

You're going to get people who can't spell, too. Some users tried to pass off *unsubibe*, *unskabribe*, *unscibe*, and *unpibspibe* as *unsubscribe*. Those "words" (if you could call them that) were taken directly from actual requests I received for removal from Lockergnome. Don't laugh . . . it's not funny. You're going to see the same kind of thing, I guarantee it. The unsubscribe directions—no matter where they happen to be placed—need to be extremely clear.

Personally, I throw the unsubscribe directions at the bottom of every mailing. It's out of the way, but not completely hidden; it's the last thing users would read in an issue. Why invite them to remove themselves from your mailing before they even have a chance to read it? You're indirectly telling them that your stuff isn't worthy enough for their Inbox. Nothing could be further from the truth, I hope.

A common "spam message header" that appears at the top of certain mailings might look like this:

Per Section 301, Paragraph (a) (2) (C) of S.1618, further transmissions to you by the sender of this e-mail may be stopped at no cost to you by ending a reply to this e-mail address with the word "remove" in the subject line. Under Bill S.1618 TITLE III passed by the 105th U.S. Congress this letter can not be considered spam as long as we include the way to be removed.

Who do these guys think they're kidding?

One of the most clever spammer tricks is to immediately tell you how to unsubscribe from their list. The message says that all you need to do is reply to the message or send an e-mail to a certain address and you'll be removed. Well, sometimes those addresses go nowhere, and other times they return to the spammer. Now, that spammer probably purchased a list of addresses and wasn't sure which ones were "alive" and which ones were dead. Chances are, the average person will want to be removed from any/all unsolicited mailings, so he'll reply and let the spammer know that he doesn't want any more. The spammer then takes the user's reply and puts it in the "address still working" pile . . . which eventually becomes a new "cleaner" e-mail database.

I never reply to spam, and I don't suggest that you do, either. You could very well be saying to the e-mail abuser that you've still got a valid address. Nevertheless, if you decide to place your unsubscribe instructions at the top of the newsletter, be very careful with your wording. And, if at all possible with your list software, let the users know which e-mail address that issue has been mailed to. One thing's for sure . . . don't tell them outright that "this isn't spam." You're right, it might not be spam, but don't tell the users what your e-publication isn't. They'll see the word "spam," and the next sound your message will hear is the click of a button as they press the Delete key.

Don't Wait

You have your topic, you have your Web site, you have your content, you have your subscribers, but do you have your International Standard Serial Number? Just as books have ISBNs, e-publications can have ISSNs. Once you've applied for and received the ISSN for your electronic serial, I recommend using it wherever possible (most likely, at the top of each mailing, along with the obligatory header information). If people accuse you of spamming them, you can point out the fact that you're an officially registered electronic publication. They may not believe you, but at least you've got the number to show for it. Those who do know and understand what the ISSN is will view you in a different, more respectable light. The application for an ISSN is free, and turnaround time is usually a couple of weeks. For more information, refer to Appendix C.

Don't Sell

If you're going to broadcast a brief message to your subscribers, don't attempt to sell anything in that space. Be explicit and clearly explain why you're mailing them (especially when you normally don't distribute small messages). If necessary, direct them to a Web page for more information.

Sadly, I'm starting to see more e-mail newsletters being distributed that are 70 percent advertisement, 20 percent useless fluff, and 10 percent content. What's wrong with this picture? Wiser subscribers will drop you like a hot potato after receiving a couple of issues if this is your regular format. Yes, it's okay to make money from your e-publication, but you need to be very careful. When you inundate the users with advertisements, they won't be around for very long. Besides that, they're probably not going to click on any link you provide. So what good has that advertising done you? Stringing more than a couple of ads in a row is usually not wise.

When a nonpersonal e-mail message doesn't have much usable content within it, a user will see it as junk—and view *you* as a spammer. So, if you're going to go with an advertising model for your e-publication, don't overdo it.

Enable Verification

When people sign up for your list, you should send them a few e-mail messages to confirm that they have been added. If you really want to add more precautions, you might be able to set up your mailing-list software to automatically verify that the new subscriber truly wants to be added to your list. When they sign up on your Web page (or through an e-mail autoresponder), your list software will send them a confirmation message. They'll reply to that message, and only then will they be added to your subscription database. This solution pretty much kills the "friend signs up an unaware friend or enemy" problem. However, it will also have an impact on your subscription count. Not everybody will respond to that confirmation message, and accordingly, will not be added to your list. But at least the subscribers have taken a second action and affirmed that they wanted to be included in your mailings.

The first document that users should receive upon joining a list is one that contains introductory information. Encourage readers to save this message for future reference. It should explain what list they've joined, what information the list provides, what their subscribed address happens to be, how to unsubscribe, how to resubscribe, and how to contact you.

The Nonbelievers

You're sending out an assumedly legitimate publication, so if certain users don't want to be on your list, don't try to convince them otherwise. They'll call you every dirty name in the book and swear up and down that you have the worst e-publication on the planet. That's probably not the case (and you know that), but you're dealing with upset nonbelievers. If they want to be removed from your database, then just remove them. The process should take no time at all, and their ramblings shouldn't bother you a bit. Why would you want to waste your time, energy, and money on sending your publication to someone who you *know* is not going to read it?

The longer nonbelievers remain on your list and receive (in their own minds) unsolicited messages, the more disgruntled they will become. Keeping disgruntled users on your list could turn into a major problem down the road; you never know who you're upsetting, and more important, who *they* know.

Dressing Up

Junk e-mail looks like junk. Seriously, I've seldom seen a spam message that didn't look like it fell out of the ugly tree and hit every branch on its way down. If you don't want to be seen as a spammer, then don't forget to have an attractive, easy-to-follow format. If your e-publication appears to have been thrown together at the last minute, replete with errors and glaring formatting no-nos, the users won't be able to read what you've written without getting a headache. (If your e-zine covers head trauma, you'll be set. But let's assume you've chosen another topic to tackle.)

Association Guilt

If you hang out with bank robbers on a regular basis, you have a strong chance of being perceived as a bank robber, too . . . even if you've never robbed a bank. The same theory applies online. If you're working with a certain sponsor (advertiser), associate program, or another company that has been known to tolerate and propagate the delivery of junk e-mail, you're going to be guilty by association. Heck, even if the jury is still out on a company, you need to be careful. If a company's or individual's service smells fishy to you, by all means: throw it back.

Yes, your stuff may be perfect. But nothing will tarnish your image and reputation quicker than if you're involved (to any degree) with a company or individual who might be seen in industry circles as untrustworthy, unfaithful, or hypocritical.

In 1997, I was contacted by a company that also ran a couple of somewhat popular mailing lists. This company wanted to help me sell advertisements in Lockergnome. I needed some sort of professional ad sales at the time, and these guys were the first to approach me. While they were able to place a handful of ads in my newsletter, to this day I haven't received a check from them. They assured me that payments were en route, but I know the U.S. postal system isn't *that* slow. It wasn't a large enough sum of money to even whine over, so I dismissed the incident quickly and moved on.

I'm a trusting sort. (My Iowan upbringing is probably to blame for that.) The president of that company approached me again a few months later and asked whether I wanted to work on a project with them. I was skeptical, but I decided to take the chance—you know, just in case this would turn into something bigger for me. I helped them launch a new discussion group, and the list was heavily advertised in Lockergnome because of my deep involvement with it.

Within a few days of its maiden issue, I was offering constructive criticism regarding the list's operation. I kept making suggestions for possible improvements and tweaks for the first couple of weeks. Then, out of the blue, the president of the company sent me a rather nasty e-mail. He said something along the lines of: "You're becoming a real pain to work with; you're complaining too much about things. I don't want to work with you anymore on this project. Oh, and, by the way . . . we only gained 2,000 members from your *alleged* database of 60,000."

Now let me point out a couple of problems with his message. He was upset because only 3 percent of my user base decided to join his list. While our two publications were similar in focus, they were operated in different ways. (Mine was an e-mail newsletter dependent on my writing skills, whereas his was a discussion list dependent on member participation.) Not everyone is interested in receiving or being involved with discussion lists, and apparently he didn't take this into account. Beyond that, a conversion rate of anything over 5 percent is considered above average (online).

Then, by using the word *alleged* in his description of my database, he was pretty much daring me to prove him wrong—by openly showing him my list of subscribers. He knew exactly what he was doing (and for a split second, I considered sending him the list so that I wouldn't lose face). But I'm smarter than that. Who knows what he and his company would have used my database for? Once your list loses its integrity, you're sunk. Protect that subscriber database from prying eyes with your *life*.

Only after I completely severed my ties with this other mailing-list company did people step forward to inform me that these guys weren't to be trusted. Had my relationship continued with them, who knows how my reputation would have suffered? Yes, the average user is not going to know the difference between a "good" and "bad" mailing-list company, but *you* should know the difference. Your e-zine's survival depends on the strategic business partnerships you forge.

Association Reassurance

The Coalition Against Unsolicited Commercial E-mail is a nonprofit group of individuals, content providers, and various companies who are determined to stop irresponsible electronic commerce. By joining this alliance, your visitors and subscribers will see that you're part of a volunteer-based, anti-spam movement. You can find a sign-up form and more information at http://www.cauce.org/. Membership is free.

Just because you've joined **CAUCE** doesn't mean you're in the clear, however; you need to demonstrate in your words, actions, and interactions that your motives are pure. It takes months (and sometimes years) to build trust.

You don't have very much time with the potential subscribers. You need to prove to people that you're not going to turn around and sell, use, or misuse their e-mail address. I have a very simple policy on my Web site, and it's worked thus far: "If something bad ever happens with the Lockergnome list, I'll gouge out my own eyes with a rusty spoon." It's a little extreme, but I think you get the picture.

Still want to provide a little more peace of mind? Swing by http://www.truste.org/ and pay to display a **TRUSTe** logo on your site. While this organization wasn't specifically designed to eliminate spam, privacy issues could potentially be squelched by showing your readers that you can be trusted with their personal information. TRUSTe has a recognizable name and logo on the Web; their approval adds legitimacy to your Internet services.

Understand, though, that in the minds of new and potential subscribers, your validity is going to be in question from the very beginning. Unless people subscribe to your list because of a friend's recommendation, they are not going to know you from Adam. Getting people to *want* to subscribe is indeed a chore, but that's nothing compared to the task of keeping them on as satisfied subscribers.

Chapter Five

E-mail and Web Sites—Natural Partners

We've established that while most people have Web sites, very few of them have e-mail publications. If you want to put all the content up on your Web site, I'm not going to stop or discourage you. However, are you honestly expecting every one of your visitors to return again and again, day after day, week after week?

You *know* that not all surfers will like what they see at your site. And out of those who do really like what you have to offer, how many will remember to come back? And even if they *do* remember to come back, how often will it be? What if they're sick for a while and miss out on something important that came and went on your Web site? If only there were a better way to keep your audience informed of your site's changes.

But what if your Web site had something that people could sign up for (with their e-mail address)? Then, every time you added something new to your site (like products, news articles, or links), you could broadcast a message informing them of the changes. You could even insert direct URLs to any one of your Web pages. Now there's an idea. Why didn't somebody else think of that before now?

You're saying to yourself, "I already did." Well, duh. Lots of people "already did." The way to ensure return visits to your site is by giving surfers an easy, accessible way to be notified of any changes. E-mail is the best possible way to keep a reader base informed of Web-site updates. Don't count on anybody to come looking for updates on his own.

Since it's important to have a Web site as a companion for your e-publication, this chapter will help you focus on creating a winning one.

What Will Visitors Do?

A user can typically join a mailing list in one of two ways: through e-mail or through a form on a Web page. While it's wise to publicize your list's "subscribe address" wherever possible, you should also have an accompanying Web site. It isn't mandatory, but I strongly recommend it. Even though most of your business is going to be handled via e-mail, how else are people going to get more information on your services? Yes, you can always set up autoresponders to handle the rudimentary explanations, but how are people going to initially discover you on the Internet?

Offliners will tell you that they want to get online for a couple of basic reasons: to send e-mail to friends and relatives and/or to surf the Web for information. It goes without saying that they're going to check their e-mail, but then what? Then it's time to fire up that old Web browser and look for something interesting.

"Ya know, my friend was telling me about aglets the other day . . . he's out of town right now. I wonder if there's more information somewhere about those things that are affixed to the ends of your shoelaces?" The guy looks around the Web for a little while, does a couple of searches, and finally pulls up the Flying Teddy Bear Aglet site. At that point, he's probably going to have all his aglet questions answered. But will he visit the site again? What's his motivation to return? How could the site owner keep him aware of any new aglet news?

What's in a Name?

I've yet to meet someone who didn't like anything of high quality. It stands to reason, then, that surfers are constantly scanning the Web for "good stuff." And you want your Web site to fall into that category in people's minds.

A company's URL is often reflective of the products or services it offers. A company with a URL like www.mrspatula.com will get much more respect as a gourmet cookie seller than, say, http://www.sprintway.com/~joe/stuff/spatula/. If you want your business to be seen as an entity to be taken seriously, you need to have your own domain name. Period. You can get by with using free Web services for a little while, but over time, without a "real" URL, businesses and other electronic content publishers might not give you the respect you deserve.

Believe it or not, some really good domain names have yet to be spoken for. This is another good reason you need to be thinking about a unique title for your e-publication. Uniqueness will pretty much ensure that your "dot com" hasn't already been taken. In fact, I wouldn't bother settling on a particular business name or title unless there was a "dot com" available for it.

The overall tone of the name that you choose is also important. Let's say you needed to find a good lawyer (one who doesn't rebill you on already-paid invoices). You discover only two listed in the Yellow Pages: Law Guys R Us and Jones & Gary Law Offices. Knowing full well that you'll need a certified, intelligent, knowledgeable person at your side when you go to dispute a case, which set of attorneys are you going to contact first? The lawyers at Law Guys R Us might be infinitely more qualified to handle your case, but you're probably not going to turn to them because their name doesn't sound very professional. If you would have turned to them first, close this book and seek professional counseling immediately.

Out to Lunch

I've been asked several times how I'm able to generate hundreds of new subscriptions for Lockergnome in a single day. I believe that it's partly because I have a good Web site to help me promote Lockergnome.

> **NOTE**
>
> *You might be wondering, "What about 'dot net' or 'dot org' or any of the other domain hierarchies?" They are fine (and I'm sure other dot-somethings will be available someday too), but everybody . . . everybody thinks in "dot com." "Dot net" sites are often overlooked by newbies. Instead of www.flyingteddybearaglets.net, a user would be inclined to look for www.flyingteddybearaglets.com. Unless you have a million-dollar budget, it will be hard to get people to notice a "dot net" site. "Dot com" has become so universal that the "com" is almost implied. Will this trend change? I don't know; I can't predict the future of domain name preferences. But until it does change, you don't want to be at an immediate disadvantage by having an address other than "something dot com."*

Let's leap into a restaurant analogy at this point. Joe Spatula is the world's greatest blueberry pancake chef. Both casual diners and crepe connoisseurs know that his special secret blend of flour and berries is extremely tasty. Mr. Spatula recently opened his first restaurant in the heart of a very busy city. He spent all his money and time getting the right tools for his kitchen. However, his entrance and dining area were beyond atrocious; tablecloths were torn, seats were missing legs, windows were broken, and worst of all—his menu had terrible misspellings (ever had a pencake before?).

People knew that his flapjacks were fantastic, but who on Earth would come into a place that looked that bad? "Oh, it's rustic," the regular patrons might rationalize. Yeah, but I don't want to lose my appetite before I eat. "His kitchen is state-of-the-art, with a microwave that'll even announce the time every half hour!" But who sees the kitchen when he's in a restaurant? "They're good pancakes!" But unless you already know about them, there's no way in h-e-double-hockey-sticks you're going to set foot in his establishment.

Can you extrapolate from this story the reason to have a nice looking Web site? No, you don't need all the fancy gadgets, any spectacular scripts, or even a gigabyte's worth of graphics to impress visitors. If the site is visually appealing, presents information concisely and thoroughly, and appears to offer what the users want, you're going to have lots of "orders from the menu." But too many site designers are out to lunch.

You want visitors to your Web site to think you're better (i.e., bigger, more successful, more experienced) than you actually are. Think about all those "important" businesspeople who are actively searching the Web for new relationships to develop. It's feasible that they will eventually stumble upon your site and/or e-publication. Their initial reaction will remain with them forever. "Looks like good stuff, but it's presented very unprofessionally" is *not* the impression you want to make.

Every day I see sites that have lots of potential, but the owners don't know how to code (HTML) very well. Having a unique, attractive site design is what gets your foot in the door. Get into the surfer's mind-set for a second: Would you be more likely to trust a company that had a bland, uninformative, unimaginative Web site over one that had an eloquent, descriptive, eye-catching, respectable one? The answer should be a no-brainer.

Take a look at what your peers are doing. There's no reason why your stuff shouldn't be better.

The Not-So-National Archives

When users sign up for your list, they're going to begin receiving issues from that moment onward (unless they unsubscribe). But what about all the other issues that were distributed before a particular subscriber had the opportunity to join? If you don't have an easy-to-peruse past issue archive set up on your site yet, do it immediately.

Not only will existing subscribers appreciate the chance to rifle through those missives, but potential subscribers will get a better idea about the kind of information you have to present. If you want to offer your content only through e-mail, that's fine. But think about those individuals who would rather see your stuff on a Web site. And consider those who want to place a link to a particular issue of yours. You might also want to set up a localized search engine for your archives so that users can find specific information.

I frequently refer my subscribers to the Lockergnome archives when replying to their e-mail queries. I don't have time to answer every question, and most of them are requests for certain types of programs that I might have covered in the past. I've got a generic signature file that tells them specifically where to look. I'm (hopefully) helping those readers answer their own questions as well as driving traffic back to my site.

Depending on which package you use, your mailing-list software could be set up to e-mail past issues directly to members using certain commands. Autoresponders work great in this situation, too. (An autoresponder is simply an e-mail address you can set up to automatically return a "form letter" document to the person who e-mailed it.)

Form Fumbles

The obligatory item on your Web site should be at least one form for new subscriptions. How else are people going to subscribe to your e-mail publication? Yes, it's possible to bypass a form completely by adding a direct e-mail link to your list's subscription address, but individuals might specifically be looking for some type of form when they first arrive. If they can't find it, they might not sign up.

This brings up another point: Don't bury that form!

When the Lockergnome Web site was first designed, the subscription form was three pages "down." First, the visitors would see Lockergnome's mission statement and basic product information; then they clicked on a link to get even *more* detailed information; and then they clicked on yet *another* link to fill out the form. Subscription rates were okay (not amazingly high, but adequate). With the first revision, the forms were moved up one page so that they would be only one click away. The subscription rates were visibly impacted by that change (nothing earth-shattering, but the difference was noticeable).

In our third site revision, we decided to move the subscription forms to the main page. This is what we should have done all along. (But at that time, there were no books on how to do this stuff. You're lucky to be learning from our mistakes.) The subscription rate went up again. However, we hadn't tweaked the form's position yet on that main page. The users had to scroll down to view and fill out the forms, and that was a little more work than was necessary. I asked my friend Michael what I could do to boost subscriptions, and he pretty much told me the obvious. Well, it was obvious to the rest of the world, but not me.

Michael told me that surfers should see everything of importance within the first screen (without having to scroll down). I replied, "Oh, so you're saying that if I move my subscription form to the top of the screen, more people will subscribe? Holy cow, why didn't I think of that!?" Since then, one of the first things people see on Lockergnome's site is that subscription form. There's no better place to have it . . . with one exception.

Easier Access

As time has progressed, Lockergnome's Web site has grown (in page count). Your site will probably progress in much the same way. Don't try to do everything at once or think that once you've done it, you're done *with* it. A new trick is always right around the corner. Perhaps you'll see a site (or e-mail publication) providing functionality that seems to work, and you'll want to implement something similar with your own content right away. Or maybe you'll just get hit with a sudden stroke of genius (which won't happen all that often).

For instance, a few months ago I started thinking that while Lockergnome's site had been more popular lately, the subscription rates hadn't changed all that much. What was the problem? I had great content, a decent design, and enough pages to fill a 10-pound catalog. Now, directly, those aren't problems. However, the only subscription form on the entire Lockergnome site was located on the main page. That meant that if users were surfing along and pulled up a page other than the main one, they might never subscribe. Oops.

Within seconds, I was pounding out a new footer for all the pages on my site. Right now, at the bottom of every Lockergnome page, you'll see a subscription form that people can use to sign up for my e-mail newsletters. I'm still kicking myself for the thousands of people I lost by not doing that in the very beginning; several visitors have used the "bottom" form instead of the "main" form.

Scripting Headaches

While you don't need to know or understand HTML entirely to get a subscription form up and running on your site, experienced users will probably have an easier time with this than will novices. I don't want to get into the nitty-gritty of designing and implementing Web-site forms (please see Chapter 12 in the book *Poor Richard's Web Site* for basic form creation). However, understand that there's more than one way to skin a cat. I'll remind you again that it's okay to post a direct e-mail link to your list's *subscribe* address (which might look something like join-listname-here@list.mrspatula.com).

You might hear people talking about CGI (Common Gateway Interface) scripts. They run on a Web server and are platform-independent mini-applications that perform specific tasks. CGI scripts work great for adding or removing subscribers to or from your database. Once you get those scripts up and running, that is. If you can't program, I suggest either finding a CGI (or Perl) programmer, asking your Web-site host to help you create a custom subscription form, or searching the Internet for a public domain CGI script archive. The site http://www.servers.nu/ offers a few "remotely operated" scripts for you to use; they can't be customized, per se, but if you're having difficulties locating other CGI resources, this site might help. Somehow you have to find a way to give the subscribers the ability to subscribe from your site.

When Lockergnome started, I couldn't find a CGI subscription script, so I had to use an e-mail form instead. Understand that when you reference an e-mail address instead of a CGI script in a Web-site form, the data that a user enters will be e-mailed to that specific e-mail address. This gets the job done, but you have to receive and deal with each request in your e-mail program. This is a pain in the ASCII. You'll also (most likely) have to add the e-mail addresses to your list database manually—this will be *extremely* time-consuming. If you do use an e-mail form, be sure to include the `enctype="text/plain"` attribute. This will ensure that all extended codes will not be included in the submitted input. Otherwise, you'll receive a message with data intertwined with gobbledygook. An example of a correctly formatted e-mail form would look something like this:

```
<form method="post" action="mailto:latenight@mrspatula.com"
enctype="text/plain">
```

You Talkin' to Me?

If you choose not to use a form to allow people to subscribe to your e-mail publication, you're missing out on huge opportunities. Not only can surfers enter whichever e-mail address they choose (instead of their default address, which might be sent along with a direct e-mail link), but they can answer other important questions. When you're working on an advertising-based model, your potential sponsors are going to want to know your audience's demographic breakdown: age, gender, geographic location, occupation, education level,

---

CAUTION

Asking too many questions up front can easily turn a user away from you. The fewer questions a surfer has to answer, the more likely he is going to answer them honestly. Exceptions to this might be when a user is registering a purchased product or entering a contest. Keep the questions to a minimum. You can always ask him to fill out a survey for you after he's been subscribed for a little while.

annual income, and so on. You can ask for this information on the subscription form.

The form you use will need to have a field for the subscribers to enter their e-mail addresses. This is pretty much mandatory with e-mail publications. Another field suggestion (my personal favorite) is a *reference point*. Ask the wannabe-subscribers how they found out about your site and/or publication. Not everyone will fill in this field (you don't need to make it mandatory), and not everyone will answer truthfully. However, you'll find that a majority of surfers will tell you how they discovered you. You can then follow up with that information and apply it to potential business strategies.

Say you keep getting surfers coming in from the "Malcolm's Moxy Mongooses" site. Who is this guy, and how is he pointing people in your direction? Upon doing a search for *malcolm moxy mongooses*, you might pull up his site and discover that he's linking to your site. Well, that was awfully nice of him, wasn't it? The first thing you should do is e-mail Malcolm and thank him for the link. Then see whether there's anything else that your sites and/or e-mail publications can do together— especially if you have a mongoose-related resource.

> **TIP**
>
> *If you want to know more about a user's background without asking too many personal questions, ask for his postal code (known as ZIP code in the United States). By disclosing his geographical location, a visitor will also be providing his general socioeconomic background (albeit inadvertently). Such information would be wanted (and oftentimes needed) by advertising agencies.*

If the users don't want to answer a question, don't force them to do so. Privacy is still a hot topic. And, of course, if you're going to collect personal information, don't share it with people not involved in your business.

About Face

Certain logos (or symbols) are associated with most successful brand names and products. You're going to want one, too. Having one isn't mandatory, but it'll enable you to start building an association between a "picture" and your product. This association will become more important over time, as more and more sites learn about your e-mail publications. You'll be able to offer other sites a unique graphic to use for linking to your site. It can be of any size, but the industry standard seems to be 88 pixels wide by 31 pixels high (otherwise known as *an 88x31*). If fitting your logo into that space is impossible, don't sweat it—just do the best you can. But you need to start with a logo—a very recognizable, unique logo. It doesn't have to be fancy; it just has to be usable in a variety of situations (business cards, Web-site graphics, invoices, etc.).

Planning on mailing your e-zine in HTML? The logo should be in there somewhere. It will provide the readers with another recognizable reference to your Web site. The format of your HTML newsletter should also be very reflective of the style of your Web site (fonts, colors, graphics, etc.). Note, however, that the HTML newsletter design does not have to look exactly like your Web site. Remember, you're trying to create and reinforce cohesion between your e-mail publication and your Web site. Uniformity is important to keep in mind, not only throughout your Web-site design, but also within the actual HTML newsletters.

Even if your e-mail publication is text-based, having a logo on your Web site is important. People will continually see your graphical presence on different Web sites that link to you and eventually decide to check you out (if they haven't done so before). Name recognition is important too, but a logo helps hammer the recognition home. Sites may change their design, fonts, colors, and so on, but their logo will generally remain the same. Nobody's forcing you to create a logo, but it's a wise suggestion that will help attract more Web-site surfers to your e-mail publication.

Oops, Wrong Number

You have to be very careful when you're pushing your agenda through e-mail. Sure, you're distributing new information to people, but nobody likes to be fed a sales pitch. If you're going to promote your products or site content through announcement lists or e-bulletins on a regular basis, give subscribers a good reason to read your mailings every single time. You might have stuff that needs to be sold, but a direct sales pitch isn't always the optimum technique. It's important for users to know that you *are* trying to sell products, but overkill (of any kind) will scare them away. If you don't give them consistent value, your e-broadcast is going to meet the dreaded delete-without-reading doom.

Subscribers might like your site, and they might like your newsletter, but if your publication sits in their Inbox for a few days without being touched, then something might be wrong. They might be busy . . . or too lazy to unsubscribe. Either way, they probably won't click on any links you've included in that mailing. Your subscriber numbers may be nothing short of phenomenal, but how many of your subscribers are active readers? Here's a quick way to tell: Include a link to a special page on your site, and publish that URL only in your bulletin. Try a few different tactics in a few different issues for the sake of argument (have one page offer a special discount, another page offer a free download, etc.). If you don't see much traffic to these pages within a day of your mailing, your other information is probably being ignored as well.

Consider adding a special "newsletter only" section, shortening/lengthening the message's content, or hiring new writers and/or editors. After you make a few major modifications, subscribers might sit up and take notice.

When you pick up the phone to dial a number, sometimes you dial incorrectly. What do you do then? Hang up and try again; it's never too late to change your ways.

Chapter Six

Configuring a Domain's E-mail Account

I know this chapter of the book is probably going to be dry, but I'll do my best to keep you lightly entertained—so don't stop reading or skip any chapters. Let's start out by reviewing some important terms that you're likely to encounter when configuring an e-mail account.

SMTP (Simple Mail Transfer Protocol): This is the modus operandi for transferring messages between servers. In other words, when you "send" an e-mail message, it's relayed via SMTP. When you set up your e-mail program, you'll need to specify an SMTP server; ask your ISP or Web-site host what that would be.

POP3 (Post Office Protocol version 3): This is the modus operandi for transferring messages from your server to your Inbox. In other words, when you "retrieve" e-mail from your server, it's relayed (moved, not copied) via POP3. You'll need to specify a POP3 server in your e-mail program as well. Sometimes the SMTP and POP3 servers will be the same. Again, check with your Web-site host or ISP for exact designations.

IMAP (Internet Message Access Protocol): Invented at Stanford University in 1986, this protocol, like POP3, is used when you're retrieving messages from your mail server. However, when you access your mailbox using IMAP, instead of deleting the messages upon retrieval, it retains a copy of them on the server. It'll pull in the headers first, and you can peruse, open, and/or delete the messages. (Once a message has been deleted on your computer, your e-mail program should also delete the copy sitting on the server.) IMAP is perfect for people who are traveling because they can check message headers quickly, download the messages they need to read, delete the ones they don't want, and keep a copy of everything not deleted on the server for when they return to their regular computer. IMAP is not as widely used as POP3 for message retrieval. While some e-mail clients will allow you to leave messages on the server while still using the POP3 protocol, IMAP will pull in only the headers so that you don't have to download an entire message if not desired. Beyond this, the IMAP folder hierarchy can be synchronized between the client and the server, and is fully (remotely) searchable. Not every mail server can handle IMAP, unfortunately; check with your Web-site host or ISP.

Web-Based E-mail versus POP3

Anybody can get a free Web e-mail address, with which you can send and receive e-mail through a Web page rather than through a real e-mail program. More and more businesses are starting to offer free Web e-mail accounts as a way to drive traffic back to their sites. It's not a bad idea for the companies providing them, but using such an account is not always ideal for the consumer.

The main advantage of using a POP3 account over a Web one is that with a POP3 account, you retain a copy of your messages on your own machine—your messages are not sitting on some Web mail server somewhere. That means you can read and write e-mail while offline, and then connect to the Internet when you are ready to send and receive. In contrast, if you're using a Web account, you have to log on to the Web mail page, wait for your account to download, read the messages online, compose a few messages online, and then disconnect. The ability to work on e-mail offline is very valuable, especially if your ISP charges you by the hour/minute, or if you're allotted a certain amount of "online time" for a given day, week, or month.

Web accounts have their benefits, too, however. They're great if you're on the go all the time because you can check your e-mail from anywhere. It's also nice to have a Web-based e-mail account to use as a backup, for times when your POP3 account is down temporarily. You can also use it if you need an extra e-mail address for testing purposes. But, if you're going to become a mailing-list manager, you'll have a much easier time with e-mail if you use an e-mail client (rather than a Web browser) as your primary e-mail management tool.

Choosing Your E-mail Provider

Let's assume you're going to be working with e-mail in a real e-mail program. The next question is: Which provider will you use for POP3/SMTP access? If you have only one ISP account and no separate host for your domain, the answer is obvious. You use what you have. But what if you have POP3/SMTP access through both your dial-up account (ISP) and your Web domain? My suggestion is that you forward all your local ISP e-mail automatically to your Web domain. The reasoning is straightforward: You may change ISPs because of moving, lower prices elsewhere, or any other given reason, but you'll probably own your domain name for the foreseeable future. Ever since I've secured the lockergnome.com domain, I've been telling people to send mail to that address.

The other good reason is directly related to how you might be perceived by subscribers, peers, and businesspeople. I'd much rather have someone see my lockergnome.com address than my Cedarnet one. (Cedarnet hosts one of my current e-mail accounts.) It's all a matter of presentation. Providing that your Web-domain host provides you with POP3/SMTP access, you should use it.

> **TIP**
>
> *It's a good idea to use a Web host that offers multiple POP3/SMTP mailboxes, as well as unlimited aliasing. That way, you can have more than one e-mail address for your domain name (for example, feedback@pirillo.com, help@pirillo.com, and so on).*

Electronic Alter Egos

When you were a kid (assuming that you're older now), did you ever have a nickname? When I was in the fifth grade, my dad told me that he wanted to name me Kit. After I heard that, I started asking people in my neighborhood to call me that. And whenever I was in a group of people with more than one Chris, I would always introduce myself as Kit. Later on (in college), after dying my hair red for the first time, people started calling me Cosmo. Well, I figured that Cosmo was a cool enough nickname to have, so I started to use that. After I started Lockergnome, some people started calling me Gnome. My fraternity brothers called me Apple. Okay, believe it or not, I'm actually going somewhere with this.

Now, when someone calls me Kit, I know that it's a person I met when I was younger. When someone calls me Cosmo, I know I met him while I was still in college. When someone calls me Gnome, I know I met that person after I started doing Lockergnome stuff. And, by the way, most of my close friends just call me Pirillo. I think my family members are the only ones who call me by my first name.

The point is this: I'm still the same person, but I can go by different names. E-mail aliases are similar. I own the lockergnome.com domain, and I have unlimited aliasing capabilities. This means I can make info@lockergnome.com mail bounce to the same mailbox as chris@lockergnome.com. I can have different types of messages sent to different mailboxes, depending on which alias they're addressed to—*advertise, joinhtml, jointext, iowa*, etc.—all @lockergnome.com. I use the *advertise* alias for advertising inquiries, and I use *iowa* for my regular Inquisitive Online Wonders and Advisories column. The *joinhtml* and *jointext* aliases are automatically forwarded to my list's subscription e-mail addresses. Not only do they look cleaner (joinhtml@lockergnome.com instead of join-lghtml-list@mylisthost.mrspatula.com), but if I ever change list providers, I'll have to change only the routing for those aliases. People will still use joinhtml or jointext, and they won't know the difference if or when I make the switch. This is another advantage of using aliases.

Most popular e-mail programs will allow you to sort your incoming mail into folders. This capability opens up a new way to use aliases to your advantage. I have my program set up to automatically send all subscriptions@lockergnome.com mails to a certain folder and all my submit@lockergnome.com mails to another one. My program will also show me how many new messages are in any particular folder, so I can tell that I received, for example, 13 submissions, 45 new subscribers, and 16 subscription-related inquires and bounces before looking at any of them.

You'll need to check with your Web host (assuming you have one) as to the configuration and editing of any e-mail aliases. Some Web hosts don't allow aliases in the first place (which is too bad, because this is a killer filtering device). I'm not going to tell you to keep shopping around until you find a host that offers the feature, but at least consider your options.

> **NOTE**
>
> *Since there are various types of servers, and various classes of virtual Web hosts, I'm not going to explain how to edit aliases on your specific account. For the most part, you should find all aliases to be set up within a simple text file; changing them doesn't take much effort. You now know what they are, so ask if you can use them.*

Advanced Aliasing Techniques

If you plan on placing advertisements in other e-mail publications, instead of using your "regular" subscription alias (like Lockergnome's joinhtml or jointext), consider creating a new, separate alias for that particular ad campaign. I might use dog-html@lockergnome.com if I were advertising in a dog-related e-zine, or leech-text@lockergnome.com if I had something in a discussion list on leeches. I would then be able to track the logs for those aliases to see what kinds of responses those particular ad buys (or trades) had. If you don't have access to your log files, this tactic won't do you any good. However, I wouldn't see a reason why your administrator wouldn't be able to show you any given statistic.

Don't be afraid to use your aliases in different places, either. On your business card, list a business alias—and publicize that address in no other place. If you are ever interviewed on radio or TV, create a special alias to give out for that appearance. Use your aliases to track how users find out about you.

You can set up some addresses to go to more than one person, too. I have set up advertise@lockergnome.com to be delivered to both myself and my current strategic business manager. Forwarding messages to multiple recipients can come in handy when you want to broadcast something simple to "everyone in the group" by mailing to one particular address (instead of CCing or BCCing individuals every single time). It's another one of those "Poor Man's Mailing List" things. However, I wouldn't put too many people on the same alias, and I wouldn't suggest running your mailing list through an alias, either. Since anyone can e-mail that address and have his message distributed to everyone in the alias, the chances of it being abused by an outside source are great. I wouldn't put more than a handful of people on any given alias, and I would put on the same alias only people who already know one another.

Setting Up Autoresponders

Not everybody has access to the Web; many people rely on e-mail for all their Internet interactions. If they want more information about your mailing list, how are you going to get it to them promptly and efficiently? While you can copy and paste from your Web page to an e-mail, automating the process by using an autoresponder is much easier.

You should be able to set up certain aliases to mail preformatted documents to individuals who request them via e-mail. For instance, if an autoresponder were set up for tellmemore@flyingteddybearaglets.com, when a person sent an e-mail to that address, tellmemore would automatically reply with predefined text. The idea is to help you automate the process of answering general and common questions.

CAUTION

It's important to remember that when information changes on your Web site, it should change in the autoresponder messages, too (if applicable).

I have not yet set up autoresponders for Lockergnome. Blame it on wanting to keep the "personal touch." I get asked hundreds of questions on a daily basis, but I'm not tech support. I simply copy a generic answer into the reply (an answer applicable for 99 percent of the questions I get asked) and hope that the recipient follows my advice.

A *signature* is predefined text that can be inserted at any point in your e-mail message. If your e-mail program can handle multiple signatures, you've already got a basic autoresponder available. It isn't completely automatic, but at least you'll save yourself some typing. When a common question needs to be answered, you can simply insert the appropriate signature.

> **TIP**
>
> *Here are some ideas of information to distribute via autoresponders: rate cards (for current advertising prices), general site information, general subscription information, past issues, or anything else you don't want to be bothered with.*

Shell: The Back Door to Your Mailbox

At times, you might not be able to retrieve e-mail from your POP3 mail account (because of temporary server problems). You might experience this problem if your account's disk quota has been exceeded or if the mail server is down. Your e-mail program might even be malfunctioning. Regardless, it's important to have more than one way to access your mailbox.

One form of alternative mail access is through what's called a *shell account*. It's basically a command line or text menu access to your mail server. If your Web host (or ISP) offers you the ability to "telnet" or dial in directly into your account (with a terminal program such as HyperTerminal in Windows), then you have shell access. Most services don't offer this capability anymore because a majority of individuals have no need for it and it poses a greater security risk than a TCP/IP connection.

If you *do* have shell access, be sure to ask the system administrator what e-mail programs can be accessed from it. Chances are, if you're set up on a UNIX server, you'll be able to use a program called *Pine* to access your e-mail through your shell account. When I run into mail problems with my e-mail program, the first thing I do is "shell out" into my Lockergnome account. Within minutes, I'm usually able to troubleshoot the problem. If the e-mail program through the shell account isn't responding, and your regular e-mail client isn't responding either, then it's most likely a mail server glitch. If the command line e-mail program is responding but your regular e-mail client is not, then something's apparently getting lost in the translation.

Whether or not you have shell access, you should browse your way over to the University of Washington's Pine Information Center and download a version of Pine for your computer (http://www.washington.edu/pine/). While versions of the program are available for UNIX, Windows, and DOS, you can find a link to a page for unofficial ports to other operating systems: BeOS, VMS, OS/2, Amiga, etc. Pine (which stands for Program for Internet News and E-mail) has been in development since 1989; while it isn't graphically driven, it works well. Think of it as an excellent troubleshooting tool for when you're having problems with accessing your e-mail. If nothing else, it makes a good secondary e-mail client.

NOTE

While the user interface is the same, the Windows or DOS version will run directly on your PC, whereas the UNIX version is run via a command prompt in a telnet session.

Chapter Seven

Subscription Management

Most subscriber databases are stored as simple text files, with one e-mail address per line. You can manage that list yourself, or you can delegate the job to a full-service list management company or one of your employees. Most of this chapter assumes that you plan on (for the time being, anyway) handling it yourself.

Some list software packages allow you to send administrative commands via e-mail, others through the Web . . . and some allow you to use either method. Since you'll probably be performing most of your list management on a virtual server from your personal computer, it is wise to find a method that you're very comfortable with using.

Upper Management

When users aren't able to unsubscribe themselves from your list, or bounces aren't being removed, or the list software doesn't check for duplicate addresses, then it's time for some good old-fashioned divine intervention, in which you take care of these things yourself.

Whenever you want to do something with your list, send commands to the list management software. This is most commonly done via e-mail. Even though a Web interface for your list management software might be available, you might find it quicker to formulate and issue your list requests in a "send immediately" text-based format.

> **NOTE**
>
> *If you're using a program on your own computer to manage your list of subscribers, then you'll need to refer to that program's documentation for subscription management procedures. However, it is more likely that you will be going through your ISP, Web host, or list host for your mailing-list management.*

Let's assume for a moment that you plan on handling the list management via e-mail. To do so, you send an e-mail addressed to the list management software containing special codes or commands that state your requests.

The commands you use will differ according to which list software you use, and may even differ according to the version of the software. You should consult the software documentation if you need guidance.

For a list of basic commands for ListProc, LISTSERV, Lyris, and Majordomo software packages, see Appendix F.

> **CAUTION**
>
> *You're probably going to be using your default mail client to issue those commands, so be sure that you're firing off messages in plain text format, not HTML. Your e-mail program should contain settings to set a default mode for messages. If you're having problems, send a message to yourself and check its header. If the attribute* `Content-Type: text/plain; charset=us-ascii` *does not appear, you should consider using a different e-mail client.*

List Management via the Web

Mailing lists predate sliced bread. Well, not really . . . but they've been around longer than the all-too-popular World Wide Web. Certain mailing-list software packages have recently been enhanced to sport a Web interface for list management, however.

What's the advantage of using the Web instead of e-mail for list management? Well, it'll pretty much remove the guesswork from routine chores. If a command prompt annoys or bewilders you, then you're better off choosing list software that can be controlled via the Web.

The trouble with working with lists via the Web is that you're a slave to your (and your Web host's) Internet connection. With e-mail, there is no waiting for pages to load. You type it, send it, and then wait for your list server to respond. An update may take seconds to complete through e-

> **NOTE**
>
> *An example of a command prompt interface would be MS-DOS; remember that "C:\" with the flashing cursor beside it? You have to know what to do there—there are no fancy buttons to guide you. E-mail management of your list is like that; you have to know what commands to issue. In contrast, Web management is more like Windows (or a Macintosh); it's all point-and-click.*

mail, but a few minutes when using the Web. If speed isn't an issue, then you don't have anything to worry about. However, you may find yourself losing valuable time when you're having to crawl through five different Web pages just to accomplish one simple update. In those instances, you might see whether issuing an e-mail command is possible with your list management software.

Copy Copy

As you probably know, computers are not always trustworthy. It doesn't matter what operating system you choose to use—it will have bugs and will crash from time to time.

Luckily, most errors you encounter will not destroy your computer's stored data. This doesn't mean you shouldn't back things up, however. Even if your list is being hosted on a server elsewhere in the world, you should do whatever you can to secure a copy of that list every couple of weeks. Remember, if that list is lost or destroyed, you'll be starting over at ground zero. Starting over might not be terribly detrimental in the early stages of development, but imagine if you've gained tens of thousands of addresses and lost them all in the blink of an eye. If your list host isn't very helpful in getting you a copy of your list at least twice a month, I'd strongly consider finding another host to work with. Most list software will allow the administrator to issue commands for extraction and e-mail dispatch of the current subscriber (e-mail address) database. Trust me, it never hurts to get a copy.

Getting a copy of your current database also enables you to keep track of how many subscribers you have. Open the list in a word processor (or advanced text editor) that will count the number of lines in a file, and (assuming that you have one e-mail address per line) you'll have your answer. This number might not be completely accurate, because you or your list software might not have filtered out bounces recently, you might have duplicate

CAUTION

Once you have a current copy of your subscriber list in hand, don't let it out of your sight. You don't have to put a ball and chain around it or anything, but don't leave it out in the open where some stranger might be able to get a copy of it easily. For this reason, I don't suggest keeping a copy of your list on a laptop (unless it is heavily password protected). If you lose that list, or an untrustworthy party gets ahold of it, you're done—game over. And remember, never share that list with anybody else—respect your subscribers' privacy.

addresses in the database, and so on. Keep in mind, too, that "real" numbers don't always tell the whole story; just because you have 1,000 e-mail addresses on your list doesn't mean that 1,000 people actually receive and eventually read what you send them.

Good Seed

So, how can you be sure that nobody has hijacked your list and used it for "evil" purposes? Well, there's no guarantee that it won't ever happen, but there's a way to find out when it does happen, so you can find and fix the security leak. It's called *seeding* your list. Seeding is easy to do and (best of all) doesn't require any horticultural experience.

You know how an individual can have lots of different e-mail addresses? Well, so can you. Spend a few hours on the Web, and you'll find many major online sites offering free e-mail accounts; take a few companies up on their offer. It doesn't matter which ones. The only thing you're going to do with these addresses is sign them up for your list—and that's all.

Name the new addresses unconventionally so that there's no way they could be linked back to you. For instance, I wouldn't use *lockergnome*, *gnome*, *pirillo*, or *chris* in any one of my seed addresses, because if someone used my list to distribute an unsolicited message, he would probably remove all addresses that might be linked back to me or my company. (Well, the *smarter* ones would do that—but we've already established that unsolicited e-mailers are dumber than rocks. A list hijacker doesn't have to be an outsider, either; someone in your own operation could potentially abuse your subscriber database just as easily.) If I chose stone211@ftbamail.com, wilbur@brianpeskin.com, and jp950432@kleckner.net as a few of my seed addresses, for example, there's no logical way you could trace them back to me. That's the idea. Nobody else is supposed to know about these addresses—*nobody*.

You shouldn't have to check these accounts every day; logging in every couple of weeks should suffice (depending on how much traffic your list gets). Whether you're writing an e-mail newsletter or moderating a discussion group, seeding is essential.

Let's say you start seeing some junk mail show up in one of your seed accounts. The first thing to do is access your other seed accounts to see whether the same junk is there. If so, then you obviously have a security problem with your list. If not, then the security of the first seed account's server might have been violated (or its owner could have possibly sold your e-mail address to spammers).

Retry, Don't Ignore (or You'll Fail)

Don't let subscription matters fall to the wayside. I've seen some list managers wait until they receive death threats before they attempt to help a subscriber on a "personal" level. Yes, as your subscriber count grows larger, spending time working with individuals and their particular problems will become increasingly difficult. One user might have a problem with his e-mail client, the other might have a problem with her mail server, and yet another one just might not understand how to go about using the information you're providing in your e-publication. However, when you don't take the time to troubleshoot subscription-related queries, you're losing a subscriber.

I see this kind of customer neglect happen everywhere I turn (and not just online). It doesn't matter whether customers are paying you directly or not— they still want to partake of your services. A few months back, I wanted to purchase an important component for my computer. I walked into one store and waited for someone to help me. Nobody came. "Oh well, I didn't have to spend my money there." I visited another similar store across town; again, nobody helped. At this point, I was starting to get fed up. I really needed to purchase this particular part, but I needed to have a few questions answered before doing so. I finally wound up at a store that I knew was overpriced—but it was well known for its excellent customer service. I wound up spending my money there because of the assistance the staff gave—not because of the product.

If you forget to pay attention to the needs of your subscribers, you can forget about being a good list manager. Don't believe that each subscriber doesn't count, because without them, there is no "you." There's no excuse for not being able to provide top-quality customer service in any given field. Some list managers will tell you that it's the subscribers' job to manage their own subscriptions to your list. This idea is acceptable in theory, but since most of your readers will be subscribed to a dozen other mailing lists, you need to make your explanations and answers as clear as crystal.

Be courteous and open with any user (subscriber or not); just because someone is rude to you doesn't mean you have to mirror his attitude. You're going to have "off days" every once in a while, but as a general rule of thumb, rise above the rudeness and there's no way you can lose. Gaining a subscriber is easy compared to retaining one.

Prompt Removals

Not removing someone who wants to be removed is stupid for several reasons. First, it can tarnish your image with the reader and/or others that he interacts with (online or off). Second, why bother mailing something to someone when you know that person is not going to read it? Just because a vacuum-cleaner salesperson knocks on my door incessantly doesn't mean that I'm eventually going to buy from him. People feel very much the same way with unsolicited e-mail (as covered in an earlier chapter). Unwelcome e-mail wastes resources, and that usually includes wasting money as well.

Subscription management starts with your first subscriber and never ends. You have to clean the database by whatever means necessary on a regular basis. Depending on how much traffic and new/old subscriptions you have to process, this could be a daily task. You'll be removing bounces with just about every mailing; don't expect subscribers to inform you of changes of address. Of course, if you consistently publish something worth reading, *trust me*—they'll remember to tell you where they can be reached. Cut out those duplicates, too; if your list software can't do that, consider picking up a word processor (or, again, an advanced text editor) that will allow you to sort the lines alphabetically and remove duplicates. Don't count on your eyes to do the work—you'll go blind trying.

What *They* Don't Know Can Hurt *You*

Your "Welcome" message is your first opportunity to educate a subscriber about your list's protocols and subscription details. A Welcome message is sent to every new subscriber, typically by means of an autoresponder. Most list software will allow you to customize the message to be automatically mailed to a user upon his subscription approval. It should be short, sweet, and to the point; tell the new subscriber what list he has joined, how to change addresses, how to unsubscribe, and perhaps (if feasible) your list's set of rules. Many list managers make the mistake of composing a Welcome message that is *too long*; the user probably won't read more than the first couple of paragraphs. Don't give your life story. If need be, point the subscriber to an online version of your FAQ.

Here's one of Lockergnome's current Welcome messages. You might glean a few ideas for your own initial list greeting:

```
<>-------------- L O C K E R G N O M E --------------<>

e-Greetings!

You've just subscribed to one of the largest & most
read e-mail newsletters on the Internet! You'll soon be
receiving the best Windows 95, 98, and NT information
```

in your Inbox on a weekly basis (every weekend). Hold onto this message!

Your Currently Subscribed Address:
[scott.hermanson@mrspatula.com]

Tell Your Friends and Colleagues about Lockergnome:
http://www.lockergnome.com/issues/

Read All of Our Past Issues:
http://www.lockergnome.com/issues/

If you did not willingly sign up for our free newsletter, simply forward this message or any issue you receive to the following address: removetext@lockergnome.com — this method is failsafe.

I hope that you'll stick around for a while and take the time to read what Lockergnome has to offer. Each issue is filled with high-quality downloads, web links, and other interesting tidbits that can't be found anywhere else online. Lockergnome has been around for over two full years.

You might have also chosen to receive our free HTML Daily newsletter. It provides information in a more easily digestable format. To receive the HTML Daily issues, you'll need an HTML-compliant e-mail program (Netscape or Microsoft products should work). Go to http://www.lockergnome.com/ or e-mail joinhtml@lockergnome.com to receive our HTML issues.

If you have any questions, please let me know. You're part of our family now... keep spreading the word about us!

Yours Digitally,

Chris Pirillo, Content Wizard: (chris@lockergnome.com)
Electronic Publisher<-> http://www.lockergnome.com/

```
FREE Windows E-mail Newsletters for the Curious User
Choose Between Our Daily HTML / Weekly Text Formats

<>-------------- L O C K E R G N O M E --------------<>
```

One bit of information is crucial and should be placed in your Welcome message: the user's subscribed address. This way, if he has more than one alias, he'll know which one needs to be deleted should he wish to be removed from your distribution. The user might not save this important informational e-mail, but if he does, it will help you troubleshoot potential subscription problems down the road. You need to assume that every subscriber doesn't know much more than his own e-mail address. And sometimes, he doesn't even know that.

I also have my subscription form set up to send me an e-mail message when someone subscribes to one (or both) of Lockergnome's e-newsletters. From this message, I discover his subscribed address, remote IP address, browser version, and how he found out about Lockergnome. This last bit of information (the reference) is possibly the most important one; from it, I'm able to uncover where many people are learning about Lockergnome:

```
From: veishea@mrspatula.com
To: subscriptions@lockergnome.com
Date: Saturday, April 24, 1999 11:07 PM
Subject: New Lockergnome Subscriber

Subscriber   - veishea@mrspatula.com
Reference    - From Windrivers.com and a friend
Sub Type     - joinhtml, jointext
Remote Host  - dial-24.nodemoe.net
Remote IP    - 165.115.105.185
Browser      - Mozilla/4.0 (compatible; Opera/3.0;Windows
               4.10) 3.50
```

Who Am I?

Expect the average user to have lots of different e-mail addresses that are all being forwarded to the same account. This makes subscription support a true nightmare. Someone will ask you to unsubscribe mooseypete@mrspatula.com when mooseypete@mrspatula.com isn't on your list. Even when you tell a user his address isn't in your database, he won't believe you. It doesn't take a genius to understand this notion: Something that isn't there can't be removed.

Most users will expect you to take care of this problem. You're likely to reply to a user with a follow-up question: "Do you have any other e-mail addresses?" Perhaps he won't reply, and he'll still be subscribed to your list. In another week, you might receive a vulgar message from the same person stating that he had already requested to be removed from your list, and if you do not comply, then he will be seeking legal action. Fine, so ask him again if he has any other e-mail aliases . . . and hope that he responds with the correct one. I recall one user who had me comb through (no joke) 23 aliases before I figured out which one he was subscribed under. This stuff comes with the territory; you have to take care of unsubscribe requests as diligently as you take care of subscribe requests.

Is this the subscriber's fault that he doesn't know his own e-mail addresses? Partly, but there are tools and tricks that can help you troubleshoot this all-too-common situation. Before you ask the user if he has any other e-mail addresses (or if the user is being unresponsive to your questions), here are a couple of things you can do to rectify the situation.

Let's say you can't find mooseypete@mrspatula.com in your database:

- Try looking for other "mrspatula.com" addresses.
- Since "mooseypete" is a seemingly unique handle, search for any addresses containing that word.
- Sometimes you'll find that the user will have an extra subdomain attached to his address (like mooseypete@smtp.mrspatula.com or mooseypete@mail.mrspatula.com). Try these variations.
- Translate parts of the e-mail message header in a user's unsubscribe request. (See the next section for details.)

I realize this list of suggestions is not very extensive, but they're all you can do if the user doesn't let you know which address needs to be removed. And don't think you're immune to this problem—it'll happen more than once, and each time will be equally frustrating to all parties involved.

Honest Headers

Another skill list managers should develop is the ability to interpret e-mail message headers. They may not be readily visible through your e-mail client, but they're there, and they can provide a wealth of information about a user. Most advanced clients will allow you to view e-mail header information. (Consult your program's documentation for instructions.)

A header is automatically generated and attached to every e-mail message. Examining the header can be helpful when it comes to dealing with unsubscribe requests as well as bounces. Here's an example of how a complete message might appear (complete with header):

```
From gretchen@hundling.com  Fri Mar 26 21:22:06 1999
Received: from llama (mail.tompepper.com
[192.41.45.139]) by lockergnome.com (8.8.5) id
VAA16047; Fri, 26 Mar 1999 21:22:05 -0700 (MST)
X-Authentication-Warning: lockergnome.com: Host
mail.tompepper.com [192.41.45.139] claimed to be llama
From: "Gretchen Hundling" <gretchen@hundling.com>
To: "Christopher Pirillo" <chris@lockergnome.com>
Date: Fri, 26 Mar 1999 22:22:54 -0600
Message-ID: <000001be7809$7c283080$588751d8@llama>
MIME-Version: 1.0
Content-Type: text/plain; charset="iso-8859-1"
Content-Transfer-Encoding: 7bit
X-Priority: 3 (Normal)
X-MSMail-Priority: Normal
X-Mailer: Microsoft Outlook 8.5, Build 4.71.2173.0
Importance: Normal
X-MimeOLE: Produced By Microsoft MimeOLE V5.00.2014.211
X-UIDL: ea93e34cb7b79315ff214cdd342d6456


Hello. I wish you would please unsubscribe me from your
list. My e-mail address is
cheesecake@youneverdothedishes.com. Thank you!


Gretchen
```

Now, at first glance, this may seem like a lot of useless junk, but let's say you can't find cheesecake@youneverdothedishes.com in your database. There are far too many users with "cheesecake" in their address, as well as people with the "youneverdothedishes.com" domain. So now what? Well, look at the message's header (which, again, might not be readily visible as seen above). I'm not going to break every section down for you, but from the above header you can find out which server Gretchen uses to send e-mail (mail.tompepper.com), what her actual e-mail client is (Microsoft Outlook 8.5, a.k.a. Outlook 98), and what that client's general settings are. Sometimes you might even be able to tell which operating system a person used to send the message.

Look at whom the message is from (hint: read the first line of the header, as well as halfway through the header): gretchen@hundling.com. Now you would search through your database to see whether you can find that particular address. If the search comes up bupkis, try looking for all hundling.com addresses. Bingo! gretchen@mail.hundling.com is there! Joy, rapture, jubilation . . . everybody can go on living as if nothing were wrong; Gretchen's none the wiser, and you don't have to play e-mail tag to follow up her removal from your list.

Who Can Help?

You're not completely on your own in terms of troubleshooting the unsubscription process. When you're shopping for list software or a list service provider, it would behoove you to choose a package that clearly displays (or has the ability to display) the e-mail address to which the e-publication is actually being mailed. The mooseypete@mrspatula.com owner might have forgotten that he had subscribed to your list using his scubapete@digitaldaze.com address, but your list software might not be as forgetful.

If you have a mail merge feature that enables you to include a subscriber's e-mail address in your publication, take advantage of it. That way, there's *no* dispute. You can instruct the subscriber with whatever directions you wish to use. For example:

```
You're subscribed to PANCAKE-LOVING-DOGS as
mooseypete@mrspatula.com. To unsubscribe, please. . . .
```

It won't get much easier than that, folks. But the buck doesn't stop there.

Deny Nothing, Confirm Everything

When users unsubscribe, they should be assured that their e-mail addresses are no longer in your database. Just as a Welcome message is important, so is a Good-bye one. Again, such a message can usually be sent automatically.

Here's an example of a current Lockergnome Good-bye message:

```
<>-------------- L O C K E R G N O M E --------------<>


e-Greetings!
We've just received and processed your request to be
removed from Lockergnome's Text Weekly newsletter. If
you did not wish to be unsubscribed, please rejoin
Lockergnome by following the directions below:
```

```
To Resubscribe Via the Web:
http://www.lockergnome.com/

To Resubscribe Via E-mail:
joinhtml@lockergnome.com

Thank you for your time, and I hope that you gained at
least one worthwhile "thing" from our free publication.
If you have a few extra moments, feel free to tell us
why you decided to unsubscribe at this time.

Yours Digitally,

Chris Pirillo, Content Wizard: (chris@lockergnome.com)
Electronic Publisher<-> http://www.lockergnome.com/
FREE Windows E-mail Newsletters for the Curious User
Choose Between Our Daily HTML / Weekly Text Formats

<>-------------- L O C K E R G N O M E --------------<>
```

Your list software might even let the user know when an address *wasn't* removed from the database. For instance, mooseypete@mrspatula.com might try to unsubscribe on his own (according to your list's directions), and he might receive a message worded something like:

```
Sorry, but the address
mooseypete@mrspatula.com
is not subscribed to the
PANCAKE-LOVING-DOGS list.
```

This message doesn't offer many troubleshooting options, but at least it lets the user know that he has not been removed at that point. Remember, too, that just because a user receives an e-mail message doesn't mean he will read it.

CAUTION

I've known list managers to send out Good-bye messages even though the particular unsubscribe request wasn't truly processed. Sorry, but that's just wrong! The user believes that he will no longer receive your mailings and is bewildered when they continue to arrive. Nobody wins in this situation—it's a blatant lie that only creates frustration. So, if possible, have your list software confirm a removal via e-mail to the unsubscribing user only when he is actually removed.

Can't We All Just Get Along?

Most of your subscribers are going to be using different e-mail clients, ISPs, operating systems, and so on. Just because your processes work in one situation doesn't mean they will work in all situations. If more than one subscriber comes forth with a problem with a certain combination of variables, you should investigate further. Offer users who are encountering problems some viable alternatives (if possible). If you know that a certain Internet mail service (or program) doesn't format your e-publication properly, let subscribers who use it know about potential incompatibility issues. You might even go as far as to contact the source of the problem (perhaps a particular ISP or the maker of an e-mail program) to see what can be done on either end to rectify the situation. I don't suggest attempting to communicate with larger services, as they will generally be unresponsive to your requests. Still, there's no harm in trying.

Delegate!

Just as every fast food joint has a manager, every list has one, too (even unmoderated lists). However, just because you own a list doesn't mean you have to manage its back end as well. Over time, you may find routine list management chores such as the ones outlined in this chapter to be a waste of your precious time. Instead of working on strategic partnerships with other online entities, you'll be tied up with the everyday problems.

When you find yourself spending more than a couple hours per day on subscription-related queries and brain-dead operations, consider bringing someone else on board. There's one thing all electronic publishers have in common: not having enough hours in the day. You're better off maximizing your "online time" dealing with development issues rather than working on tasks that just about anybody with a keyboard and a mouse could do. After you master the list management yourself (and you should definitely know how to do it in case of emergency), consider passing off the responsibility and focusing on other matters.

> **CAUTION**
>
> Be sure to pick someone to help you who will do a good job. Don't entrust your customer service to someone who lacks skills or motivation. List management, though routine, is an important part of the e-publication puzzle.

Chapter Eight

Publishing E-mail Newsletters

E-mail is quick, slick, and costs virtually nothing to distribute. This is probably why the medium is so easily abused, and why you must take extra precautions to ensure that you're providing an informative, articulate, and straightforward newsletter.

Select Your Software

You probably rely on some sort of postal service to transport mail from your home or business to another location. In the same light, you're going to use some sort of list software to distribute your e-mail.

E-mail clients are perfect for distributing your publication when you're just starting out. You'll find a list of them in Appendix E. However, they're not incredibly powerful or efficient when it comes to mailing to more than 25–50 people at one time. If you want to really run a mailing list, you'll need to do one of these things:

- Download or purchase list software to be run on your own computer. This is probably the best option for individuals who are using a very fast Internet connection (56k modems don't count), who use one of their computers as their Internet/Web server, and/or who are extremely knowledgeable with e-mail and/or Internet applications.
- Ask your ISP (Internet Service Provider) if it offers any list-hosting services with your account. These services are typically limited as to the number of subscribers, which is okay if you don't plan on growing your list over 20,000 subscribers or so. Remember, too, that if your ISP doesn't concentrate its efforts on providing excellent list service, you run the risk of it not knowing everything it should know regarding professional high-volume e-mail delivery.

- Ask your Web host (the company that provides the hosting for your Web site) if it offers any list-hosting services with your account. Yeah, it's pretty much the same story as when you talk to your ISP. However, Web hosts are typically more responsive to your needs and understand more about the underlying technologies of the Internet.

- Go to a company that provides only list services to its customers, or one that has dedicated list service resources. This is probably the best route for most e-publishers; if you find the right team that provides competent service and uses top-notch software, you'll be set for a long time.

No matter which route you decide to take, Appendices A, "Service Providers," and B, "Mailing-List Software," can help you with your ultimate decision.

You can always change list hosts later, although that can get rather complicated and messy (and wind up costing you a few extra dollars). Imagine telling all the people in the world that they can subscribe to your newsletter by sending a blank message to chubby-bunnies@lists.horizonlists.org for months and then suddenly switching to a new list host that uses a different subscription address. All that time you spent hyping the original address will have gone to waste unless you can arrange forwarding with your old list host.

> **TIP**
>
> *One fantastic way to avoid this problem altogether would be to set up an alias for all subscription inquiries. This way, if/when you change list hosts, the users won't know the difference. For my lists, potential subscribers would always be e-mailing subscriptions@lockergnome.com. Ya gotta think ahead, people.*

Choose Your Weapon

All software is buggy; you'll encounter headaches no matter which list software you use to distribute your e-publication. They'll all get the job done, although each package will vary in speed, efficiency, and subscriber/administrator benefits. Some will cost a pretty penny, and some will be more robust than others. You will more than likely be dealing with "list stuff" on a regular basis, as described in Chapter 7. When something isn't working the way you need it to work, you'll need to either fix it or find someone who can fix it for you. The more tools you can find to make your job as list owner/administrator easier, the better off you're going to be. Unless, of course, you thrive on stress.

I'll discuss the most popular programs in the following section. But popular or not, every list software package has its share of benefits and drawbacks—feature classifications are for *you* to decide. Talk to other list owners, join electronic-publishing-related discussion groups . . . remember that you're not alone. You'll discover that software isn't a textbook industry; just because a product or service says it will work in a certain fashion doesn't mean it always will. When you outgrow your current means of distribution, don't be afraid to explore your options.

The Big Three

If there's one piece of list software an ISP or Web host probably has installed already, it's Majordomo. But keep in mind that Majordomo really wasn't designed to handle larger lists efficiently; there are headaches associated with the administration, distribution, and maintenance of your list when using it. It's very popular, though, because it is usually free (or costs very little), and is perfect for e-publishers who don't have or plan on having a large subscriber database. It's been around for a long while, and Internet veterans are familiar with its structure and e-mail command set.

Another very popular program is LISTSERV. Traditionally used for discussion lists, LISTSERV has been around since the beginning of the electronic publishing industry (if you would call it that). The word "LISTSERV" has inadvertently become a generic term for mailing lists in general. If you plan on hosting a discussion group (moderated or unmoderated), understand that LISTSERV was designed expressly for the management of interactive e-mail communities. Unless specifically customized for a site or host, this software accepts commands via e-mail. It's simple, and it gets the job done with a good degree of accuracy.

And then there's Lyris, another major player. I have yet to interact with an e-publisher who didn't think that Lyris was top dog. Arguably one of the more complete, hassle-free list software packages available to the average Joe, Lyris is quickly becoming the list software of choice for both experienced and novice list administrators. It will generally cost you a bit more to run your list using Lyris, but after being spoiled by its features, you'll find it difficult to use anything else. If you're more budget-conscious (not wanting to spend thousands of dollars on software), Lyris probably isn't for you at this time.

Pegasus: More Than a Myth

"I don't want to spend any money on list software or services. I just want to maintain a small list on my own computer. Isn't something out there easy to use and free?"

Open almost any mythology book and you'll find your answer. No, there isn't such a thing as a mailing-list god (although, at times, I wish there were). You're going to find satisfaction by using Pegasus Mail, an e-mail client that runs on both the Windows and Macintosh platforms. Pegasus has been used for years in networked environments, and has been in perpetual development. System administrators have always appreciated how it handles small distribution lists without hassle. Subscriber databases can be edited easily, mailings can be dispatched with the click of a button, and it doesn't take up that much hard drive space.

When I first started Lockergnome, all that "list software stuff" was confusing for me. I just wanted to publish my information promptly and without too many problems. For the time I used it, Pegasus didn't disappoint me. If you're still unsure that you want to do a mailing list, I'd encourage you to use Pegasus (rather than spending too much time and money on other products and services). It runs well for list owners with fewer than 2,000 subscribers in their database, but once you pass that number, you should certainly start using software specifically designed to handle larger lists. Remember, too, that with most programs, all subscription requests must be handled manually; you'll have to manage subscribes, unsubscribes, bounces, and duplicates. There are only a couple of programs that *can* handle subscribes and unsubscribes (and one of those happens to be Pegasus). We'll look at that next.

Nuts-and-Bolts Setup Stuff

After you have chosen the software you want to work with, you'll need to set up a few features the way you want them. For example, you'll need to set a valid reply-to address, specify who can mail to the entire list, find out whether you can do mail merges with your software (and decide whether you even want to!), and more. Check out the following sections for some pointers.

Handling Subscribes and Unsubscribes

It may be possible for you to load e-mail addresses from incoming messages directly into an address book. There are two programs that can do this: AK-Mail (http://www.akmail.com/) and Pegasus (http://www.pegasus.usa.com/). There was another, Postmark, but it seems to have been taken off the market. Note also that AK-Mail, while still available, does not appear to be in development any more (there have been no updates since October of 1996).

In order to do this little trick, you have to create filters. Filters look at incoming messages and act on them accordingly. Most e-mail programs have filters that will, for instance, move a message to a particular folder depending on the From name, or perhaps delete the message or play a sound file to let you know that it's arrived. But these two programs have a very handy feature. Their filters can add the address from which the message was sent to an address book (or distribution list, as it's called in Pegasus), or remove the address from the address book.

You could, for instance, set up an e-mail address to accept subscriptions and cancellations—KiteNewsSub@TheBigKiteStore.com, for instance. You can then set the filters so that when a message arrives for that address, with the word "subscribe" in the subject line, the address from the incoming message is automatically added to the discussion group's address book. When a message arrives with the word "unsubscribe" in the subject line, the address is automatically removed from the address book. Then you'll need to set up another e-mail address—KiteNews@TheBigKiteStore.com—to be used for the mailing list itself.

This is a trick that Peter Kent used for his *Poor Richard's Web Site News* newsletter, in its early days, and he reports that it worked very well. Still, after a while the list can grow too big to handle well—after he had 2,000 subscriptions he switched to the Lyris software. The problem is that a simple subscribe/unsubscribe system like this only works well if people follow instructions properly . . . and many don't. The bigger the list, the more time you'll spend fooling around fixing people's subscription problems. At that point you need to switch to a proper list program.

Setting Your Reply-to Address

Every legitimate piece of e-mail has a specified sender *and* receiver. Your subscribers are evidently going to be receiving your e-mail newsletter, but from where will that e-publication originate? Will it appear to come directly from your personal e-mail address, a general address from your Internet domain, or a third-party service? You don't want to confuse your subscribers—especially when it comes to replying. Make sure they understand where (or to whom) their message is being delivered. When a user wants to be removed from your list, his first instinct is to hit that Reply button. In most e-mail clients (and, indeed, in most list software packages), you will be able to designate a specific reply-to address. It can be just about any e-mail address, but I suggest that you set up an alias to have all replies/bounces sent to the individual who handles subscription-related queries. You should be able to set up your software so that any reply to your list automatically gets processed as an unsubscribe.

But while some users will respond to your issue requesting to be unsubscribed, others will send you innocent comments regarding that particular missive. You don't want them to be processed as unsubscribes. In addition, a user may have subscribed to your list with a different address than what he normally uses for replies (which will most likely result in a nonprocessed unsubscribe request). You may consider informing subscribers outright that another address should be used for questions or comments, rather than encouraging them to reply directly to the mailing.

The worst thing you could possibly do is use a nonexistent e-mail address for replies. For example, if you set up subscriptions@mrspatula.com as your reply-to address, be sure that alias is valid. The user will receive a bounce and become frustrated when he replies to your issue. I've seen list owners sit there and try to explain that it's not their job to unsubscribe people who don't know how to do it themselves; they'll purposefully use a nonexistent e-mail address for replies. Pardon me, but that's moronic. I realize that nobody likes to lose members from their list, but that's no excuse for avoiding support problems. How frustrated do you feel when you contact someone via e-mail and receive an immediate reply stating that the user does not exist? Everybody is annoyed by bounces, but it's now your job to handle them (or find someone to handle them for you). Failing to do so will create confusion and aggression. Again, you might consider setting up one specific e-mail alias for all subscription-related events.

Preserving Privacy with Broadcast Controls

One of the list administrator's first duties should be to turn off the broadcast feature of his list software so that no one can send unauthorized messages to your list of subscribers. (The only exception would be for unmoderated mailing lists, where subscribers need the ability to freely broadcast messages to the entire list.) Depending on your software, this also might be referred to as *setting* (or restricting) posting privileges. Without this block in place, anybody with e-mail access could potentially send a message (including junk mail) to your subscriber base without your permission.

Blocking the broadcast ability can also save users from making embarrassing gaffes accidentally. A user might reply to the mailing and inadvertently send a personal comment to everybody on your list.

TIP

For added security, you should also protect your subscriber database from being viewed by anyone other than the administrator (this switch can be toggled with most mailing-list software).

Mail Merge Madness

Lately, there is a lot of buzz about customizing and personalizing online products and services, to make messages seem like they were personally composed. It's the online equivalent of a mail merge in a word processor.

Personalization is a good idea in theory, but I don't see the real-world practicality of it. I never believe the envelopes that read "Chris Pirillo has just won $3 gajillion!" so why would I believe a message that starts out with "Hey Chris Pirillo, are you feeling healthy today?" I know that the sender of this message doesn't know me well enough to ask that question, so I know it's just a trick.

Having the ability to invoke mail merge commands can add personalization to your electronic publication, which some of your subscribers might think is a cool thing. But, as with any useful instrument, personalization can be overused. For instance, let's roll with the "Hey, Chris Pirillo" example. First off, nobody calls me by my full name (except my mother scolding me—in which case, I would also hear my middle name). And second, it looks hokey. I'd be inclined to delete such a message without reading any further. While using a user's real name may make the message appear more personalized, it could potentially be a turnoff too, depending on the recipient's attitude.

> **NOTE**
>
> *Upon receiving a personalized message, the recipient's first question might be "So how does this company know who I am?" Well, that company doesn't necessarily know who you are; it may only know a few select facts about you, such as your name, gender, or state of residence. It might have gathered information from you when you signed up for services on its Web site or on someone else's site who then sold that company your data.*

However, mail merge can help you do one *very* useful thing: Insert the subscriber's e-mail address in the message, so each person will know which e-mail address he has used to subscribe. That way, he can unsubscribe more easily, without having to guess at the address used. (Chapter 7 detailed those woes, remember?) You could also potentially mail merge the time, date, or any other collected user information.

Consider the benefits of mail merge to your situation, but don't overdo it. Consult your list software's documentation to see whether mail merge commands are available and how to use them.

What's the Frequency?

After you've made up your mind what you want your e-publication to cover, you need to decide how often you want your missive to be published.

It's a virtual crapshoot when it comes to planning and sticking to a distribution schedule. Yes, you need to keep your personal interests in mind when you sit down and figure out a number, but it's also important to take into account your subject matter. Once you've established a schedule, do your best to stick by it. No, it's not mandatory to be regular, but your subscribers should know when they can expect to see their "favorite" newsletter (yours!) show up in their Inbox. You can always change your mind (and your schedule) if your original plan doesn't work well for you or your readers.

The last thing you want to be is forgotten by your subscribers. For this reason, most list owners choose to deliver issues once a week. A daily distribution can be a bit excessive—especially for novice e-publishers. You don't want to burn yourself out before you have the chance to get the ball rolling. If weekly is too often for you, consider going twice a month. Or, if you don't have enough information to present that often, move up to a monthly schedule. I don't advocate anything less frequent than that; when a user doesn't remember who you are or doesn't see you often enough, he will be much less likely to read and act upon your offerings.

Great Opening Lines

Before users have the opportunity to open or read your message, they're probably going to read the subject line. With the right subject line wording, users will immediately recognize who you are and know what that particular issue will be covering. The more intriguing you make that single line, the more likely you are to pique your subscribers' curiosity. Of course, that translates directly into more people taking the time to read your newsletter. Something like "Ferrari Fascination Fiasco" might work better than "Car Stolen." Yeah, it's sensationalism—but sometimes you have to get people's attention the hard way. Maximize the efficiency of that subject line; I've seen it underused too many times.

It all depends on how you want your users to react when they see your message show up in their Inboxes. If your name alone trips their trigger, then that's all you need to use. In the beginning, however, you're going to need to be a bit more creative.

How Much Should I Say?

There is a perfect amount of information to provide to a given audience on a given topic. But what is it that perfect amount? There's no easy answer, of course.

Too Much of a Good Thing

In high school, I remember having to memorize the periodic table of elements. Of course, all that information is virtually worthless to me at this point in my life, but hey—I needed a passing grade. My teacher encouraged her students to learn the chart column by column. It was either that or attack the whole thing in one sitting—which you could assume would have resulted in failure. The more information you throw out at one time, the less likely someone is to remember everything you covered. If I sat here and rattled off 50 names of important industry professionals, you'd probably remember the first few and last few . . . but virtually nobody in between. Keep this point in mind when you start compiling your issues. Believe it or not, information overload is more of a problem than the lack thereof.

When I used to publish on a biweekly (twice per month) basis, my issues were crammed with total substance. It was all "good stuff," but my subscribers forgot about or ignored half of it because there was *too much* good stuff. If you find yourself holding onto an overabundance of sharable information, consider publishing more frequently. You'll enjoy a candy bar much more if you eat it bite by bite, rather than shoving the whole thing in your mouth at once.

Not Enough of a Good Thing

Choosing a subject close to your heart is very important; but it's also essential for your publication's long-term survival that your chosen area allow for insight and development. Your newsletter doesn't have to tackle the hottest topic on the globe, but it shouldn't be so incredibly microtargeted that you struggle to fill up space in every issue. Check to see what other kind of related resources are available online before you commit. You may be filling a void if there's not enough information, but that also means you'll have to work harder to provide content for your readers.

I watch companies (large and small) distribute e-mail newsletters every day. However, I *know* that most of their subscribers aren't reading them. Why? Because nothing of value is included; companies suffer from providing virtually the same information in every one of their mailings. Subscribers will quickly develop the "if I've seen it once, I've seen it a thousand times" syndrome. There is no known cure for this disease. Prevention is simple: Keep your e-publication lively, informative, and worthwhile.

Chapter Nine

Working with Text Newsletters

Get ready to enter a world where the animated logo doesn't exist. Perish the thought! "You mean to tell me that I can actually get my point across without having to resort to using cheesy graphics?" Yes, Virginia, there really is a way. You can capture someone's attention quickly and easily through simple text. This low-tech solution doesn't necessarily have to be low-key, by any means.

Point Blank

E-mail is known for its speed and efficiency; you don't need to say a lot to convey a lot. A carefully crafted sentence can say more than an entire page of words.

So, get into the mind-set that you don't have to explain *everything* in order to be viewed as a wonderful, worthwhile resource by your subscribers. You mustn't have too little information, but you don't want too much of it either. The proper balance depends on your audience and subject matter. "Heavier" topics should be covered in "lighter" issues, and vice versa. Use your best judgment—and if all else fails, ask your readers!

I Feel Pretty

Just because you're using text-based mail doesn't mean that your publication has to look boring. While the bulk of your newsletter will be taken up by words, you shouldn't throw every paragraph or section together like they had just been run through a trash compactor. Or else, well . . . your newsletter will look like (for the lack of a better word) trash. I don't care if you're the smartest person in the galaxy with the "bestest" ideas around; if your publication isn't easy to read, you're going to disappoint more than a few existing subscribers and scare away potential ones. The formatting of an e-mail newsletter is just as important as its actual content.

Here are a couple of extremely truncated Lockergnome issues—provided only to illustrate what you should avoid when formatting your text-based e-publication. Each example has the same basic content but is (obviously) presented in a different format. Keep this analogy in mind as you read them: How do you eat a regular-sized candy bar—bite by bite or all at once?

Example #1

HERE IS TODAY'S LOCKERGNOME ISSUE!!!!!!!!!!!! >>>>>>>
you can visit us on our web site at
www.lockergnome.com!!! or you can e-mail me at
chris@lockergnome.com at anytime!!!!!!!!! Copyright
1999. Today is March 29th, 1999.:) :) :) :) :) :) :) :)
:) :) :) :) :) :) :) :)
Program: Metapad--------
http://members.tripod.com/~aadavids/metapad.zip or you
can visit the web page for it -------------
http://welcome.to/metapad/o/metapad/
What!? Another NOTEPAD replacement? Okay, so what makes
this one different? Well, it's smaller than the Windows
Notepad, runs (seemingly) quicker, comes with search
and replace functionality, remembers window size and
position, has more keyboard shortcuts... and if those
options don't win you over, Metapad was also created by
a Lockergnomie! It still has a memory limit (like the
Windows Notepad), but you'd only want to use this
editor for simple tasks anyway. Notepad has been
permanently replaced on my machine.
FAVORITE web site: CE Desktop------
http://www.cedesktop.com/ PDAs running Windows CE are
all over the place (gotta love 'em). Who do you turn to
for the latest CE-related news, software, and tips?
Springing onto the CE scene is CEDesktop.com (along
with CEShopper, CEGlobe, CENewsletter, and CESearch).
In this network, you'll find message boards, hardware
reviews, product information, and much more. It's
organized, well presented, and (most importantly)
original. Oh, and don't worry—they've got downloads,
too. "CE" you there!ere!
HERE IS TODAY'S TIP----------Lockergnomie Davis Straub
(co-author of the best-selling book Windows 98 Secrets)
told me about a killer trick for a major Outlook 98 &
Outlook Express annoyance. Have you ever seen those
solid lines to the left of your reply text in HTML-

formatted messages? Here's Davis's way to get rid of
them: "after you click 'Reply' and get the vertical
line(s) on the left, move your text cursor to the spot
where you want to insert a response and press 'Enter'—
this will extend the line. Next, click the 'Paragraph
Style' button on the OE format bar (notice that there
is a dot next to normal). Click 'Normal' and the lines
will DISAPPEAR! Be sure to check out
www.davisstraub.com for the entire OE chapter!
Thanks for reading this issue again!
--------<<<<<<<<<<<<<<<<<<<<<<<<<<<<<<<<<<<<<---------
>>>>>>>

Example #2

The following issue contains the exact same content, but is formatted much
more clearly and attractively.

<>----------------------<>----------------------<>

Lockergnome's Daily Windows 9x/NT Snippet
http://www.lockergnome.com/ <> chris@lockergnome.com
(c)1996-99, Lockergnome LC <> ISSN: 1095-3965 <>

<>---<> G N O M E P R O G R A M <>----------------<>

<> Metapad v1.0 [18k] W9x/NT FREE

http://members.tripod.com/~aadavids/metapad.zip
http://welcome.to/metapad/

What!? Another NOTEPAD replacement? Okay, so what makes
this one different? Well, it's smaller than the Windows
notepad, runs (seemingly) quicker, comes with search
and replace functionality, remembers window size and
position,has more keyboard shortcuts... and if those
options don't win you over, Metapad was also created by
a Lockergnomie! It still has a memory limit (like the
Windows Notepad), but you'd only want to use this

editor for simple tasks anyway. Notepad has been permanently replaced on my machine.

<>---<> G N O M E F A V O R I T E <>---------------<>

<> CE Desktop

http://www.cedesktop.com/

PDAs running Windows CE are all over the place (gotta love 'em). Who do you turn to for the latest CE-related news, software, and tips? Springing onto the CE scene is CEDesktop.com (along with CEShopper, CEGlobe, CENewsletter, and CESearch). In this network, you'll find message boards, hardware reviews, product information, and much more. It's organized, well presented, and (most importantly) original. Oh, and don't worry—they've got downloads, too. "CE" you there!

<>---<> G N O M E T I P <>-------------------------<>

Lockergnomie Davis Straub (co-author of the best-selling book Windows 98 Secrets) told me about a killer trick for a major Outlook 98 & Outlook Express annoyance. Have you ever seen those solid lines to the left of your reply text in HTML-formatted messages? Here's Davis's way to get rid of them: "after you click 'Reply' and get the vertical line(s)on the left, move your text cursor to the spot where you want to insert a response and press 'Enter'—this will extend the line. Next, click the 'Paragraph Style' button on the OE format bar (notice that there is a dot next to normal). Click 'Normal' and the lines will DISAPPEAR! Be sure to check out www.davisstraub.com for the entire OE chapter!

<>-------------------------<>-------------------------<>

Night and Day

Which example would you rather receive in your Inbox: #1 or #2? I'm starting to sound like an eye doctor here, but you don't need 20/20 vision to walk away with an upset stomach after viewing the first example. And believe it or not, there are newsletters being published today that look a lot like it. Scary? Yeah. But you can't call other people's baby ugly—they have to see the ugliness themselves. Before you even start with your newsletter, I suggest you look at various other e-publications—whether they're related to your subject matter or not. Good formatting typically isn't topic-specific.

But be careful . . . I'm not advocating that you copy and/or emulate other e-publishers' styles. There aren't many e-mail publications that hold copyrights or trademarks (even when they say they do), but that doesn't make it any less wrong to steal. And that, in essence, is what you would be doing if you borrowed heavily from another publication. It's okay to further develop minor ideas set forth in other e-publications or be inspired from someone's great-looking newsletter, but don't lift formatting directly from someone else's design. That author/designer (most likely) had to work diligently to come up with a style that worked for his newsletter. The last thing you want to do is make an enemy instead of an ally. It's a mistake far too many novices make.

If you like the way a fellow e-publisher does something, tell him! Then, if possible, ask if he would help you create something (especially if you're not incredibly confident in your text-formatting skills). The worst thing he can say is "no." By establishing contact with a compliment, you're creating a positive relationship instead of ripping the person off.

Some publishers might help, and others might not. Just because people choose not to help (or can't) doesn't mean that they're big meanies and shouldn't be dealt with again. Understand that you're not the only one trying to do this; it takes time, energy, and patience to publish a quality e-publication on a regular basis. Of course, you should recognize this when you first contact an e-publisher whom you admire.

> **NOTE**
>
> *On the other hand, I wouldn't suggest buttering a person up too much in your initial correspondence. Explain who you are, what you're doing, why you're writing, and how you'd like him to help you. If you have something to offer in return, by all means, say so. But don't get too big for your britches; if you just started out and are talking to someone who's been in the game for a long time, he isn't going to be terribly impressed with your 10 subscribers.*

You don't admire any e-publishers yet? Wait until you're in the field for a while; then you'll start to see certain individuals doing things that you wish you had done. Especially when it comes to formatting and style.

The Art of Formatting

I look back on my earliest Lockergnome issues and cringe. I hadn't quite mastered the art of clean and attractive e-mail formatting. I can't go back and erase the past—but I can learn from the mistakes I've made. This is where you're way ahead of the game . . . you can learn from *my* mistakes. But don't get ahead of yourself—there are plenty of mistakes just waiting to be uncovered.

If a style isn't working for you (or too many of your readers are complaining), change it! Unless you're using a really, really, really old computer, your formatting isn't carved in stone. You'll probably change a few things over time. Your style will most likely develop and grow in direct proportion to your publication's reach. It's rather cool, actually . . . compared to a print publication, changing the style, layout, or format of a text-based e-mail newsletter is simple.

> **CAUTION**
>
> *Be careful—don't go changing the way your newsletter is presented too often (twice per year is a maximum). When you want to add a new section, add a new section. But don't change the way your entire publication appears in every other issue. Readers won't know what to expect or where to find their favorite bit.*

Separating Sections

You need to visibly separate the sections of your newsletter through characters or blank spaces. Spaces are okay, but somewhat mundane. Instead, consider creating lines. Dozens of keyboard characters (when placed together) will create interesting patterned lines for separating sections. Just about any keyboard symbol character works well, such as dashes or asterisks. Get creative with them!

You can use just about any of the 254 ASCII (extended) characters, but for maximum compatibility, I'd advise against using any symbol not found on your keyboard. Older text e-mail clients can't handle extended characters. Of course, if you're writing in a language other than English, you're going to be working with those extended characters anyway. Stay away from the Tab key, too. Each user's client will potentially interpret them differently, and you'll wind up with 43 different "versions" of the same newsletter; use the space bar, instead.

Extra lines can work wonders too to build your publication's structure. Don't be afraid to throw in an extra space or hard carriage return every once in a while to separate sections. I wouldn't suggest using too many of them, but as long as you're consistent throughout your document, your readers shouldn't mind. Moderation is the key; don't overdo any particular part of your newsletter.

CAUTION

Use lines tastefully. When one line of percent signs will suffice, don't use four. "Simple" is sometimes the best route; having too many formatting gimmicks and not enough content is a good way to ensure that subscribers will delete your missives before reading them.

Font Formats

Depending on the e-mail program subscribers are using to read your mail, they may see your newsletter in either a monospaced (fixed width) font or in a variable-width font. A monospaced font's characters each take up the same amount of space, whereas a variable-width font's character spacing is uneven. The first example below is rendered with a monospaced font; the second is done in a variable-width one:

```
Wilbur's Wheelbarrow
```

Wilbur's Wheelbarrow

Note how in the monospaced font example the lowercase *i* takes up the same amount of space as the uppercase *W* does. This isn't the case in the variable-width font example.

You should always format your text newsletter as though your audience will be using a monospaced font to read it. That's because everyone can read monospaced text (although some folks may need to set up their e-mail clients to do so if they don't by default), but not everyone can read variable-width text. I've always used a monospaced font in my e-mail client, because it ensures that everyone, even people using old command-line e-mail programs, will be able to see my newsletter as I intended it to be seen. A newsletter formatted for a monospaced font but viewed with a variable-width font looks a lot less "disgusting" than vice versa. For more information on the uses of monospaced fonts, swing by http://home.bsu.edu/prn/monofont/. As a side note, you'll have noticed that all the text examples in this book have been rendered in a monospaced font.

Those Darn URLs

How can you think of sending out an e-mail newsletter without including at least one URL? Ya know, a Web address . . . those thingies that usually start with http://? They're all over the place, and you should use them wherever *probable*. But use them for a reason—not just to take up space. Nobody's going to be impressed with your list of 50 links if 20 percent of them don't work and 70 percent are Web sites that everybody's already seen. URL overkill could potentially be a problem. Putting too many links in an e-mail newsletter will decrease the probability of your user clicking on many of them.

Have you ever noticed when people send you a Web address in a text e-mail message that it is automatically "hot"? That is to say, you can click on it with your mouse, and the location will load up in a browser window? If not, then I strongly urge you to download a newer client that will do that for you; it is extremely helpful. Providing a hot URL does a great service for the recipient; instead of having to copy the URL from the message and into the browser, he just has to click (providing, of course, that the URL was entered correctly and the e-mail reader makes the URL "hot").

An e-mail message doesn't have to be formatted in HTML to have working hyperlinks in it. A lot depends on the client a subscriber uses, but it's safe to assume that most of your readers will have "hot" links. The only exceptions to this rule are usually found when the readers are using an e-mail program not specifically designed for the Internet. These users are typically found in a corporate environment (on a network at their workplace). Still, you should be careful as to how you present any URL to your subscribers:

- If you're using the URL in a sentence, you could enclose it in angle brackets. This isn't mandatory, but it's a nice touch:
  Good: <http://www.mrspatula.com/>
  Bad: http://www.mrspatula.com/>
  Bad: >http://www.mrspatula.com/<

- Other than enclosing in angle brackets or ending with a slash, *never* place any other character immediately before or after a URL, or it might not read properly in the subscriber's mail client. If you need to place a character alongside a URL, be sure there is at least one blank space between it and the resource. Examples of what *not* to do:
  http://www.mrspatula.com/.
  http://www.mrspatula.com/pilot.html,
  http://www.mrspatula.com/—
  (http://www.mrspatula.com/greatamerican.html)

- Be sure to use the correct address and character conventions with URLs. Here are a few often-seen mistakes. Although some of them are subtle and difficult to see, they can still cause problems in the reader's client. Can you tell what is wrong with each of these?
  htpp://www.mrspatula.com/
  http:/www.mrspatula.com/
  http;//www.mrspatula.com/
  http://ww.mrspatula.com/
- When you're referencing a Web site, be sure to include its complete header (http://, ftp://, gopher://, et al.). Without it, certain e-mail clients might not make the links "hot."
  Good: http://www.mrspatula.com/
  Bad: www.mrspatula.com
- When the URL isn't referencing a specific page, you should add a trailing slash to it. The hyperlink will work either way, but it appears cleaner (formatting wise) with the slash:
  Good: http://www.mrspatula.com/
  Bad: http://www.mrspatula.com
- Always double-check your URLs to make sure you have typed them correctly and that the sites being referenced are still in business at those addresses. If you don't have time to do it, then have someone else do it for you. Otherwise, you'll get flooded with people telling you that a certain link didn't work. I realize that sometimes there's nothing you can do—for example, if a site goes offline the day after you link to it— but do your best to cover your bases.
- Be careful with long URLs. If you have your e-mail program set to word wrap at a specific column number, a URL can get cut off and only the first part of the URL will be hot. This will lead the subscriber to an incorrect Web page unless he copies or pastes the entire string into his browser. One way to prevent this from happening is by turning off the automatic word wrap in your mail program (or word processor, if that's what you use to compose your newsletter). Try to keep that lengthy address on one line if you can at all help it. If your list software asks you whether you want it to word wrap for you, just say no.

Take It from the Top

While the subject line is an important part of your message, it will not be found in the actual body; a text header (like a title or a headline) will typically precede your content and contain more than one line. All magazines have covers, and all text e-zines should have headers at the top, the first thing users read when they open your message. You can put whatever kind of contact and/or publishing information you deem important up there—just not *too* much. The title, your name, the date, the particular issue volume and number (if any), and your Website URL are a few pieces of information you could report. Take a look at the type of information that other e-mail newsletters are putting in this space. It's designed more for the new reader, but your "older" followers might appreciate it as well (although most of them will ignore it and get on to the "guts" of your mail).

Some users would rather read your information on the Web, so consider posting an HTML version of each issue on your Web site and including a URL for the issue toward the top. The Web version should contain the same content as the mailing.

If you're going to put a missive on the Web, be sure that you're not just uploading it as a simple text file. Downloadable utilities are available for most operating systems to translate plain text into HTML (which will also automatically make URLs "hot"). The HTML doesn't need to be fancy-schmancy, but it should be pleasant to the eye and include features such as large bold headings and a page title.

> **NOTE**
>
> *If you have created dividers using repeated characters in your e-mail, you might want to remove them in the Web version of the issue, perhaps replacing them with graphic lines.*

Depending on how much content you produce in a particular issue (and how much extra time you have on your hands), you might consider inserting a table of contents right after the obligatory header information. With the table of contents, a user can skim to see whether anything is worth looking at. That can be a double-edged sword, however; you don't want readers to decide not to read a particular issue based on the table of contents.

I used to have a table of contents for Lockergnome issues, but I found that it made users more likely to skip sections and reviews that didn't have interesting titles. By *not* putting a TOC in there, I'm pretty much forcing subscribers to take a look at each review to see whether they'd like to check out the resource.

Final Words

In closing, I just want to say . . . good luck. Oh, wait—the book isn't over yet? Well, you know it's going to end eventually. When that page comes, I'll attempt to bow out gracefully—just like you should with every issue you distribute. Any words of wisdom? Interesting tidbits of info that you want to pass along to future generations? Extended copyright and/or subscription information? They are all perfect items to put at the closing of your issue.

If you really want subscribers to read the entire newsletter, you have to give them a good reason. Toward this end, I have found that the "saving the best for last" strategy (believe it or not) really works. One of the most popular parts of my newsletter is my Tips and Tricks section. So, consequently, it's at the end. Sure, the users might scroll all the way to the bottom of every issue to read it, but at least I know they're interacting with me.

You can also use extra little items to entice readers to read certain editions or to check out the Web version. For example, I used to put a little "fortune cookie" at the bottom of every weekly text issue to give those who read that far a little treat. They don't appear in *Lockergnome's Text Weekly Digest,* so people have to subscribe to the daily version to get those. I also post them in the Credits section in the sidebar of *Lockergnome's HTML Daily,* though, so people can visit the Web site and read them if they want to. No, something this insignificant won't make or break an e-publication, but I do know that people look forward to reading those completely random maxims. Besides, I eventually plan on putting small graphic advertisements in the *HTML Daily* sidebar; subscribers' eyes will be looking for a saying, so the advertisement will stand a better chance of getting noticed.

I've covered this point before, but you must put unsubscribing and/or resubscribing information either at the beginning or the end of the message. Some electronic publishers place "how to subscribe" information in both places. That way, if a subscriber forwards the issue to a friend, the friend will be sure to have the subscription information included in his copy. That's a valid idea, but results will vary. First, these publishers are assuming that subscribers are passing along their stuff. (This is a nice thought, but don't bank on it.) Second, they're assuming that *if* a subscriber forwards their stuff along to someone else, the subscriber will forward the *entire* issue; this isn't likely to happen. Readers will often find one or two things that they appreciate and then copy and paste those items into a completely new e-mail—bypassing the "how to subscribe" information entirely.

For this reason, I've chosen to add a Web page link for users to recommend Lockergnome to friends; I place this link at the top and at the bottom of each *Lockergnome's Text Weekly Digest.* Not only am I able to track how many times my site/newsletter is recommended in a day, but I have (almost) complete control over what is sent to the potential subscriber. You don't have to take this route, but consider it as one of your options.

How Should I Say It?

While I try to stick to the standards of the English language, every once in a while I might write something completely unconventional. I willingly accepted a few failing grades in college because I refused to change my writing style to fit the teacher's criteria. Lo and behold, life went on. I hope that nobody is going to hover over your shoulder and tell you how to write your e-mail newsletter. Your style is going to come shining through every single time—as well it should.

But you need to remember that your subscribers might not appreciate (or understand) your methodologies. I've offended users by using *proggie* instead of *program*, or *yr* instead of *your*. Over time, I've had to develop a more professional presentation in my newsletters. I try to make sure that my language is *very* clear when I foresee potential confusion.

Since I do a lot of my editing on-the-fly, "proofreading" doesn't exist in my vocabulary. Then again, I haven't had too many complaints thus far. If there isn't a problem, nobody will complain. As long as very few of your subscribers become vocally infuriated over your writing style, don't change a thing. I'm from the "as long as you're consistent" school of thought.

Nobody's perfectt.

Advertising Acceptability

When you watch television, do you find yourself changing the channel when commercials come on? It's a safe assumption that most people don't like being on the receiving end of a sales pitch. Unfortunately, if your list offers free subscriptions, you're going to need to find a way to pay for it. Sure, in the beginning when your subscriber base is relatively small, you can afford to do things for free (or cheaply). But over time, if you're consistently *not* bringing in money, you'll find the frustrations will outweigh the benefits of electronic publishing.

The good news is that the number of companies willing to advertise in text-based publications is growing by the day. A few years ago, nobody would consider purchasing an advertisement if it didn't involve a graphical banner. I knew this model would eventually die (and, indeed, the traditional Web banner ad is in its death throes as you read this). Click-thru rates just aren't there. Plus, as I mentioned before, nobody likes to sit and listen to advertising. So how can you make your advertisers and readers happy?

My biggest suggestion is for you to make the line between advertising and editorial content very clear. Use a header labeled "Sponsor" or "Advertisement" to set off the paid announcements from your regular content. Failing to do so will confuse your subscribers and make them lose respect for you. Imagine if you made an advertisement sound like it wasn't an advertisement and didn't place it under an "advertising" label. Your subscribers wouldn't know the difference between what you're "telling" and what you're "selling."

Another potential subscriber annoyance is seeing too many advertisements in proportion to content. The biggest offenders in this area have generally been Internet marketing newsletters. Not only are most of them filled with an overabundance of "sponsors," but they also don't clearly draw that line I outlined in the preceding paragraph. The subscriber will read one (possibly two) issues filled with nothing but advertising tripe, and either unsubscribe or remain subscribed and delete the e-mail in the blink of an eye. When someone subscribes to an e-mail newsletter, it typically means that he wants to learn more about the subject matter that it promises to cover.

> **NOTE**
>
> *What's the difference between those two words—telling and selling? As far as you're concerned, nothing; they're pretty much one and the same. But, to the end user, "This issue sponsored by" sounds better than "Please support our advertisers." Is it a word game? You bet it is.*

So, what's the magic number for ads? It depends on how extensive your issues are; the number of advertisements in an e-mail newsletter should be directly proportional to its length. Feel free to experiment in the beginning, but don't overdo it. I'd say the average e-zine should have no more than two or three advertisements in each issue. The closer to the top they are, the more you should charge for them. Remember, with text-based newsletters, the user doesn't have to wait for any graphics to load before reading the first line. I'd suggest putting the first advertisement immediately underneath your header. Let readers know who you are before you show them who's helping you keep their subscription free.

There's no universal template for the size and content of a textual advertisement. A good rule of thumb is to keep it between three and six lines and to include a URL if possible. You should always reserve the right to rewrite the text that advertisers want you to run. This way, if their wording is a little off (or if they can't write very well), you don't wind up getting stuck with a lousy-looking advertisement. Besides, you know your publication's audience better than they do (I'd hope).

Editor du Jour

You'll need to use your e-mail client (or the Web) to initiate the mailing of an issue. But this doesn't mean that you need to compose and edit your missives online (or even in your e-mail program or Web browser). If you use a word processor, be sure that you're editing and saving your work in text (ASCII) format. Word processors offer various "text" options (Text Only, Text Only with Line Breaks, MS-DOS Text, and so on). While they'll all create basic text file output, your best bet is to stick with the most basic format: Text Only. The best way to ensure that you're getting Text Only is by using a simple text editor for composition; you'll avoid any potential problems and/or incompatibilities.

Even if your editor of choice doesn't offer a spell check, be sure to run it through some sort of "checker" before you actually submit your issue for dispersion. Go over the spacing, spelling, grammar, formatting, and so on to ensure that everything is as it should be. Handing it to a knowledgeable friend always helps, too; a friend is more likely to catch mistakes than you are. Errors will always slip through the cracks, but the fewer you have, the better. The editing stage is important, and unfortunately a step that too many e-publishers skip.

Dump the Word Processor

Actually you're probably better off dumping your word processor, and using a text editor. The problem is that word processors these days like to drop in special characters—curly quotation marks, special typesetting characters for ellipsis (. . .) and em dash (—), and so on. These characters can mess up your e-mail message very badly. Have you ever seen e-mail messages that are littered with the characters =20? At the end of each line, for instance, you may see =20=20.

This problem is caused by an e-mail server getting a little confused when it sees some of these weird little word-processor characters. The only way to completely avoid the problem is by being absolutely sure that none of the characters creep into your newsletter.

Before you send out your newsletter, it's a good idea to send it to yourself, and then look at the message header (remember, most e-mail programs hide much of the message header, so you may have to use some kind of "Show Header" command to view the entire header). Look for lines like these:

```
Content-Type: text/plain; charset=iso-8859-1
Content-Transfer-Encoding: 8bit
```

You may also see something like this:

```
X-MIME-Autoconverted: from quoted-printable to 8bit by
bigbiz.com id UAA26184
```

Oops, you've got a problem! The `charset=iso-8859-1` piece, and the `8bit` on the second line, and the `Autoconverted` line, all indicate that the message has been converted, because it contains these weird non-ASCII characters. Rather than `charset=iso-8859-1`, you want to see `charset="us-ascii"`. And rather than the `Content-Transfer-Encoding: 8bit` line, you want to either not see the line at all, or see something indicating that it's 7-bit.

Now, if you send a `charset=iso-8859-1` message out, most recipients will see it just fine. But a significant portion—all your America Online subscribers, for instance—will get the bad message, the message with all the `=20` characters.

So there are two things you must remember. First, it's a good idea to stick with a plain old text editor that doesn't create these types of characters. But secondly, if someone sends you text to include in the newsletter, you're going to have to check it carefully. For instance, if someone writes an article to include in your newsletter, or sends you an advertisement, make sure you replace all the quotation marks, apostrophes, ellipses, em dashes and en dashes (the en dashes are shorter dashes, used between numbers in a series) with plain old text characters. You should also look carefully for such special symbols as ®, ©, and ™.

What if you send out your test message and it comes back as 8-bit? If

What's =20?

=20 is the hexadecimal code for a space. For some reason some mail servers, when they receive an 8-bit message, get a little confused and display the hexadecimal code for a space if there are no other characters to the right of the space except another space or a carriage return. (If a space is followed by a word, it's okay, but if followed by another space and then a carriage return (that is, a break to a new line), or immediately by a carriage return, it becomes =20.)

you were using a text editor, then perhaps you've copied text from elsewhere, and that text contained a special character. How, then, do you find which character is bad?

Split the message into two parts and mail again, and see which half is converted to 8-bit; then split that half in two and mail those two pieces, and see which is converted to 8-bit, and so on until. Eventually you'll be able to split things down until you find the bad character.

By the way, if you look carefully you'll find some excellent text editors, programs that have lots of the features of word processors but that save the text without word-processing characters. Peter Kent, the publisher of *Poor*

Richard's Web Site News (and of this book), who provided the foregoing tips, recommends a program called TextPad (http://www.textpad.com/), for instance. Macintosh users may want to try a very popular program called BBEdit (http://www.barebones.com/).

The International Archives

Once you've published a newsletter (text or HTML), you should also have an easily accessible copy of it on your Web site. You could upload your text newsletters as text, but it would be wiser for you to pick up a "text to HTML" converter and have that program automatically turn the issue into a Web page for you. Several shareware utilities of this kind are available, such as the following:

Text2Web (Windows)

http://www.virdi.demon.co.uk/

AscToHTM (Windows, OpenVMS)

http://www.yrl.co.uk/~jAF/asctohtm.html

Text2Html (Windows)

http://www.cyber-matrix.com/txt2htm.htm

ARWPC (Windows)

http://www.trah.co.uk/welcome.htm

text2html (Perl)

http://www.isys.hu/c/verhas/progs/perl/text2html/

Text to HTML Conversion Utility (Web)

http://com.org/hb/Text_to_HTML.htm

txt2html (UNIX)

http://www.thehouse.org/txt2html/

Text file to HTML converter (UNIX)

http://www.beard.demon.co.uk/software/tohtml.html

HTML Markup (Mac)

ftp://ftp.switch.ch/mirror/info-mac/text/html/

TextToHTML (Mac)

http://sunsite.doc.ic.ac.uk/Mirrors/info-mac.org/text/_HTML/

Even if you choose not to transmogrify your text, a "past issues" archive is obligatory. You might be able to set up your list software to enable your subscribers to retrieve any given issue by issuing certain commands via e-mail. If you don't have a Web site yet, consider this method as an alternative.

Chapter Ten

Working with HTML Newsletters

While plain-text e-mail newsletters currently represent a larger piece of the "e-zine pie," it's only a matter of months before the majority of e-mail publications will be created and distributed in HTML. I field inquiries about e-mail publishing on a daily basis, and the most frequently asked question is: "How do I do an HTML newsletter?" After responding to this query for the umpteen billionth time, I thought that someone ought to write a book covering the subject . . . well, at least a semiextensive chapter. Even if you don't plan on publishing in HTML right now, this chapter will help you develop other elements of your electronic objective, so don't skip it.

HTML stands for Hypertext Markup Language. It is a hypertext document format, in which bracketed codes (called *tags*) are inserted into a plain text document so that the text will be formatted in a certain way in Web browsers (and HTML-capable e-mail and other programs). Over time, HTML has been expanded to include not only formatting codes but also codes that display graphics, codes that run applications, and codes that provide hyperlinks to other Web pages and e-mail addresses. All Web browsers have been designed to work with HTML documents, but not all e-mail clients will at this time.

When I started *Lockergnome's HTML Daily* newsletter in the summer of 1998, the only other HTML e-mail publications were being managed by the "big boys" of the industry. Since then, lesser-known e-publishers have made the leap to rich-text formatting (messages with colors and/or text-formatting enhancements).

The difference between rich-text and HTML messages boils down to the number of formatting options available. Whereas HTML messages can include any number and just about any configuration of HTML tags on top of text formatting, rich-text messages only allow you to manipulate the text part of the message. While you may use tables, inlaid graphics, and advanced scripting (like JavaScript, Java, or DHTML) in HTML messages, you will only be able to bold, italicize, or underline fonts in rich-text messages.

You'll find that as newer e-mail clients are released, more will be able to handle HTML messages (Microsoft Outlook Express, Microsoft Outlook 2000, Microsoft Outlook 98 Internet Edition, Netscape Messenger, etc.); many corporate clients will only handle text or rich-text messages (Microsoft Exchange, Outlook 98 Corporate Edition, etc.). Some e-mail clients are set to handle HTML messages, but only via a limited internal viewer or by calling upon an outside browser. For instance, Pegasus Mail has an internal viewer that renders HTML messages, but very poorly; however, it also allows you to use Internet Explorer 4.0 and above to view the same message. The Eudora e-mail programs also have similar features.

New HTML newsletters are popping up every day. The expanded availability of HTML-capable e-mail clients has a great deal to do with this growing trend, although some traditional text-based e-publishers will probably never cross over into this new format.

And there's nothing wrong with that; textual e-mail newsletters can be just as good (if not better) than HTML ones. The advantages of using HTML mail are endless, however: You can format the document in any way you see fit, use various fonts, add a splash of color here and there, and so on. Plus, advertisers like HTML newsletters, because banner ads can be inserted into them. Of course, with these extended options comes the potential for incompatibilities and headaches. Just because an e-mail program or Web site says it is capable of sending and/or receiving HTML mail doesn't mean that your HTML document is going to look the same in every subscriber's Inbox. And just because a subscriber thinks that he can handle HTML mail doesn't mean that he can.

Pirillo's First Law

Pirillo's first law of HTML e-mail newsletter distribution clearly states: Just because it *can* be done doesn't mean it *should* be done. Ask yourself this question: What's the purpose of sending out an electronic message in HTML instead of plain text? You had better have a good reason.

Scores of users will make your ears bleed if they see anything but a text message in their Inbox. And, from the way I've seen HTML mail abused, I can't say that I blame them

CAUTION

Most traditional discussion lists are strictly plain text because of the potential headaches that would be involved in making sure that all participants can use HTML. I advise against trying to start an HTML-formatted discussion list.

for feeling so defensive about not wanting to receive it. E-mail has traditionally been distributed as plain text, and with good reason. Plain text is universally readable and takes up very little space. Nothing is more annoying than opening up an 87k message that contains one sentence (less than 1k's worth) and a gaudy background image that consumes the remaining 86k. What was accomplished by sending that message? Sure, the receiver might have understood what the sender was communicating, but he was also pelted with a useless background image that wound up not being related to the reason for that particular e-mail.

When an HTML newsletter really isn't offering something that a text one could not, then please do yourself (and your readership) a favor and stay away from HTML.

Is Your Software Up to the Challenge?

Before you start distributing in HTML, you need to be sure that your list software can handle the format. If your list software of choice cannot handle HTML messages, then you obviously need to move on to another package (or give up the idea of publishing in HTML). A common fallacy is that all HTML messages are somehow sent as HTML: This is not quite correct. HTML messages are sent as text. Remember that HTML is merely a markup language—it's text-based. That is, an HTML document is a text document, containing special codes that tell the browser—or, in this case, the e-mail program—how to display the message. So when you send an HTML message, you're really sending a plain text message. So you need to do two things. You must make sure that the message is sent as text. But you must make sure it's sent as a particular type of text, as HTML text.

You need to be sure the message has the appropriate content type set in its SMTP header—the stuff that appears at the top of a message that directs how the message wends its way through the Internet. (Most mail programs display the From, To, and Subject lines, but hide most of the other header lines, things such as Message-ID, Return-Path, and Content-Type) This is not something you can do with most e-mail programs; the program will create the header for you. If you're using special mailing-list software, though, you may be able to modify it.

On the other hand, if you're using an HTML-capable e-mail program, chances are it will set the header correctly. But as we'll see a little later in this chapter, there are reasons why you may not want to use one of these programs.

The e-mail program reading your message—assuming it's an HTML-capable program—can display your message in one of two ways. It could display it in the way you intended, as an HTML message: using the appropriate colors, the images, the font formatting, and so on. Or it can display it as plain text; that is, the reader will see the actual HTML tags inside the message, the "raw" HTML. The program determines whether a particular message should be displayed as HTML or as plain text by reading the Content-Type line in the message header. The e-mail program will view a message as plain text if the following message header is included:

```
Content-Type: text/plain; charset="us-ascii"
```

Plain text is the default for text-based messages, so if the message does not contain a Content-Type header at all, the message will be interpreted as plain text. Therefore, without a specific type of header, your HTML message will not show up looking like a Web page. Instead, your recipients will see the HTML code itself. The way to ensure that an HTML-capable e-mail client will view your HTML message correctly is by using the following header lines:

```
MIME-Version: 1.0
Content-Type: text/html; charset="us-ascii"
```

These header lines specify two things. The first line informs the recipient e-mail program that the message contains more than just plain text. And the second line states that the text is HTML text. That is, that the text is intended to be viewed as an HTML document.

Ask your list host or consult the documentation for your list software to see how to force this header to be included in all outgoing messages. If you don't add this header, the receiver of the message will not be able to see it in all its HTML glory, even if he does have an HTML-capable e-mail program.

Generally speaking an HTML-capable e-mail program will add the correct header lines automatically. If you don't use any special formatting, it's sent with the Content-Type: text/plain; charset="us-ascii" line. Use the special formatting tools, and it's sent with the Content-Type: text/html; charset="us-ascii" line. (To complicate the issue, it's possible with some programs to send the message with both plain text and HTML text—Eudora, for instance, asks if you want to send it Plain, Styled, or Plain & Styled. Pick the latter, and Eudora includes the Content-Type: multipart/alternative line.)

If you have an e-mail program that allows you to format the message, then it will probably be sending it out with the correct header lines (but check to see what the received message looks like—you can't send HTML messages from AOL or CompuServe, even though those systems allow you to format e-mail). However, while HTML e-mail clients will allow you to perform rudimentary formatting (add graphics, change font size, color, and face, etc.), most will not allow you to use advanced formatting (such as working with tables). For that, you'll need to create the HTML code in an HTML editor or a text editor, and import the code in a text message.

My Current HTML Procedure

When I first started the *Lockergnome HTML Daily* newsletter, I created a template—a plain text file containing HTML tags—that I could use for each message (using Notepad as my HTML editor); all I had to do was drop the day's text into the correct part of the message.

I also configured my Lyris account using the Web interface. Lyris is a very sophisticated system, and allows you to add or remove any header line you want. I made sure I was using `MIME-Version: 1.0` and `Content-Type: text/html; charset="us-ascii"` for this particular list.

Now, here's the procedure I follow when I send out a message

1. Using the template as my foundation, I insert that particular day's content (again, using Notepad as my editor).
2. Still in Notepad, I copy that issue's HTML code to the Clipboard.
3. I fire up my Web browser and log into my Lyris account.
4. I navigate my way to where I'm able to paste the HTML code into the mailing form.
5. I click the Send button (in my Web browser, still logged in to my Lyris account).
6. I sit back and wait for the issue to be distributed by Lyris.

HTML and File Size

HTML files, especially those containing images, can get really large, really quickly. I'm not saying that you can't use images in your messages, but try to keep the message's total size below 20k if possible. If you go over that amount, consider resizing your graphics or cutting them out entirely. Most e-mail clients will readily display the size of an e-mail message sitting in your Outbox. It never hurts to check; the last thing you want is an upset subscriber.

Certain HTML e-mail clients and HTML composition/editing programs will "bloat the code," adding extraneous codes that can turn a 14k message into a 60k message without changing how the document appears onscreen. You need to decide which method works best for you and your situation. I'm an old-school coder, though; I still do everything in Notepad (or any given "vanilla" text editor). Yes, you can find great WYSIWYG (What You See Is What You

Get) HTML programs out there, but they're not very efficient with HTML and can wind up creating unnecessarily large files.

You'll have more control over your document if you use an outside HTML editor and import your code as either an attachment or a template. If you're looking to compose HTML messages on-the-fly without having to worry about bloated code, steer clear from Microsoft products at this time (Outlook 98, Outlook 2000, and/or Outlook Express); they're the worst offenders. Netscape Communicator comes with an able client, which will allow you to import HTML (and will not change it in any way). You can also compose a message within Communicator, but again, you'll be dealing with a little bit of extraneous code.

If you go the route of using an "outside" HTML editor (that is, something other than your e-mail client to compose your HTML), check the size of the HTML file before and after you send it. When you discover a major discrepancy in size, I'd strongly advise you to find a new way to distribute your issues. If you start out with 6k worth of HTML code and your subscribers receive a 50k message, you have a problem. The e-mail client you used to send your message may have inflated the code by adding proprietary tags or extra spaces to it.

Who likes to receive messages over 100k in size on a regular basis? Not everybody has a fast connection to the Internet, and the world doesn't have that much bandwidth to waste. On top of this, some e-mail service providers charge according to the size of the message you send. The smaller they are, the less you'll have to pay.

I've watched e-publishers use their e-mail clients and/or HTML editors to create and distribute messages 100k (or more) in size. In certain instances, I showed them that their HTML code shouldn't have been much over 30k. Shaving 60 percent off *anything* is substantial. I did this simply by mailing their message using three different methods (using list software directly, and by using two regular e-mail programs). The size was simply reduced by using the most direct method (using the list software, which didn't alter the HTML code at all). If you've got money to burn, and you don't think that your subscribers will care about larger messages, then you're in the clear. However, I'd wager to say that you're not in that boat.

TIP

If it's doable, have someone develop an HTML template for you to use; finding a coder who understands the intricacies of HTML in a plain text editor is a major *plus. Those individuals are more likely to cut out the extraneous tags and keep your HTML documents manageable in size.*

Would You Like an Attachment with That?

If you can't get your list software to handle HTML mail outright, you might check to see whether it will accept messages with file attachments. A subscriber won't need to have an HTML-capable e-mail client to read a message with an attached HTML document. Your e-mail will pop up, and the receiver will be informed that a file (or multiple files) is attached to it. From that point, he should be able to save and/or view the HTML file in his Web browser of choice.

The only marketing concern with this method is that it requires the receiver to take an extra step in order to access your information. Sure, it's only a matter of clicking and viewing, but there is a far greater convenience with HTML mail that shows up directly in the e-mail window without involving any user interaction. I suggest attaching only as a last resort; poll your subscribers if necessary to find out if they would find it helpful or annoying.

CAUTION

Understand that not everybody appreciates attachments with mail messages, and not every e-mail client can handle attachments in the same manner. Some users have their e-mail clients set up to automatically reject messages that include attachments.

Image References upon Request

There are two ways for you to put images into your HTML mail messages. You can attach them directly into the message; that is, the image is carried along with the message, it's actually transferred with the message and placed onto the recipient's hard disk. Or you can link to the image from the message. The image itself sits on a Web server somewhere, and when the user views the message his e-mail program will retrieve the image and display it in the correct place. In other words, the image file is *not* transferred with the message; rather, it is retrieved across the Internet when it's needed.

Unfortunately, neither method is perfect. If you attach the image to the message—if the image travels with the message—it won't work properly in many recipients' e-mail programs. On the other hand, if you link to the image across the Internet, the viewer has to have his Internet connection running when he views the message, or the image can't be retrieved.

Linking to an Image

Linking to an image from an HTML e-mail message is no different from doing so in a Web page; you simply use the IMG tag. The actual image, however, should be located somewhere on your Web server. Don't make the mistake of linking to an image on your hard disk! If the image source sits somewhere on your personal hard drive, ask yourself: does the world have access to your computer? No. So while this first example would work:

```
<IMG
SRC="http://www.lockergnome.com/images/lockerlink.gif">
```

This would not:

```
<IMG SRC="C:\My
Documents\Newsletter\Images\lockerlink.gif">
```

This tag will attempt to find the image locally—on the reader's hard disk—when the HTML mail is read.

I'd advise that you link to an image, not attach it to the message. The message size will be smaller, which may well save you money (if you're using a list service, the more you send the more you spend). And, as you'll see in a moment, attaching images is a real problem anyway. But you can't make everybody happy. Not everybody reads e-mail while online (especially those not from the United States). Many individuals choose to compose and read their messages offline, if only to keep that phone line freed up for important calls.

Certain dial-up configurations will enable a user's modem to immediately initiate a connection when an HTML message is trying to access an image on the Web. If a dial-up session does not initiate, the user could be pelted with error messages (a message for each image that can't be loaded because there's no network connection). These messages are annoying to the users, to say the least. You might encourage users to tweak their dial-up networking settings to *not* automatically connect to the Internet when an online object is being referenced while offline. A "LAN" setting usually works well but isn't always an option. Should a user continue to complain after exhausting the dial-up networking options, encourage him to view your issues while still online, to subscribe to a text

TIP

You can keep the same coding for an image in each issue, yet change the actual image. For instance, let's say you reference a graphic called 'billandpam.jpg' and you plan on changing the image frequently. You can upload new versions of the image to your Web server without having to change the HTML code of your message.

version of the same newsletter (if available), or to view the newsletter at your Web site.

Also make sure that the image to which you're referring actually exists. There's nothing more irritating than a broken image link. When you put images on your own Web server, you shouldn't have too many "broken image" problems (as you should have control over what is and is not uploaded into your account).

Attaching Images to HTML Messages

It's possible to attach images to the message, so the image travels with the message and thus does not have to be retrieved from the Web when the message is read—it's already on the recipient's hard disk. However, you probably won't use this method, for a variety of reasons.

First, how do you create HTML mail messages with attached images? You'll need a WYSIWYG graphical mail program such as Eudora or Outlook. For instance, if you're using Eudora, you can simply copy an image into the Clipboard and then paste it into a message where you want it by pressing Ctrl-V. Or use the Insert Object button-menu on the toolbar, and choose Picture; then you can select the image file you want to insert into the message. (You may have to set up various configuration options to get the program to send the images properly—take a close look at the program's documentation, and experiment a little.)

If you're using a nongraphical program, you probably won't be able to attach the image anyway. For instance, if you're using the Lyris list software, there's really no way to attach an image to the message and have it appear in the message. So there's a good chance that once you've got a really big subscriber list and you switch to a heavy-duty list program, you won't be able to attach images to your HTML messages.

So, let's say you're using a WYSIWYG program, and you paste an image into the message. When you send your message, the image travels along with it. But what happens when it gets to the other side? It may not be displayed, depending on the program being used and how the recipient has set up the program. Some programs that are capable of displaying images inside the message may not do so if the user hasn't chosen a particular configuration option. The image may simply be saved on the recipient's hard disk as an attachment—the reader would have to open the attachment in order to view it, hardly what you intended.

In general I'd say that you're better off linking images, rather than attaching them. If you attach it may not work. If you link, it will. And if subscribers don't like receiving messages with linked images, well, those are the people who are better off with the text version of your newsletter anyway. You simply can't please all of the people all of the time.

Playing in Traffic

Another advantage HTML newsletters have over their text counterparts is your ability to easily track how many times a particular issue is viewed. If you have a statistics package running in conjunction with your Web server, and you load in an "invisible" image from the Web within an HTML newsletter, you should be able to count how many times that particular graphic was loaded during any given period of time. Your graphic doesn't have to be invisible, but make sure you're not referencing it anywhere else but in your HTML newsletters. Or, if you want to take that idea to the next level, use different "invisigraphics" for each individual issue or each day of the week/month. The image has to be only 1x1 pixels in size and saved in whatever format you choose. While some users might not be connected to the Internet while reading your missives, this will still give you a better idea as to how many eyeballs are actually staring at your scribblings.

Maximum Compatibility

Naturally, we all use different computers that have different configurations. For the most part, this isn't a major problem. But when you begin to explore advanced operations (like the publishing of HTML e-mail newsletters), incompatibilities start to pop up like dandelions on an Iowan lawn. You may not like to use the "other guy's" software, but that doesn't mean your subscribers feel the same way. Don't download every e-mail program known to humanity simply to examine your HTML e-mail's appearance in each one. Get ahold of the "biggies" first and work your way down. It's safe to assume that the e-mail clients bundled with Web browsers are popular choices. When your HTML document shows up fine in one but not in another, check to be sure that your code is correct. I wouldn't suggest limiting your audience to using only one e-mail client. Unless, of course, your subject matter revolves around the use of said program.

Not all formatting that you use on a Web page is suitable for an HTML e-mail message. Stay away from using frames, anchors, and advanced elements (DHTML, JavaScript, Java, etc.). Tables are fine, but remember that not every user will be running in the same resolution. If you have a table's fixed width set at 400 pixels, keep in mind that some people are running in 640x480 resolution and may have to scroll horizontally to see your message. Avoid placing too many table width limitations in HTML newsletters (as you might do on a Web page).

Having to scroll vertically through an HTML document is customary, but having to scroll horizontally to see the entire page is often seen as a nuisance. Anything you can do to help your reader avoid having to scroll horizontally is good, and not setting width limitations is a good start. It's safe to assume that the width of the viewable message will be somewhere between 300 and 500 pixels wide (depending, again, on the user's screen resolution).

Step outside your own computer for a while, and look at how other people are seeing your messages. You might even consider soliciting screen shots from subscribers that show how your issues appear in their Inboxes.

Finding the Look

E-publishers often make the mistake of not presenting their content in an easy-to-read manner. Do you recall the two examples of text newsletter formatting from Chapter 8? The potential for bad formatting is increased when you're using HTML because you have more design elements to tinker with—images, colors, and fonts. If one of those elements is out of line, your whole publication could suffer.

You might already have a style for your newsletter; look at your Web site. The two don't have to be the same in every respect, but if you use the same colors, fonts, and graphics, you'll be establishing a subtle (and somewhat direct) relationship between your Web site and e-mail newsletter. Once you decide on a design, make sure you apply it consistently. For instance, if a heading is bold in one section, make sure it is bold in another.

> **TIP**
>
> *If you're not incredibly familiar with HTML, then consider finding someone who is somewhat proficient with it. He'll be able to fix rough spots, clean up the formatting, and make your newsletter appear professional.*

When you're planning your design, remember also to reserve space for subscription guidelines. If you rely heavily on tables, consider putting administrivia in a "sidebar" of sorts. Also be sure to leave room in the design for advertisements. You may not have any in the beginning, but get your subscribers used to the fact that there will (eventually) be something there.

Choosing the color scheme for your publication is also an important planning step. Before you make use of graphics, before you play with fonts, before you mess with the document's layout . . . decide which colors you'd like to use. For example, what color background do you want and what color text? Do you want a colored bar down the side or across the top? Colored bullets? Different-colored headings? Most readers prefer dark text on a light background, but you are free to experiment with all combinations.

And what about images? You have probably visited Web pages that had a textured graphical background behind the text; such backgrounds are available for HTML e-mail too. You could use a background graphic in your publication (nobody's stopping you), but remember that *more* doesn't always mean *better*. If a background graphic adds functionality to, or doesn't detract from, the user's overall interpretation of your content, then you're safe. The graphics you'll most likely be using in HTML mail are for banner advertisements, screen shots, and/or your logo. Adding a graphic without a valid reason, however, isn't worth the effort. Assume that your readers have subscribed so that they can get information, not so they can appreciate your newsletter design panache. Eye candy is important, but functionality should take precedence in most instances.

What about the fonts? Not only are the actual typefaces you use important, but their sizes and colors are adjustable characteristics that will allow you to accentuate certain elements of your HTML newsletter. Your "content text" should be at a medium (regular) size and in a color that properly contrasts with your background color. The section headings should be a larger font size and possibly a different color. As a general rule of thumb, don't use more than three typefaces in the same document; two distinct fonts are plenty.

The typefaces installed on your computer are probably not the same as the ones that your subscribers have, and if you use a font that someone doesn't have installed, that person will not be able to see your message as you intended. Some generic font (such as Times New Roman) will substitute for the missing one on the other user's PC; your publication might end up looking worse on that person's screen than if you had used a more ordinary font to begin with. If you want to ensure that every user is viewing your HTML message with the same font (or something similar), stick to the basics: Use Helvetica or Arial instead of Shulba Regular, Courier New instead of Gerrard 074, Times New Roman instead of Waitress Bacon, and so on.

Cookie-Cutter Templates

Have you ever tried to make gingerbread men without using some sort of cookie cutter to help shape each great-tasting guy? I don't care if you're no good in the kitchen—you should have caught my analogy loud and clear. Instead of sculpting each cookie individually, you'll save time by using a predefined mold to define the borders and characteristics of each one. By stripping down an issue's format to its barest essentials (when you're finally happy with whatever style you choose) and using that as a template for every subsequent issue, you'll save time in the e-zine construction process and retain consistency amongst your issues. This holds true for both text and HTML e-publications.

It's easier to use HTML newsletter templates when you edit your code "by hand" (that is to say, in a simple text editor). This way, there will be no guesswork as to where you'll need to insert content. With WYSIWYG HTML editors, it is often difficult to maintain a consistent look throughout the same document. Spacing will typically turn out not to be equidistant, and you'll most likely be bloating the HTML code a bit by not going directly to the source. If you view or edit the HTML source, however, you'll be seeing simple text—which, of course, will contain HTML tags. There's no conjecture involved with using text-based templates.

You can always change what your template contains; it doesn't take much time to tweak. A little nip and tuck job every once in a while typically yields positive results—as long as you'd be making subtle changes more often and sweeping changes less often. The following is the part of the code I use for *Lockergnome's HTML Daily* (before I insert the day's content):

```
<!– PROGRAM –>->
<p><hr size="3" color="#990000" noshade><font
   size="5">GnomePROGRAM</font><p>


<!– SYSTEM –>->
<p><hr size="3" color="#990000" noshade><font
   size="5">GnomeSYSTEM</font><p>


<!– CANDY –>->
<p><hr size="3" color="#990000" noshade><font
   size="5">GnomeCANDY</font><p>


<!– DESKTOP –>->
<p><hr size="3" color="#990000" noshade><font
   size="5">GnomeDESKTOP</font><p>
```

If you'll notice, there are two blank lines between each section; this is done so that I can quickly locate the spots where I need to paste information.

Midstream Modification

Are you already publishing a text newsletter? And you don't want to start all over again with a new HTML one? Well, you might not have to . . . as long as your new creation isn't too dissimilar from your original one. You can continue to offer your traditional text publication but also offer a new, "improved" HTML version. I had to face a major decision about this in the summer of 1998. Up until then I had been sending out Lockergnome in plain text every other week. I wanted to make radical changes in my publication's circulation and configuration; at that point, I created an *HTML Daily* missive alongside the "classic" text version. I stepped up the pace 200 percent, but doing so has opened many doors for me.

As I've noted before, not many small companies are distributing HTML newsletters at this time . . . let alone on a daily basis. When people ask how many individuals are on the Lockergnome editing team, I answer quickly: one. People are surprised, but I really don't see why. I have the same essential information in my weekly text issues as I do in the daily HTML versions—they're just being distributed in two completely different styles. Lockergnome had good click-thru rates before I switched to this new (seemingly frantic) publishing schedule. After I made the change, I saw my readership satisfaction and name recognition skyrocket.

Now, instead of offering a killer issue every other week, I was entering Inboxes on a daily and/or weekly basis. Because my subscriber database was well over 100,000 before the switch, and I didn't want to start over again from scratch, I decided to copy the list to a separate database and send *Lockergnome's HTML Daily* to it. This was a bold move, and I was initially curious as to how my readers would respond. They had been receiving Lockergnome as text for the longest time, and here was this radical new style. Not only was it more frequent, but also in a different format.

Yes, some subscribers were up in arms, and some just silently unsubscribed from the HTML version and stuck with the text one. Over a period of six months, I watched my subscriber numbers stagnate, but they eventually started to grow again. I knew this would happen, but it was a risk I was willing to take. I didn't change the content of my newsletters, so I assumed that most subscribers wouldn't be totally turned off. You're better off starting out with different versions from the start—this way you won't have to face a similar "splitting" decision. I was successful, but that doesn't mean every publisher will be.

I've faced a few headaches from managing two separate (but similar) e-newsletters. Individuals sign up for both, unsubscribe from one, and are upset when they continue to receive the other. Some get annoyed with one format (typically the *HTML Daily*) and unsubscribe from both versions without hesitation. But, for the most part, I've had few complaints.

Secret Instructions

When I copied the classic text subscriber database over to HTML, I realized that not every user would have an HTML-capable e-mail client. For this reason, I included a "hidden" message at the top of each HTML issue that could be viewed only by individuals who couldn't receive HTML mail. Here's an example of what I'm currently using within *Lockergnome's HTML Daily*:

```
<!--
Read today's newsletter online for FREE:
<a href="http://www.lockergnome.com/issues/daily/
19990323.html">
http://www.lockergnome.com/issues/daily/19990323.html
</a>
To unsubscribe, please e-mail the following address:
$subst('Email.UnSub')
Don't worry about anything else below this paragraph.
It's for those with HTML e-mail clients. Just go to
the above listed web address to view this issue
perfectly in your Web browser. Thanks again! -->>
```

You'll notice arrowlike patterns at the beginning and end of this section; anything between them will be completely hidden from view if the user is using an HTML-capable client (or browser). This allows me to "talk" to the subscriber who can see plain text only. I further entice that user to view this particular issue online at a specific URL. I wrapped the Web address within an HTML tag for the benefit of AOL readers, who can't see HTML in an e-mail message but *can* see URLs. So, no matter what program a subscriber is using, he can still read my daily stuff easily.

The next item you'll notice is the unsubscribing directions. Since the average user will see the following HTML code as "garbage," he needs to know how to be removed from future *Lockergnome HTML Daily* mailings.

You'll also notice a weird-looking code (`$subst('Email.UnSub')`. This is a mail merge command that my list software (Lyris: http://www.lyris.com/) will translate into a unique address that the user can e-mail to be immediately removed from the *HTML Daily* database. I could also include each subscriber's actual e-mail address (to which the issue is being sent), but I want to keep this section as small as possible. When the user is able to view the newsletter in an HTML-capable e-mail client, he will see both the unique unsubscribe address as well as his actual subscribed address.

Finally, I advise the subscriber that he can stop reading. Who knows if people actually do? But at least they know that there's "nothing else to see here." After closing the "hidden" comments with the right-pointing arrow pattern, I insert about 25–30 blank lines . . . again, just to give the appearance that there's nothing below the instructions worth noting. (When the message is viewed in an HTML-capable mail program, the blank lines are omitted, just as they would be in a Web browser.)

The Lost Clients of Atlantis

A few e-mail clients out there don't render HTML issues correctly in the user's Inbox, nor do they enable the user to easily view the "secret instructions." These programs fall somewhere in between "text only" and "HTML-capable." Usually corporate users, whose companies use some proprietary e-mail program, fall into this category.

Just because an e-mail client can handle rich-text formatting (like underlined words or font color modification) doesn't mean that it can handle all forms of HTML mail. You know this, but most end users don't. Some individuals want to subscribe to something that's a bit prettier than plain text but don't have the right software for the job. This scenario is important to remember when users approach you with certain formatting inaccuracies.

When I started to do HTML mail, I was thrilled because I could include longer URLs without having to worry about them wrapping incorrectly in the subscriber's window. So instead of clicking on a link that looked like this:

- `http://www.altoonalibrary.com/users/michael/robertson.html`

The user would click on a link that looked like this:

- `Visit Site`

This wasn't a problem for people who viewed the issue "normally" in their Inbox or on the Web, but subscribers with "middle of the road" clients couldn't see the URL, nor could they click on it to load it in their browser. This was a minor problem that was easily solved. I reverted back to providing the full URLs for most of my featured links as well as posting the online URL for that particular issue within the HTML newsletter (much like I had done in the "secret instructions"). That way, *any* reader could easily do a quick copy/paste job to visiting any given URL. I'm always shooting for maximum compatibility, and so should you.

Chapter Eleven

Working with Discussion Groups

Why do an e-mail-based discussion list (as opposed to publishing an e-mail newsletter)? Simple: Lists bring people with common interests together. Individuals are able to share their resources, ideas, and opinions in a straightforward, familiar format. Who doesn't know how to send and receive e-mail? Even my technologically dumbfounded parents have mastered that skill. It doesn't take too much more knowledge to grasp the basic concepts of e-mail discussion groups.

While newsletters and bulletins are generally one-sided, discussion groups are interactive. In fact, a user may be more inclined to remain subscribed if he plays an active part in your list's existence. In a discussion list, any member of a group may "post" (that is, send a message to the rest of the list members). Then anyone else may respond to that post, and that's how the action gets generated. You might think that running a discussion list would be less work than publishing a newsletter because other people are generating the content for you. But it isn't necessarily so. The workload is not lighter; it's just different, as you'll learn in this chapter.

> **NOTE**
>
> *Before we go further, you should note my take on whether or not this format should be identified as discussion groups or lists. "List" may refer to the actual physical property, whereas "group" refers to the people using the list. In essence, however, I believe the two words are (at least in the minds of your subscribers) interchangeable.*

Electronic Societies

Everybody's talking about the creation of Internet communities. I see businesses spending lots of money on Web design trying to build profitable communities, thinking that pushing glitz and glamour is the way to attract loyal community members. It could happen—and monkeys could fly out of my floppy drive. There are very few "successful" online communities today, and 80 percent of them can be found in either the Usenet newsgroups or e-mail discussion lists. What does that say to you? It says that online communities can work, but not because someone threw millions of dollars into them. Communities work because they provide user interaction.

Ever try to have a one-sided conversation? It gets boring—real quick. Or, have you ever been in a situation in which one individual monopolizes the discussion? Most people will respect that kind of enthusiasm, but too much talking becomes more of a negative than a positive. There *is* a happy medium, and finding it is dependent on several variables. Anyone can have the right tools in place, but without a well-mannered user base supporting the discussion, no amount of money will be able to help. This is why many multimillion-dollar business plans are destined for delivering disappointment from the word "go."

The Software Side

You'll find that most popular server-side software can handle discussion groups easily. A reader will send a message to the list address and one of the following will take place:

- If it is a moderated group, the moderator will be asked to accept or reject the posting, or
- If it is an unmoderated group, the posting will be distributed to the rest of the list without human intervention.

That's the process in its purest form; it doesn't sound too difficult, eh? Understanding the basic concepts of discussion lists takes virtually no time. But not surprisingly, learning how to be a good list manager does take a *little while* longer.

Discussion lists will generally require more e-mail addresses than a newsletter does. You need one for the list server, one for the particular list, one for subscription requests, one for the moderator, and possibly one for each subscriber. All those addresses can be confusing, so make it as easy as possible for your users. You should set up your list software to automatically append instructions to the bottom of each post, after the primary content. If you do so, you'll receive fewer questions about basic operations. Ever hear of the KISS method? It stands for "Keep It Simple, Stupid." If you're not a good KISSer yet, you'll learn to be quickly.

You can control which address is used in replies to posted messages by setting a reply-to address. If Don posts a question, and Juan replies to Don's post, to which address is Juan's reply being sent? Is Juan's reply sent directly to Don, to the list server, or to both? Replies should default to the list when a person hits the Reply button, and not to the original post author. However, you need to make sure your subscribers are aware of this default, so they do not accidentally send personal messages to the list by mistake.

The Discussion Group Culture

Imagine walking into a library and screaming your lungs out. Yes, you'll get people's attention—and you'll also (in all likelihood) be removed from the premises. Being quiet in public libraries, out of respect for other patrons, is an unwritten rule; it's a guideline that very few people ignore. Very few people are unfamiliar with the function and role of these literary sanctuaries, so you wouldn't expect to see very many obnoxious outbreaks in these institutions. However, mailing lists are fairly new, and not everybody understands that each one has (most likely) developed its own ethos.

Before you establish your own discussion group, join a few others (related or unrelated to your preferred topic) to see how they operate. Observe how the users interact with one another and react to certain types of posts. Their responses may be indicative of what you will experience with your own list. Different subjects will lend themselves to users with different communication styles, but the community standards for acceptable behavior will, by and large, be comparable. To review the basics, simply refer back to Chapter 2's Netiquette section.

It's likely that you'll establish your own rules for the list as it develops—don't try to use someone else's policies. You can base your regulations on another set, but remember you have a different group of people on your list (with different interests and annoyances). Customize the ground rules to fit your readers' preferences, and you can't go wrong. At the same time, remember that you're still the one in charge.

If you don't have clear-cut rules in place before too long, users will find themselves drifting away from your list. Setting up an FAQ of sorts will help. You might require that all your new users read it before joining. (Although they might not actually read it, at least you've made it clear that such a document exists.) This way, they won't waste the existing users' time and resources with questions that have already been answered many times.

Interacting with List Members

You might have a discussion group set up to talk about the usage of duct tape in the home, but until you find enough active and interested users, you'll have nothing. This is the proverbial thorn in a discussion list's side. You can guide— not drive—the content in this kind of electronic publication. All activity depends on the quality and quantity of your members' discourse and disclosure. Too little, and users will not be inclined to post; too much, and your users will be overwhelmed.

When you haven't seen posts to your list for a little while, think about "throwing a log on the fire." Sometimes that's all it takes; push a few hot buttons, challenge the status quo, make people sit up and think. But don't be too overbearing if/when you decide to moderate or post to a list. Nobody likes being on the receiving end of an intimidating message. You're obviously in charge, but don't throw your weight around too much; a frightened user will be less likely to publicize his thoughts on your list. Be kind, courteous, and (above all else) open minded.

Not every user will come to your list with the same experience level. Some will be two-week-old "newbies" who don't know the difference between a Web page and a cucumber; others will be die-hard Internet wizards, hell-bent on putting everybody else in their place. Bringing these two wholly dissimilar subscriber types together in the same forum can be both a blessing and a blight. Advanced users might be very willing to help those who are less educated; they also have the potential for being a bit condescending in their public and personal responses. On the other side of the coin, novices may admit that they're new and incredibly enthusiastic to learn more; conversely, new users can be overtly unwilling to "go with the flow" and follow well-established Internet etiquette conventions. There's no perfect mix of personalities in discussion groups, but as long as your readers aren't complaining too much, you need not be concerned.

You'll come to love (and loathe) certain users; there will be those who post more than others, or who say something just for the sake of reminding the world that they're still alive. You want your lists to stay active, but don't be afraid to force those subscribers back on track when they start to stray. If your list is about chocolate pudding, and a discussion starts heading down the "pie" road, be quick to remind your subscribers that the pastry department can be found right around the corner.

Moderated or Not

As a child, when you needed permission to do something, which parent did you turn to first? Who was more conservative or liberal with judgments? In my house, Dad would usually let us get away with just about anything, whereas Mom would think about it for 2.3 seconds and then give her *final* answer. Not to say that Dad didn't love us more than Mom, just that he wasn't quite as cautious.

Remember that a moderated list is led and controlled by one party (either an individual or definite group of people). This format offers more control over discussion direction and development, and message formatting, and is generally used with lists with more than a few dozen readers who might not know each other intimately. On the other hand, unmoderated lists are not censored by a central figure, cater to hundreds (or thousands) of subscribers, and have the ability to become unruly at a moment's notice. "Unmoderated" is not necessarily the same as "unstructured." They aren't always "out of hand," but it doesn't take much to throw a discussion list's harmony out of whack.

Do you want to operate a moderated (Mom) or unmoderated (Dad) list? Ask yourself what kind of user you plan on attracting, and how much time you want to devote to being an editor. Moderated lists will usually take more time from your day than unmoderated lists.

While it is possible to switch between these two formats after you start, you want to make sure that your readers don't become alienated with the change. It isn't easy to move from moderated to unmoderated and vice versa. Individuals may be used to speaking their minds and having their opinions heard without asking or waiting for approval; equally, those used to seeing some form of structure in place may not take kindly to a glut of unsuppressed and/or unrelated messages.

A Sizeable Law

Your subscriber base will grow in size over time, and so will the amount of activity. So don't be concerned when a large company comes along and tries to do what you're already doing (or plan on doing). If you have a dedicated following, then what are you really worried about? Besides, you'll find that (especially with discussion groups) your user base is not going to grow very large. And that's okay.

Are you familiar with the law of diminishing returns? This isn't necessarily an enforceable law, but it holds true for discussion groups. In the beginning, you probably won't have more than a few users contributing to your list; you'd assume that as your subscriber base grows larger, so would the number of posts. This is true, to a certain degree.

Imagine that you presented a question to a list that contained 1,000 members. Would you really want (or expect) to receive 1,000 responses? Chances are, you'll get fewer than 10—both personally and publicly. It is safe to assume that the mentality of any given user is: "Someone else will take care of it" or "Someone probably already took care of it." You might have over 10,000 people in your discussion group, but not everybody is going to post, and not everybody will want dozens of messages streaming into his Inbox on a regular basis. Once a user's question is answered publicly, it will probably not be answered again more than a couple of times (even if you take lag

NOTE

"Lag time" refers to the time it takes for a message to get from Point A to Point B when it experiences congestion in between. More often than not, electronic communications are instantaneous, but sometimes networks go down.

time into account). The amount of comment repetition also depends on how you have your list set up. Obviously, unmoderated lists will not automatically delete repeated information, whereas moderated list administrators will be able to pick and choose from the best responses and let them pass through to the group.

Subscriber's Digest

Whereas e-mail newsletters are always broadcast to the entire subscriber database at one time, a discussion group member may choose to receive posts as they come in or in a regular "digest" format. A digest contains all the messages posted in the specified period (daily, weekly, or some other interval), one after the other, in a single message. Depending on the abilities of your list software, digests can be automatically compiled or put together by hand.

You should give your new members the option to receive either form of mailing. For most users, a digest is the more attractive option. That way, they aren't bombarded with posts every time they check their e-mail. Digests are less intrusive (and, therefore, less annoying) to people who may want to read the discussion but not participate in it enthusiastically every day.

Other people prefer the immediacy of receiving individual messages throughout the day and the ability to respond to a post right away instead

TIP

The digest version may become more and more popular as the traffic in your discussion list increases over time. When the regular number of posts exceeds a reader's tolerable limit, he may want to change his subscription. Make this as simple for readers to do as possible (either through e-mail commands to your list software or via a form on your Web site).

of waiting until the next digest. Your most active list participants will probably want to receive messages this way.

Digests are easier to archive than individual messages, so you will probably want to create a digest for archival purposes even if you don't offer it to your subscribers. (Although if you've created a digest version, why *not* offer it?) The digests probably won't take up much less disk space than the individual messages, but instead of thumbing through 100 different documents to find a particular posting, a reader might need to look at only 10.

There is also the option of having your discussion list published *only* in digest format. This will give it a more "e-mail newsletter" like appearance, although the content will still largely be provided by your subscribers. You'll need to be wary of formatting issues in this case as well. (Turn back to Chapters 9 and 10 for hints about that.)

Text Only, Please

The first HTML message you post to nearly any discussion group will more than likely be your last because you'll probably be harassed unmercifully by other group members, or at the very least bawled out by the moderator. Think I'm kidding? Try it.

Unless you're subscribed to an established "HTML only" list, all your posts should be Text Only format. Check your e-mail client's settings to be sure that you're not broadcasting in "rich text" or HTML by default. Not doing so could prove fatal for you and your reputation. Thousands of lists have been around longer than you've probably been online, and more often than not, each one of those members will openly combat all forms of nontextual e-mail.

There is a time and place for HTML e-mail, but discussion group users are generally not ready for this new format. Since your list's survival depends on the activity of its members, it would be wise for you to follow the already-set conventions for this type of e-publication. Don't try to rewrite the book— especially when you're depending on other people for your list's continued existence. The fewer headaches a reader has, the more contented he will be with your service. Keeping HTML e-mail out of the picture as often as possible will help ensure continued subscriber satisfaction.

Unmoderated Madness

In the first chapter, I likened an unmoderated list to a room full of sugar-injected preschoolers. Fortunately, this isn't always the case—but if you don't keep a watchful eye over an uncensored group, your list can quickly degenerate into a complete waste of bandwidth and resources.

Allowing your users to "moderate themselves" is one viable solution. For the most part, you'll encounter few problems with smaller, microtargeted lists. Every once in a while, however, you'll bump into a mischief-maker. When that happens, interject and get the ball rolling in an agreeable direction again. As a list owner, you have the right to permanently ban users from joining or partaking in your list (moderated or unmoderated).

All unmoderated messages are automatically transmitted to all list members, so if you go the unmoderated route, your list members are probably going to continually experience certain minor annoyances. Making subscribe/unsubscribe instructions blatantly obvious on each post can help, but it won't solve the problem entirely. As I've mentioned before, even if you tattoo simple "unsubscribe" directions on your users' foreheads, some people still won't follow them. A user might wish to be removed from a list, and instead of following the correct procedure, he will broadcast his request to the rest of the group.

Then there's the dreaded "me too" virus. This is all too common, and should be stopped before it can infect too many subscribers. *Exemplum Gratis*: Copeland tells the group that he can't wait for the release of a new poetry anthology; Baughman chimes in with a brief agreement; Fehlman follows soon after with an even shorter response; Cawelti feels like he needs to concur; and so on. None of these members are adding anything worthwhile to the conversation. It's okay for subscribers to agree with other subscribers, but it's even more important for them to expound upon their thoughts. Encourage all the subscribers to spill their guts whenever possible.

> **TIP**
>
> *Your list software might be able to block messages sent from a particular user until he has been on the list for a certain period of time; this could very well weed out "mindless" posts typically seen only after a user first joins a discussion group. Again, you're trying to keep your existing readers happy.*

As list membership becomes larger and increasingly unwieldy, you might consider turning to a moderated format to cut down on the number of "useless" posts. Understand, too, that a discussion group that attracts people interested in a very specialized topic will typically encounter fewer user-centric problems than a discussion group that appeals to the masses.

Flame Wars

One user might post something that sets another user off, and before you know it, you've got what they call a "flame war" on your hands. Nobody wins in these situations. You'll encounter flame wars no matter which type of discussion list you choose to develop. The question is: Do you want to step in and break it up, or do you want to let them duke it out? I suppose your answer depends on your mood at the time.

Remember, however, that there are other users on your list, too. Not everybody appreciates getting caught in the middle of an argument and having his Inbox overwhelmed with largely pointless bickering. A list moderator should not let things get too far out of hand; unmoderated list owners might intervene only when the discussion falls into the realm of "off topic." It's like any group of people (virtual or in real life); you're going to have individuals who feel a certain way about an issue and others who will be diametrically opposed to those opinions. With luck, your list will attract every kind of user; the more diverse your readers' backgrounds are, the more dynamic your discussions will be.

Quality Control

Although the content in a discussion group is not driven by the moderator, it is very important to maintain a level of excellence in your list's content. If post after post is unreadable or unintelligible, you'll find yourself losing subscribers. Understand, though, that not everybody is gifted in the writing department. You're walking a thin line when you start picking and choosing posts. A user may become offended and believe that you're discriminating against him for some unfair reason, when in fact you just feel that he's not contributing anything worthwhile to the group. If someone confronts you with claims of unmitigated expurgation, explain to him why you chose not to let his post pass. You should always have good reason for your actions as a moderator; you never know when you'll need to defend yourself. A post may be cut because it is irrelevant, doesn't carry a solid argument, or repeats something that has already been expressed. A post should never be cut just because you "feel like it" or dislike the writer's point of view.

You will likely appreciate subscribers who can compose their thoughts coherently, but don't forget about those who can't compose a single intelligible sentence. When you run into this kind of user, contemplate doing a minor translation (or on-the-fly editing) before passing the post along to the rest of your list's members. Your grasp on grammar, spelling, and language syntax is going to translate directly into a more trouble-free time when it comes to weeding out lesser-quality material. This doesn't mean that an incoherent user doesn't have the right to take part in a discussion, just that a list's members will want to spend their time reading stuff *worth* reading.

To avoid potentially offending a user, before you distribute his "doctored" post, ask him if you can edit it first. Then, before you actually post the edited message, ask again for his final approval. Or, to avoid this interaction altogether, you might consider rewording his comments in a post of your own and giving him credit for the thought. His original point should still come across, without being clouded with poor writing skills. A wise woman once said to me: "The moderator should be more a policeman than an editor." Sometimes, however, you have to play both roles.

Once you have a good understanding of the types of material your subscribers enjoy responding to, you should start accepting only the posts that cater to their tastes. Ascertaining a group's desires is an innate ability; developing the skill will take time and can only be learned through hands-on experience. A good rule of thumb is to tolerate only what *you* enjoy reading or learning about. It's *your* discussion list, and it's obviously going to be covering your interests. Don't get to the point where you're accepting every bit of information that passes across your desk; having too much information can be just as disadvantageous as not having enough. The more subject-knowledgeable people you can attract to your list, the better chances it will have for long-term survival.

As the list moderator, you may also be able to control the formatting used in each posting. No two e-mail clients are exactly alike, nor are the people using them. Some users prefer to have their automatic word wrap set at an extremely low number, whereas others don't bother to set it at all. Depending on your list software, you might have the opportunity to edit each message as it comes in to ensure that all list messages appear the same onscreen.

You might also want to establish submission guidelines, so your participants can do their part to ensure that the postings are consistent and correct. You might request that your subscribers use a spell checker before submitting if you're tired of seeing misspelled words in every single post. Or you might define a standard for how public replies are to be formatted. If a message arrives that does not conform to your guidelines, you can correct it yourself, reject it, or return it to its author with a note explaining what needs to be fixed.

These are all quality control issues and should not be viewed as any less important than any other aspect of your discussion group. Nobody said that maintaining compatibility and consistency was going to be simple. The more variables you introduce to a situation, the more difficult it will become to manage. Control freaks will probably have a more difficult time trying to keep tabs on every aspect of their discussion list. Understand, however, that no matter what you decide to do, this is *your* e-publication. Your name and reputation are on the line, and you have the right to allow nothing to tarnish them.

The Web Page Complement

In earlier chapters, I've stressed the importance for having a Web site to complement your electronic publication. While it isn't mandatory, e-mail discussion group members (whether the group is moderated or unmoderated) would waste less time if they had a place to which they might turn for basic list information. Instead of posing a basic query to the group, they could flip to the online FAQ; rather than asking subscribers to introduce themselves, they could visit your "meet the members" page; instead of asking where to find "X," they could peruse your links to related resources. Your list's subscription instructions, charter/mission, and archives could also be placed on its Web site.

But such a source of information is important for prospective users as well. Before deciding to join your discussion group, they might want to read some of the more recent posts. Your Web site will act as the perfect gateway for attracting new, qualified readers. Let them know everything there is to know about your list, and you'll find that the overall dissatisfaction rate will be relatively low.

Some might say: "Why subscribe to a publication when you can get all its information via the Web?" This may be a valid point for newsletters, but you can't take part in a conversation without being a subscriber. A complementary Web site will do nothing but draw more subscribers to your discussion list.

It's possible to use the Web site as a "teaser," providing just a taste of information to try to entice people to subscribe and get the full version. However, "holding back" will hurt nobody but yourself and your list. By providing complete archives and full information on your Web site, you are showcasing your product (that is, your list) in its best light. Provide subscription directions (and perhaps a subscription form) conspicuously on your Web site, and visitors will want to subscribe.

When users finally join your discussion group, you might ask them to introduce themselves immediately to the rest of the list's members. This request can (and should) be delivered in the Welcome message that users receive upon subscription approval. New members will feel welcome, warm, and ready to participate, and existing members will possibly make a new friend or contact.

Directing the Discussion

It's not only important for the moderator to keep subscribers focused, but to inject new topics on a regular basis as well. Keeping content fresh and exciting is just as important for discussion groups as it is for e-mail newsletters (and, for that matter, for Web sites). When you stumble upon something interesting, share it with the rest of the group. Gauge their response; monorail trains might not be as exciting to them as classic locomotives. Continuing to post matter that nobody else seems interested in is not the best plan of attack. Sure, it's *your* list—but you're not the only one responsible for keeping people interested. Without user interaction, all you have is an e-mail newsletter or bulletin.

Beware also of jumping on the "me too" bandwagon. When every other Web site and e-mail newsletter is covering a certain story, it doesn't necessarily mean that you need to discuss it too on your list. Hype is a major problem in this industry; the last thing you want to do is allow your discussion group members to fall victim to it. When a product or service hasn't been released yet, don't spend too much time talking about it. Sure, it's a hot topic, but can you bring a unique perspective to the table? Covering popular issues is okay, but you should present them cautiously. Instead of simply telling your readers about an event, let them know what happened and how you feel about it.

As conversation threads begin to sound mundane and nothing new is being presented to the group, toss in a cherry bomb. That is to say, introduce an idea or concept to the group that is guaranteed to elicit a reaction. I used to be afraid of covering controversial and questionable topics, but I've found that more users will sit up, listen, and respond when someone comes along and shakes things up. Touch a nerve in readers, and (trust me) they'll be more than willing to take the time to respond to you. I'm not saying that you have to start contradicting every statement made in every single post, but by all means, stir up a hornet's nest every now and then. For example, you could start talking about a new feature in a foreign car in your moderated list that covers domestic autos.

Silent Scoldings

I don't know if it was something in my genes, but every time I went into a grocery store with my mother, I'd do something silly and get slapped. I don't know which felt worse: the actual smack, or the fact that the smack took place in front of other people. It's embarrassing when people chastise you in public, and the same holds true for being berated in discussion groups. As a moderator, you're viewed as the person in charge. As soon as you lay down the law, people will (assumedly) listen. Do *not* abuse this power.

When a problem arises, the last thing you want to do is ignore it. When someone steps out of line (and someone *eventually* will), don't make an example of him. Castigate him privately, and ask that he not repeat the offending behavior. Punishment need not be harsh, and your severity should depend completely on the context of the situation. More often than not, the subscriber will apologize and all the subscribers will be able to move on with their lives. From time to time, the troublemaker will refuse to repent; in this situation, don't feel guilty for banning the person from future list activities.

Marketing Mayhem

Everybody has an opinion, and it is assumed that most subscribers will be ready to share theirs at the drop of a hat. Nevertheless, it would behoove you to mentally note the relevance and ultimate usefulness of information a user posts on a regular basis, to make sure that nobody is taking unfair advantage of your list to promote himself.

Every once in a while, a member may talk about how he accomplished some amazing feat with his own online endeavor. If the information is relevant to that particular situation, there shouldn't be cause for alarm. But when every one of his posts is filled with self-glorifying tripe, it's time to become concerned. That user might be chiming in only when he can convey his own agenda. While he might be helping the other list members, chances are, this user is helping nobody but himself. It's a marketing trick (and a clever one at that), but other subscribers don't always want to be presented with this kind of "hidden" advertising. Again, watch for emerging patterns underneath the surface of readers' posts; don't cry foul if it happens once or twice within a dozen messages. The subscriber may very well be providing a solid example of how a tip or technique may be applied, but if his motives are habitually questionable, it's time to intervene.

Keep an eye on users' signature files, too. When someone posts to a discussion list (moderated or unmoderated), chances are, he'll have a signature block at the end of his message. Anything between 4 and 6 lines is customary; the signature should contain fundamental contact information like real name, occupation and/or title, traditional contact details, e-mail and Web addresses, and possibly a blurb concerning his "habitat" on the Internet. This space can easily be abused, though; a user may try to sneak in a URL or two that clearly aren't part of his personal or professional endeavors. Effectively, he could be using your list to make money for himself! This is completely unacceptable, and I suggest you put a "zero tolerance" policy in place in regard to nonrelated links in users' signatures. I've seen more new users trying to get away with this than older ones; they probably picked up some Internet marketing book that suggested it was okay to do this. I hope they can get a refund.

Chapter Twelve

Finding a High-Powered List Service

At the outset, most e-publishers will be comfortable with using software on their personal computers to distribute and manage their lists.

The only resource this home-based approach might save is money; it certainly won't save time. Since most users are not on a dedicated (or fast) Internet connection, and since most no-cost mailing-list packages aren't very powerful, you'll spend extra time and energy on completing crucial administrative tasks. Even if you believe you'll have hours to spare, that time *will* get sucked up without warning. Situations that will demand your immediate, undivided attention will unexpectedly arise. The more support you have on the back end, the fewer headaches you're going to encounter. When you're running distribution software on your own computer, you're pretty much your *own* support team.

Sooner or later, you'll find yourself searching for something more robust. You always have the option of purchasing your own server, bandwidth, and software, but with that (again) you're going to have to rely on yourself for support. This is okay for those who understand the Internet and it's various technologies, but the majority of e-publishers shouldn't waste their time putting out little fires and dealing with issues not directly related to their mailing list's management and/or content. Fortunately, hundreds of list service providers are vying for your attention. (See Appendix A for a condensed list.) But finding a company that works well with you, your subscribers, and your list is not a cut-and-dried undertaking. Many "gray areas" need to be cleared up before you sign on with any company that provides list services.

Cheap Stuff

Your wallet loves free lunches, but those meals don't always taste good. Your list doesn't have to be the biggest in the world to be "too big" for free list services. It is extremely important for you to think long term before you settle with any company in particular. Your subscriber base will be small in the beginning. Some e-publishers will want their member numbers to grow exponentially, whereas others will never allow their list to grow too large. Generally speaking, free services were not built for those of you who want to turn electronic publishing into a full-time job. They're great for part-time, nonprofit, weekend hobby lists, but I don't recommend attempting to start a professional, for-profit distribution through a free list service. It is quite possible to begin your venture with an all-purpose service and later move it to a more dedicated server, but try to remember your long-term goals before you make your decision.

You'll find yourself having more control, more stability, and more options when you pay for list hosting. However, the maxim "you get what you pay for" doesn't always hold true with list service providers. *Top dollar* doesn't always equal top service; again, take your time and do some comparisons. You don't want to pay out the nose for limited functionality with "X," when you know that "Y" gives you exactly what you need for much less money. Even if all your friends recommend a particular provider, their reasons for choosing it might not match yours.

Put That in Writing

Before you send out your first mailing through a list service, have a signed contract in hand. If it's "not their policy" to issue contracts, simply tell them that it's not your "policy" to work directly with businesses without some form of legal protection.

Said contract should contain expectations on both the server and the client side; you'll be responsible for not spamming people, and they'll be responsible for not sharing or abusing your list. Naturally, the contract should outline more expectations, but the key is to at least *have* a contract. Everybody involved should be protected from liabilities.

Bear in mind that you should be able to change providers at any time. Make an effort not to lock yourself down into a time-specific contract. Performance is what you should be seeking, and when "X" constantly fails to deliver in any aspect, it's time for you to start looking for "Y."

Ask and Get Answers

The questions in this chapter are not all-inclusive; use them as guidelines for what you should be asking potential list hosts. If you have a question, by all means, ask it! Demand full satisfaction with the responses to your queries. If answers aren't clear enough for you, continue asking until you completely understand. When a service provider is lax in its reply time and not very descriptive in its explanations, that may well be a sign of things to come. You're going to be relying on "Company X" to deliver your e-publication; *that company* works for *you*, and you shouldn't let it forget that point. Don't be snooty about it, but at the same time, don't let the company bully you. Plenty of other businesses would love to host your list.

Making a final decision in a single afternoon after speaking to only one list service provider is shortsighted; research is exceedingly important. Talk to other list owners who have used certain services and/or software, but remember that not every list (or list owner) is going to have the same needs. Compare software, services, and most importantly, experiences. That's exactly why the industry stories were included in this book. You're not the first person to do this, and I daresay you won't be the last.

Important Questions

Run through this list and choose the questions that are the most important to you (and to your list). Then customize those questions according to your needs and present them to the potential list providers; there is no minimum or maximum number of questions you can ask. (E-mail is a great medium for making the contact.) With luck, you'll hear back from a customer service individual within a few days. If you wait longer than a couple of weeks, I strongly recommend not using that company for list service. You need a list host to be prompt, honest, and direct. These questions will help you ascertain its level of competence and willingness to work with you intimately.

How long have you been around? Running list services?

You want to be sure that you're not hooking up with some fly-by-night operation. Start-ups are fine, but be sure it has the ability to pull things off. Find out what kind of experience it's had in dealing with its list software (and list-related issues) specifically.

What kind of list software do you use?

This may not seem important in the very beginning, but your list is only going to be as powerful as the software it is running on. Find out what the service's software can do for you, whether it has been customized, and whether you can ask for possible future customizations.

How will I be able to administer my list? Through e-mail, the Web, or either?

How comfortable are you with using the Web? Are you a point-and-click person, or would you much rather enter commands by hand? Sometimes it's good to have both options available to you. Classic list software will have e-mail command capabilities only, but Web interfaces have been created to be backward-compatible for interaction with those older packages. Administration is a daily task; if you're not comfortable with the process, you'll burn out quickly.

How extensive are your list software's options?

Assume that any list software's primary function is to mail messages to subscribers, but take note of all the bells and whistles at your disposal. Tweaking is practical; while beginners won't mess much with configuration, eventual exploration could very well unearth several possible opportunities. You will most likely never take advantage of every feature offered, but it's much easier to work with robust (as opposed to limited) packages.

Can I run multiple lists on the same account? Will this cost more?

One list is sufficient for now, but what if you would like to start another list at some point in the future? Is it even feasible for you to do, and how easily will the list software handle all your lists? Would it sit in the same account and use the same resources? You may not be thinking much past the operation of your first list, but you should never rule out the possibilities of future expansion.

Does your software have digest capabilities?

Discussion list administrators will probably be more inclined to ask this question, but you never know when automatic archival will come in handy. It is also important to ask where and how your mailings will be stored (to be retrieved via e-mail or through the Web).

Do I have the ability to use autoresponders?

Covered in earlier chapters (5 and 6), this feature will allow a user to e-mail a specified address and receive a document automatically within a few minutes. It is useful for setting up hands-off retrieval of past issues, essential subscription-related documents, and frequently accessed information.

Do I have the ability to use mail merge commands?

Covered in Chapter 8, the ability to use these codes will further enhance the subscriber's understanding of his list membership. You will be able to automatically insert a subscribed e-mail address, the date and time your mailing left the server, possibly a unique unsubscribe code, and so on. Out of all the mailing-list features, this is quite possibly one of the most powerful.

Is scheduling of delivery available?

Say you won't be in town for the next three months and your next few issues are set to be published. Instead of having to lug around a laptop and find an Internet connection, you might be able to have each issue distributed at specified days and/or times. This is useful even if you're going away for a few days.

How much will it cost me to distribute issues based on my schedule?

No two e-mail publications will be alike; while some will be under 10k in size and delivered on a weekly basis, others will be 25k in size and delivered on a daily basis. Find out what it will cost you to run your particular configuration through the service.

Can I send HTML messages? If so, can you show me exactly how?

Here is (quite possibly) the most frequently asked question. Even if you don't plan on distributing HTML messages in the near future, at least you can find out whether the option is available. Most likely, the service will refer you to the list software documentation. If you can't find the answer there, try locating the software's creator. HTML distribution will probably require only a few extra steps.

On what platform does your list software run?

Are you totally sold on a particular operating system and don't want to see your baby running on anything else? Are you already familiar with a certain list software package and/or platform? For those moving from one list service to another, this is a very prudent inquiry. You'll want any transition to go smoothly; if you're familiar with an operating system's peculiarities, moving to a similar system will minimize troubles. This isn't a question a novice will typically ask (as remote operating system selection is virtually meaningless for new users).

What is the maximum number of subscribers your software will handle?

Your list might have only 631 subscribers today, but you should expect growth. Even if you don't plan on having your database get much larger, you need to find out what the list software limitations are (if any). If the service is unsure of its "cap," just hope that you're not the first to discover it.

How large is the largest list you host at this time?

If the "Flying Teddy Bear Aglets" list has 45,000 subscribers and has been running smoothly for a year and a half on the service's server, and your list currently has 3,000 subscribers and isn't growing very rapidly, you should have nothing to worry about. However, if its largest list is 800, and yours is five times that amount, you may be hitting a few brick walls over the coming months.

What kind of bandwidth will my list have access to?

Most would stop at asking what kind of Internet connection a company has; unfortunately, the answer won't always tell the whole story. This is why you must ask specifically what kinds of resources your list can make use of. The bigger the bandwidth, the faster (and possibly the more efficiently) your mailings will be distributed. This concern will affect larger list owners especially (with 30,000 or more subscribers). Try to get an honest and direct answer. The service may have an OC-3 connection to the Internet, but its list software may have access only to the equivalent of a 56k modem.

How quickly will my list messages be delivered?

One hundred per hour? 1000 per hour? 10,000 per hour? Just how powerful is the service's list software, and does it make effective use of its bandwidth? How long will it take when you approve a document before you see it posted to my list? You may be surprised at the answers you get. Again, this will become a concern once your database starts registering in the five digits.

With your list software, how *exactly* are messages delivered to subscribers?

Older software tends to send out one message to one chunk of subscribers at a time. This means that if an address is caught within a problematic "chunk," that user may receive duplicate issues—if he receives the issue at all. Other list software will distribute *one* issue directly to *one* address. This method may take more time to complete and be more resource intensive, but delivery problems will shrink dramatically.

Do you tolerate unsolicited mailings?

You don't plan on sending out junk, and you certainly don't want to associate with anybody who has a relationship with someone who does. The service's answer should be either yes or no; there are no shades of gray here. A no-tolerance "junk e-mail" policy is like a golden ticket for legitimate e-publishers.

How available and able is your technical support?

When you're stuck at 2 a.m. on a Sunday morning, who will be there for you? And, more importantly, will that person understand the problem and be competent enough to assist? Is the service's "24-hour tech support" merely an answering machine that's plugged in all the time? If you have a serious question and someone doesn't know the answer, he should at least point you in the right direction or refer you to someone who might understand.

Will you let me know when there is a problem with my list or your server? How quickly?

After I pay someone to take care of a task, I expect to be notified when that task is not completed suitably. It's inevitable that you'll run into problems with your mailing list, so you need to identify the dedication level of your service provider. Will it fix the problem? Will it sweep the problem under the rug and hope it doesn't happen again? And, most importantly, will it let you know what's going on before you become aware of the problem?

Who are your other list clients?

You may very well be the service's first customer—and there's nothing wrong with that. However, a company should not be afraid to tell you who else has been using its services. It doesn't matter if you don't recognize any names. Converse with other list owners to see whether any "red flags" are associated with your potential list host.

What kinds of features does your software have to make my job easier?

Know your options up front. If the list provider hands you the manual, read it. You may work on a task for five days only to discover later that it could have been completed in five minutes. Don't make things more difficult than they need to be. Does the list provider know of any tips or tricks that will make your administrative duties more comfortable? Has it designed any proprietary software for its list owners to use?

Do you perform backups? If so, how often?

Crashes happen. If you lose your entire subscriber database, you're pretty much thrown back to ground zero. I would like to believe that every Internet service provider makes regularly scheduled backups, but this isn't always the case. Should the server experience an unrecoverable crash, you'll want to *know* that there is a very recent copy of your database somewhere else.

Can I get a copy of my subscriber database at any time (upon request or without intervention)?

I prefer to have fresh copies of my list databases sitting on my own computer. Not only are certain aspects of subscription management made more simple, but I'm less likely to lose that data entirely in the event of a server problem. You never know what is going to happen on the other end—especially if you're not familiar with your list service company yet. As your database grows larger, the importance of having your own copy will increase. That's your baby!

Can I easily import an existing list? Export? What's the file format?

Change is inevitable. If (or when) you need to move from one service to another, it's good to know of any potential incompatibility issues. I've found that most lists are stored (or can be exported) as simple text files, with one e-mail address on each line.

Can demographic data be included within my subscriber database?

When someone signs up for your e-publication, you may ask for his real name, country, ZIP code, etc. Will you be able to store this information alongside the user's e-mail address? You might need to manage those statistics separate from your actual subscriber list. This is more of a "convenience" question.

Will you show me how to add new subscribers to my list with a Web form?

Each mailing list has an e-mail address that can be used to add or remove users from the database. However, many list owners choose to use the Web as the main source for subscription-related inquiries. It is probably wise for you to consult your Web-site host regarding the construction of a Web form. The host may very well point you toward free script archives elsewhere on the Internet or suggest that you locate a programmer if you're not familiar with CGI or Perl.

Can you help me sell ad space?

You'll find (for the most part) that list services won't deal directly with managing advertisements in their clients' publications. Nonetheless, it never hurts to ask; they just might know someone who might be able to help you. And having a few more contacts will seldom hurt.

What makes you different from (if not better than) the other list services?

Every company thinks it is the best—but let it tell you in its own words. Can the company do anything truly special for you or your list? Will it bend over backwards to keep you as a client? This is a rather direct question, and the answer doesn't necessarily have to weigh heavily on your ultimate decision to use the company's services. You're just trying to find out what its mentality for hosting happens to be. Does the company think it can't be beat? Can it put its money where its mouth is?

Can you guarantee that my list will stay private and not be sold or used elsewhere?

A handshake isn't good enough for this one; you *need* to have the service's declaration in writing. Even the most trustworthy of sources should not be fully trusted. You never know who's going to want to get ahold of your list. Even after you have a signature, take whatever precautions possible to ensure that your list is not being used for mailings other than your own. Remember the "seeding" trick from Chapter 7?

Will you ensure that someone else can't "break in" and steal my subscriber database?

Find out what kind of security elements the service has in place on its server. Armed guards aren't necessary, but you'll want a certain degree of reassurance that your confidential data will not be seen by anyone other than those directly involved with the maintenance of that list.

Does your software have a record of sending an issue more than once to the same address?

It's very frustrating when you have multiple users tell you that they have received your most recent issue five times. "One is enough." Well, duh! Sometimes the user has duplicate addresses in the same database, sometimes the user's ISP duplicates the mailing, and other times your list software will get caught in a small loop. Pull out your troubleshooting tool belt! Duplicate deliveries are common; should they have a problem, ask what can be done to stop or curb it. This may be the only flaw for an otherwise exemplary list service provider.

How is bounced mail handled by your list software?

Do bounces trickle in as problems are encountered? Or are all the bounces reported in a single message at the end of the day? You're going to deal with bad addresses no matter where you turn. The larger the list, the more bounces you're going to receive. This may not be a concern initially, but the task could turn into a huge time waster in a short time. The more "automatic" cleaning the service's software will do, the happier you're going to be.

Can I get a report on mail bounces?

Having 100,000 users in your database is a wonderful feeling. Then again, if 20 percent of them are bad (or duplicate) addresses, you're fooling yourself and wasting resources. By knowing exactly how many bounced messages your list experiences on average, you can get a better idea about the true size of your subscriber database. If the reports tell you which addresses bounced (and for what reason), you can keep your list squeaky clean. It's a never-ending job.

Will I get regular delivery reports?

Who got what . . . and when? Were there any problems? To how many addresses was this issue successfully distributed? Keeping tabs on these statistics never hurts. The more you know about your list, the more confident you'll be about its foundation. And sometimes you need to know the numbers (especially when advertisers come a-knockin').

Can I send attachments with your list?

Some e-publishers would rather send HTML documents as attachments than "inline." In addition, if you choose to attach images to your issues, your list software will need to handle them. Keep in mind, though, that not every user enjoys receiving messages with attachments. Attachments will usually bloat the size of your mailing and could (consequently) increase your costs.

Will the list administrator be protected from being removed from the list?

This seems like a silly question, but it has been known to happen on occasion. You should have this security measure in place before broadcasting your first message. The last thing you need is an angry user trying to remove you from your own list. You're in charge, and you should remain in charge.

Can the administrator be the only one allowed to post to my list?

Unless you're managing a discussion group, you'll definitely want to set up an automatic block on all "outside" messages. Otherwise, any user (member or not) could send a message directly to your subscribers—without your consent. It's like leaving the key in your car's ignition . . . with the windows rolled down.

Can I block specific (if not all) list information from the public?

Without certain switches in place, it is possible for any informed user to acquire highly confidential list information *without* your knowledge or consent—including detailed statistics and the entire subscriber database! Every list administrator should take the steps necessary to discourage prying eyes. Protect yourself up front, and you should have nothing to worry about. Ask your list host which specific "bases" need to be covered.

How do subscribers interact with your list software?

Users have the right to know how to be unsubscribed from your e-publication, or simply how to change their e-mail address. These tasks can be carried out via e-mail or on the Web. Subscribers shouldn't have to burn off too many brain cells when trying to complete these basic subscription-related queries. For this reason, you should give serious consideration to list hosts that offer Web-based interfaces for end-user subscription management. There's virtually no guesswork in a point-and-click environment.

Can I make the headers appear as though I'm hosting the list on my own server?

For some professionals, this may be a very sensible question. Depending on the flexibility of the list host, this shouldn't be too much of a problem. Headers and domain names are significant, but as long as they're not getting in the way of your subscribers' contentment, I wouldn't worry about changing them.

What formatting issues do I need to be aware of in relation to your list software?

Will it wrap lines automatically at a specific column number? How large a document can it handle? You will need to recognize the limitations of the software (if any). The host may not be aware of any quirks; you'll probably stumble upon most of them on your own. Communicating with the host's other clients might clear up these kinds of questions; list administrators deal with the software from a real-world aspect.

Can you handle lists in foreign languages and/or with foreign characters?

Not everybody speaks English, and every once in a while you'll need to use an accented "i" or a *schwa*. The list software may not be able to handle extended characters. Generally speaking, you shouldn't run into any major problems with this, but it's still a question worth asking.

Chapter Thirteen

Guerrilla Promotions

Aspirations will vary from publisher to publisher; some are in this industry for the thrill, some for the experience, some for the notoriety, and yes, some are in it for the money. There is no ultimate objective that every electronic publisher struggles to achieve. However, most of us have one thing in common: the need to be recognized. Simply publishing a marvelous e-zine and then waiting for the world to read it ordinarily isn't good enough. You need name and product recognition; you need subscribers; you need a marketing strategy.

Sometimes you have to turn right to go left; the immediate route isn't always the greatest or easiest way. This is the idea behind guerrilla promotions: achieving your goals by means of an indirect marketing campaign. Don't walk in the front door—use the back or side door.

Low Cost, High Return

Few e-publishers have either access to a sizable budget or the desire to work with venture capitalists and/or loan officers. There's nothing wrong with either of these two situations, but there's no point in wasting money. Too many Internet start-ups ultimately regret funneling thousands of dollars into campaigns when they could have easily achieved the same results without dropping a single dime. Sure, sometimes you'll need to spend money, but when a cheaper road exists— you should consider taking it. Especially if you're publishing independently and don't have much liquid capital on hand.

Subscribers: Your Greatest Resource

Look outside the lines for a moment. You've got capable list software, quality content, and a pretty darn good Web site. What's missing from this picture? What is the one element essential for your e-publication's success? *Subscribers*—without them, you're nothing.

These aren't simply e-mail addresses in your database—they're real people. Your mission should be not only to keep users subscribed to your list, but to turn them (eventually) into *loyal* readers. By offering users continual satisfaction, you're building a relationship that will not evaporate on a whim. Strive to maximize the time they spend reading every one of your mailings. Without a doubt, they're your greatest resource.

Subscribers should definitely be involved with certain, significant decisions you make. At one time, I approached Lockergnomies with the idea of doing an audio show. Since I had no idea what its focus would be and how long it should last, I asked them for their candid opinions. The response was tremendous and very telling of what the average Lockergnome subscriber would like to hear. That informal poll will eventually help me focus on developing a show my readers want—and avoid the features my readers do *not* want. I didn't hire a market analyst, as most companies might have done. You'll be able to craft your own publication to suit your readers' desires over time by simply asking them questions. This strategy will show them that you're willing to keep an open dialogue. Do not allow their feedback to fall on deaf ears.

Peer Endorsements

You may not realize this, but you *need* a glimzorp. Even if you don't know exactly what one is, commercials keep telling you that life is incomplete without one. You've seen this product advertised dozens of times; it looks interesting, but you just can't see why or how it will do you any good. Suddenly, your good friend Byron stops by your home and shows off this amazing new tool. Wow, a good friend recommended it . . . now are you a little more open to getting a glimzorp of your own?

Your list may be obtaining dozens of new subscribers per day, but how are those readers finding out about your publication? Did they discover you through the search engines? Was there a link on some random Web page they recently visited? Or, did a friend take the time to recommend your site to them? By far, the most desirable new subscribers are the ones who received an endorsement from a close friend. These new members will be less likely to unsubscribe because they knew exactly what to expect from your publication before they joined. "I trust Byron. He says it's good, so it must be good." Compare this thought to: "Oh, a newsletter. I think I'll try it."

You can (and should) ask your readers to recommend your e-zine to friends, family members, and co-workers—but don't count on them doing it in droves. Some e-publishers will ask that subscribers forward an entire issue to someone else, which in theory is a good plan but doesn't usually translate into mass results. So how can you get people to start suggesting your work?

Free scripts and services available on the Internet will allow you to set up a recommendation form on your Web site. You can send traffic to the "recommend" page by providing a link to it in every issue, in the Welcome message, and in your e-mail signature. You can find one of the better CGI scripts for this purpose at http://www.willmaster.com/. Or, if you don't know much about programming, you might consider using a free service such as http://www.recommend-it.com/. Most free services will append their own form of advertisements along with a user's "recommend" message, and they usually do not allow for tweaking (like customizing fields, questions, and output format). The advantage of serving up your own script is that you can customize it to suit your needs and be able to track its usage in detail.

With Lockergnome's recommend script, a user fills in his name and e-mail address, the name and e-mail address of his friend, and possibly some personal comments. Then, upon completion, the script redirects to a page containing the same form—asking him to recommend Lockergnome to *another* friend. Out of the blue, I'm asking the user to suggest Lockergnome to another friend while his mind is still in "sharing" mode. And, to top it off, his name, e-mail address, and personal comments have been carried over from the first recommend form he filled out. All the user has to do is think of someone else and press a button. Kablam! I just turned one solid recommendation into two or more. It's potentially a never-ending loop.

Here's the e-mail message the recommender receives:

```
From: Chris Pirillo [chris@lockergnome.com]
To: Byron Fleaman
Subject: Thank you for recommending Lockergnome!


Thank you for recommending Lockergnome to Wayne Halibut
today. We hope your friend will enjoy Lockergnome as
much as you do. If you want to recommend Lockergnome to
another friend, visit:


http://www.lockergnome.com/recommend.html


Please keep spreading the word about us!
```

Yours Digitally,

Chris Pirillo, Content Wizard: (chris@lockergnome.com)
Electronic Publisher
Award-Winning Windows 9x/NT E-zine
http://www.lockergnome.com/

Here's the e-mail message the recommendee receives:

From: Byron Fleaman [byron@mrspatula.com]
To: Wayne Halibut
Subject: Byron Fleaman recommends Lockergnome!

Byron Fleaman (byron@mrspatula.com) wants you to check
out Lockergnome's FREE Windows 95/98/NT e-mail
newsletter.

Byron notes: "Hey, since you liked the glimzorp,
I thought you'd like this, too!"

http://www.lockergnome.com/

Keeping current with the newest Windows 95/98/NT &
Internet stuff is a full-time job—so let Lockergnome do
the work for you! We'll e-mail our FREE e-mail
newsletter to you— packed with the latest 32-bit
downloads (freeware & shareware), Web sites, games,
sounds, fonts, updates & patches, themes, tips &
tricks, computer industry news, and much more. Get
either our HTML Daily or Text Weekly versions for FREE
TODAY.

Again, visit http://www.lockergnome.com/ to subscribe
for free!

We trust you'll enjoy receiving Lockergnome as much as
Byron Fleaman does. If you do not know this person,
please ignore this message or report it to
abuse@lockergnome.com.

Here's the e-mail message I receive to notify me of the recommendation:

```
From: Chris Pirillo [chris@lockergnome.com]
Sent: Saturday, October 3, 1998 2:00 PM
Subject: Lockergnome Recommendation

    Date: Saturday, April 10, 1999
    Time: 14:43:18
  Visitor: Byron Fleaman (byron@mrspatula.com)
   Friend: Wayne Halibut (jester@butterflypumpkin.net)
  Message: Hey, since you liked the glimzorp, I
           thought you'd like this, too!
```

I don't recommend moving forward without having some sort of recommend form set up on your Web site. Even if you don't "do" e-mail publications, it is a valuable guerrilla promotions tool that shouldn't be overlooked.

The Precarious Post Boast

In Chapter 11, I discussed the serious nature of discussion list abusers. Don't be one of those.

However, one excellent way to get your e-mail publication known is by taking an active part in Internet discussions. The key word here is *active*. You're welcome to post whenever you have a question or an answer, but don't address the members of a group only when your interests are blatantly served. Advertising your services without some logical connection to the conversation is considered rude . . . and some would go as far as to call it spamming. Your best bet is to sit back (lurk) and watch the regular users interact with one another. Then start answering questions confidently without mentioning your e-publication outright. After a while, you'll be seen as a "regular." Ask the moderator (if there happens to be one) if it would be okay for you to tell the members of the group about your resource. Who knows? You just may set up a strategic business partnership simply by asking!

You don't need to shove your subscription information down people's throats at any given opportunity—especially on mailing lists, the Usenet newsgroups, or Web forums. When you post to a group you're unfamiliar with, be very careful as to how you construct your message; every experienced nose has a built-in BS detector. If you're trying to get people to visit your site, don't come out and ask (or tell) them to go to it. Instead, contribute to a few conversation threads and place your URL/subscription info in a four-line signature of sorts (or underneath your real name if you don't have a "sig"). It's generally safe to speak when spoken to; you appear more legitimate when answering someone's question than you do by merely volunteering seemingly unrelated information. It's not your content as much as it is your technique in presenting it.

You want group members to trust you, as much as you need your subscribers to trust you. Unfortunately, this takes a lifetime to develop and only a moment to destroy. Still, the more familiar users are with you, the more they'll let you "get away with." Out of posting 100 times over the course of a year, two messages may have been a little off topic. Compare this with posting 3 times over the course of one hour and having two messages be off topic. There is *no* comparison.

The Adventures of Links

A few years back, not very many "Windows" e-mail newsletters were in existence (a primary reason for Lockergnome's inception). I contacted major shareware-related Web sites to inform them that I had started distributing a free Windows e-mail newsletter on a regular basis. This announcement was intended to establish possible relationships with other content-oriented Internet resources. However, very few site managers paid attention to my blurb. I was the new kid on the block, desperately in search of the right stuff. To a certain degree, it is still difficult to get my foot in the door since I don't operate on a Web-centric model. I've seen subpar sites receive recognition and phenomenal e-mail newsletters thrown to the wayside. This is a frustration that comes with the e-territory for the time being. Still, there are ways of getting your foot in the door with existing Web sites and/or e-mail publications.

I began by offering reciprocal links to related Web sites. If they would place a link to Lockergnome on their site, I would do the same for them on mine. This worked for a while, until my list of links became unmanageable. Having a "reciprocal links" page is great for sharing resources with other site owners. By asking someone to swap links with you, you're effectively announcing your e-publication's arrival to the Internet. I strongly suggest focusing only on working with sites directly related to your subject matter; there's practically no advantage to having a kite newsletter link on a motorboat site (and vice versa). Yes, every link counts, but concentrating on strategies that will get you more recognition in your field is paramount.

It's also important to note that most FFA (Free For All) links pages do not work in the short or long run. At first, it may seem attractive to have your link on thousands of different pages, but recognize that your link will be lost amid hundreds of other links that are (more often than not) wholly dissimilar to your online resource. You stand a better chance of getting hit by a meteor than you do having someone discovering your link on an FFA page and actually clicking on it. If you really want to be listed in a directory, shoot for Yahoo!. You'll find that a listing in Yahoo! will, by far, bring you the most visitors. If you're smart enough to use the right keywords for your description, the chances of "user click-thru" will be even higher.

Design a Logo

Web surfers need to know who you are and what you do. If they see a link sitting on a Web page, it should be descriptive and/or intriguing enough for them to click on it.

One way to help with name recognition on the Web is by designing a small logo. A standard graphic format for logos measures 88 pixels horizontally by 31 pixels vertically. This "button" can be animated or not. When Web sites approach you for a "button swap," they're most likely looking for this 88x31 image. Just about any graphics application will help you create a simple one; download an image-editing utility from your favorite shareware site if you don't have one yet.

Web Ringmaster?

You may have heard of "Web rings" before; as a rule, they're a waste of time and space. The idea is to link a handful of related sites together to form some sort of "virtual donut." If you stumbled upon a leather knapsack site that is a member of the leather knapsack Web ring, you can see other leather knapsack sites with the click of a link (in theory). Here are the problems:

- Member sites might belong to more than one Web ring.
- A member site might not display the Web ring link in a highly visible area.
- Member links can change at a moment's notice, consequently disrupting the circle.
- There are usually no solid standards for member sites.
- It just doesn't look very professional.

You're better off working with a select group of sites if you want to create some sort of "network." You'll have more influence over implementation and be better acquainted with your affiliates. For example, if you have a "low carb" discussion list and know of someone who has a "low carb" e-mail newsletter, you may consider working together. After a user subscribes to your list, he could be automatically directed to sign up for that related newsletter. Of course, you'd expect to see a similar referral after a user signs up for the newsletter. It's a ring of sorts, but in a more controlled environment. You'll all walk away as winners.

Sit Up and Give Notice

I knew that it would take a while for the world to recognize Lockergnome. So I decided that when I featured a resource in my newsletter, I would contact the authors to let them know that they had been formally recognized. I did this for a few different reasons: (1) it was courteous, (2) they probably wouldn't have known otherwise, and (3) I was hoping that they'd want to set up links on their sites pointing to Lockergnome's site. On the whole, authors have been very receptive to (and thankful for) these enlightening messages, such as the one below:

```
From: Chris Pirillo [chris@lockergnome.com]
To: Michael Robertson
Subject: Upcoming Lockergnome Coverage

Your site, or selected software on your site, will be
featured in two upcoming Lockergnome e-mail
newsletters. Our HTML Daily is mailed out to readers on
weekdays, and our Text Weekly Digest is sent out on
weekends. Your resource will be seen in both
publications. The Web version can be found here:

http://www.lockergnome.com/issues/win95nt/19990417.html

This e-mail newsletter, with a readership of over
150,000 users, informs individuals of new Windows
95/98/NT downloads, fonts, themes, audio applications,
computer-related news, tips & tricks, and a little bit
more. You'll find your hit rate increasing over the
next couple of weeks—Lockergnome's review might be why.
Ask your "shareware friends" if you don't believe the
validity of my statements. Please feel free to link
back to us:

 Light: http://www.lockergnome.com/images/lg_light.gif

 Dark:  http://www.lockergnome.com/images/lg_dark.gif

 88x31: http://www.lockergnome.com/images/lockerlink.gif
```

```
You can visit Lockergnome's site and subscribe to our
newsletter(s) at any time. Lockergnome only chooses the
best of the best... you're definitely noteworthy! If
you have any other questions, please let me know. :)
Again, congratulations on providing such an excellent
resource!

Chris Pirillo (chris@lockergnome.com)
Electronic Publisher
http://www.lockergnome.com/
```

This is something that I've continued to do, and I advise that you do the same. You're consistently building qualified relationships that will (in turn) help build your publication. But Web sites ought not be your only focus.

Oranges and Oranges

Let's take the concept of reciprocal links a step further. If you have (or will have) an e-mail publication—you're not alone. But your subscriber base is almost certainly unique, just like everybody else's is. Wouldn't it be fantastic if you could hook up with other e-publishers and exchange advertisements at a moment's notice? You can, and you should! This is a great way to legitimately gain access to a potentially fresh audience. And you don't necessarily need to have the same number of readers in order to swap with someone else. Here's the math: Newsletter A has 30,000 list members, and newsletter B has 55,000 list members. It's possible for newsletter A's host to approach newsletter B's and request a 2:1 advertisement swap (and vice versa). Even if newsletter A's subject matter is radically different from newsletter B's, both subscriber bases are used to receiving e-mail publications—and will consequently be more likely to subscribe to another one.

In fact, it's usually better if ad swaps are done with unrelated newsletters. This way, the subscriber bases are almost guaranteed to be completely unique. A graphic-design e-zine swapping with another graphic-design e-zine might not yield too many new subscribers, as there might be a high amount of duplication between the two lists. However, if a graphic-design e-zine were to ad swap with a newsletter covering cell phones, the chances of each publisher walking away with more subscribers are higher. I've found that there's no better campaign for getting new subscribers than to work directly with other e-publishers. Forget about press releases, forget about prestigious awards, forget about trying to do things on your own. By sharing resources with others in your industry, you're playing smart. It's okay to be independent, but don't let these opportunities pass you by.

On the flip side, seemingly worthwhile ad swaps might not be as fruitful as expected. Remember that subscriber count is not always representative of the number of regular readers. In an e-publication with over 100,000 e-mail addresses in the database, only 70,000 might be verified as "good." And, out of those 70,000 working addresses, only 20,000 might actually read the publication on a regular basis. So don't let the numbers fool you. If someone approaches you with a phenomenal subscriber count, be very leery. Not every e-mail publication is well read. Find out what kind of response their issues usually elicit (if possible). You, too, should be honest when approaching other e-mail publishers; the chances for disappointment on either side will be far less.

I realize that approaching other electronic publishers can be daunting, especially if you're just starting your own e-mail publication. Should you wish to initiate a relationship with another mailing-list manager, consider featuring his e-zine in your e-publication prior to contact. This way, when you finally do get in touch with that list owner, he may be more willing to work with you—especially if your mention had a noticeable impact. Understand, too, that often a well-written review from the list owner holds much more weight in a subscriber's eyes than does an advertisement. Method and presentation are important factors to bear in mind.

> **TIP**
>
> *When you do swap ads with other e-publications, be sure to include subscription information. A Web site and e-mail address should suffice. Leaving either of these two things out completely nullifies the reason for doing an ad swap in the first place. Be descriptive, focused, and as thorough as possible.*

Get On, Stay On

When someone sees a URL while he's still online, he's more likely to visit it than if he would have seen the same URL *offline*. A user might be visiting a Web page, viewing a newsgroup post, or reading an e-mail message, but he is in "online mode." Suppose people see a flyer in the grocery store and become interested in your resource. At that point, they're far away from their computers—and will probably forget your URL by the time they get online again. Now, what if they had seen the same URL while they were sitting in front of their terminals? Chances are, you'd have new subscribers.

Operating a business on the Internet can help keep your costs low, but you need to get out of the "traditional" mind-set before you begin. Stop doing things *offline*—start doing things *online*. By focusing your efforts on Internet-related resources, you'll find your benefits far outweighing the drawbacks. Instead of posting flyers around town, it would be simpler, cheaper, more focused, and less time-consuming if you were to post a single message in a related newsgroup or mailing list. The Internet is global—and you need to use it to your advantage. Thinking small will produce small results. Though your focus may be strictly on people in your locale, expect that others from around the world will want to know more as well.

And travel down those online avenues first! You shouldn't have business cards printed until you have a professional Web page up and running; don't think of getting T-shirts printed until you have an interested subscriber base who will buy them; why have personalized pencils made if you never plan on handing them to people who would be interested in your e-publication? You can use other great promotional items to help create awareness of your online venture, but you should reserve them for use at trade shows, conventions, or speaking engagements. If you have money to burn, I suggest spending it on creating and fostering relationships with other e-mail publishers first.

Whatever you decide to do, make sure you do it for a reason. If you don't have to spend money to get something, then don't. I'm sure you'll discover on your own that online pursuits—targeted or not—will generate more results than anything done offline. Lockergnome has been featured in countless print publications with millions of regular subscribers, but e-mail newsletters with fewer than 2,000 members have helped me more. You wouldn't expect that, but again—there's more than just one variable at play here. The largest variable is the environment in which the URL is seen: online, rather than offline.

Offline Offensive

Don't get me wrong—it's okay to have items imprinted with your name and URL. But don't hand them out to unqualified strangers without a good reason. There are millions of people who have yet to jump online, and not all of them are going to be interested in what you have to offer once they get there. Still, I understand the thrill of seeing your logo or name on everyday objects. If you have a culinary e-zine, think about having customized placemats printed—then give them freely to restaurant managers. If you have a fitness e-mail newsletter, what about customized duffel bags to be given away or sold at gyms? Dental discussion list moderators should have toothbrushes in hand. First aid list owners would want bandages. You get the idea.

Business cards *are* important to sport at all times. When you need to explain your e-publication to someone—but don't have a lot of time—give away a card. Let people visit your site and discover more on their own. Yes, it will probably be a few days, weeks, or months before they swing by, but if you *personally* give them a compelling argument as to why they can't live without your e-zine, they shouldn't quickly forget. The actual design of your card is completely up to you. However, keep in mind that you hand out these cards primarily to drive traffic to your Web site and/or e-mail publication, not just to show people how to get in touch with you. Your URL should be the most noticeable object on your business card. Specific subscription instructions could be included, but remember that such instructions are prone to change over time.

Develop Writer's Cramp

Assumedly, you would like to have your e-mail publication be as popular as dish soap. While it probably won't be lemony fresh, you want people to know that you exist. When I started writing Lockergnome issues, my forte was "how to find cool stuff for my computer using the Internet." Virtually nobody knew who I was, and it was difficult to prove my worth to the world on my own. I would have had an easier time at building a name had I written articles in other electronic publications.

If you have a way with words, I strongly encourage you to do what I (and others) failed to. This bit of extra writing would have given me experience, visibility, and the opportunity to (once again) cultivate strategic relationships. Freelancing may not be your style, and the pay may not be exceptional, but you should do whatever you can to get your name and e-publication better known.

Don't pull yourself in so many different directions that you neglect your regular administrative or editorial duties, but if a simple opportunity arises, you should take it. Not having enough time may be an issue. In that case, a simple syndication model might be worth pursuing with similar e-mail publications. The syndication idea is further explained in Chapter 14, but the concept revolves around writing something one time, and seeing it show up in several places. It's relatively easy to swap content with other e-zines; you wouldn't be writing any more, and you'd be getting more content for your own mailing list. The same benefits would be seen for the other e-publisher, if he is willing to work with you in this capacity.

Unrelated Relations

Having a Web page for your e-mail publication is important for several reasons. You can use it for just about anything you'd like—including for "stuff" not exactly associated with your e-zine. Having a domain name works best for this tactic, as it is more recognizable for indirect association.

For example, suppose our friend Mr. Spatula registered http://www.mrspatula.com/ with the intent of publishing a free weekly e-mail newsletter reviewing syrups of the world. The people who would most likely be interested in his offering would be pancake or waffle lovers, breakfast eaters, chefs, et al. But what about other people who might not be surfing specifically to uncover scrumptious syrups? They'll probably never visit http://www.mrspatula.com/.

Imagine that Mr. Spatula has another hobby—collecting bottle caps. He could easily make a separate section on his site using a subdirectory: http://www.mrspatula.com/bottlecaps/. This would be designed, operated, and marketed much differently than his staple content (the syrup newsletter). Those interested in bottle caps would most likely visit his bottle caps page before they'd visit his main page.

It would be wise for Mr. Spatula to put a link, subscription form, or subscription instructions for his syrup newsletter on his bottle caps page. And did you know that Mr. Spatula also enjoys creating wallpaper images of baby seals? He might provide those for download at http://www.mrspatula.com/babyseals/. Are people interested in bottle caps or baby seals going to be interested in syrup? Quite possibly!

The only drawback to this technique (as I see it) is in the outcome of your intentions. Visitors to the bottle caps page might believe that the subscription form is for a bottle caps newsletter, not a syrup newsletter; they'll probably wind up being disappointed. Notwithstanding, you should be attracting a different audience to your newsletter—simultaneously giving your URL more "airtime" in diverse venues.

Pressing Introductions

After you distribute your first e-mail publication, you're a member of the electronic press. Your job is simple: to inform. The more people you inform, the more your publication will be worth in your industry. Now, how can you start getting companies to sit up and take notice of your online venture? Let them know two things: (1) you're alive, and (2) you want to work with them in a mutually beneficial way. There is no better person to whom you should divulge this information than a public relations (PR) professional or press contact. These people thrive on publicity. When you want to speak with someone, be sure you're barking up the right tree.

With luck, you're not the only person in the world interested in your chosen subject. You're going to have opportunities to cover topical events and/or review related products without having to spend a dime. For instance, let's say

Katie has a recycled-products discussion list. Company XYZ manufactures a mouse pad made from 100 percent recycled materials. Katie wants to give this accessory a whirl, so she uncovers a press contact and blasts off an e-mail message to that individual:

```
From: Katie McHenry [katie@recyclereceptacle.com]
To: Leslie Arturotronopolis
Subject: Potential Press Coverage
Greetings,

My name is Katie McHenry; I'm the moderator for the
'Recycle Receptacle' discussion group. This list has
more than 2,000 active readers who regularly talk about
recycling issues. I discovered today that you had
released your Envirotelligent Mouse Pad Plus. I'm sure
my list's readers would be interested in hearing more
about it; do you have a press kit or demo unit to send
my way? I appreciate your help.

If you would like to check the validity of my Web site
and its contents, simply swing by
http://www.recyclereceptacle.com/ — thanks again for
your time!!

Katie McHenry
Electronic Publisher
katie@recyclereceptacle.com
1203 Ayefee Drive, Suite #21
Christiansen Falls, IA  54321-9876
```

Her message might have included more background information on the Recycle Receptacle mailing list, but saying very little is often as good as saying more than enough. Katie may never get a response from this company contact (or receive an evaluation unit), but at least she's introduced herself. If she decides to review the product, a link to the Recycle Receptacle might be placed on Company XYZ's Web site—potentially sending subscribers in Katie's direction. Understand, too, that the more expensive a product or service is, the less likely you will be to receive a "copy" of it.

Sweeping Idea

Some e-publishers have organized sweepstakes (of sorts) for their subscribers. Although not everybody has something of value to give away, it's possible to set up cross-promotional offers with other businesses. Recycling this example: Katie doesn't make products, but Company XYZ does. Once Katie has established a relationship with that company, she might offer to run a contest in conjunction with them. In essence, she would be pitching XYZ's products in her mailing list for free—in exchange for a few units for a few selected subscribers. Who wins? Katie gets coverage, the Recycling Receptacle subscribers get the chance to win, and Company XYZ gets to have its recycled products showcased in the mailing list. The most difficult part is finding a company willing to work with you. For more details (and legalities) on running contests online, check out http://www.adlaw.com/RC/rf_sweeps.html.

You can promote your list in thousands of ways; you'll discover more on your own over the coming months. As long as you don't compromise your integrity, you should be in the clear. Respect yourself, respect your subscribers, and respect other list owners. In marketing your list, keep your ultimate goals in mind. Don't feel that you need to take advantage of every possible opportunity, either—some may not work particularly well for your list. It's great to have an e-mail publication and to know how to promote it efficiently . . . now, how do you make it float? That is to say, how can you keep it running without running your wallet into the ground? It's time to answer the age-old question: *How can you make money with your mailing list?*

Chapter Fourteen

Money from Your Mailing List

Wipe those dollar signs from your eyes; e-mail publishing is *not* a major cash cow at this time. Yes, you can make an adequate amount of money over time, but instant financial success is virtually impossible. Good money will come as a result of creating a powerhouse e-publication.

I'm hopeful that Chapters 1 through 13 have provided you with enough insight to develop a mailing list that you (and your subscribers) can be proud of. While it's important not to lose money through electronic publishing, I don't suggest setting "wealth" as your ultimate goal. Your publication will almost certainly suffer. Subscribers are to publishers as students are to teachers; they can see right through you when you lie or mislead them. And remember, without subscribers, you've got bupkis.

I didn't start Lockergnome to make money; I started it to make waves. Any financial gains I *do* make from Lockergnome are merely icing on the cake. I'm a young college graduate with massive student loans who just got married and bought a house—I'm *anything* but well off. In spite of those drawbacks, I've continued to publish a high-quality e-mail newsletter and driven my subscriber base higher than many of my contemporaries'. Here's the kicker: I've been profitable! It hasn't been much, but at least I'm not "in the red." Look around and you'll find businesses losing money left and right on the Internet—but there's no reason why *you* should be in the same unsuccessful boat. Keep your costs extremely low by sharing and bartering resources, employ cost-effective ground-level techniques, and listen to your subscribers. You'll be infinitely more satisfied—guaranteed.

Click Here to Make Money

"Yeah, but the Internet was made to make money!" No, it wasn't. It was created for the electronic distribution of information. Financial geniuses and marketing wizards decided that it was the next frontier for commerce. Consequently, too many underinformed and inexperienced users are logging on to line their pockets with "easy" money. We're in the middle of an electronic gold rush, and disenchantment hangs heavy in the air. I keep seeing circular arguments: *Make money by clicking here to make money by telling people to click here to make money by clicking here* . . . and so on. There's no content, there's no purpose, and there's no way you want to get involved in that game.

You may choose to found your publication on the principle that advertising will *never* be accepted. This is admirable, but not always realistic. Can you foresee how popular your mailings are going to be? And who knows how much it will eventually cost you to distribute? By keeping your subscriber base small, you will avoid most financial annoyances. But not every e-publisher wants to restrict growth in that fashion. There's the possibility for you to start doing a separate sponsor-supported e-mail publication—providing you have the time, energy, and resources for it.

The Free or Fee Decision

Face it: Revenue has to come from *somewhere* to keep your enterprise afloat. The obvious solution is to charge for subscriptions. But the average Internet user isn't ready to pay for services or subscriptions online yet. Some surfers are a bit more capricious with their cash, but for the most part, users will pass you by if you start asking for their money up front. It's okay to offer your e-mail publication for a fee, but you probably won't get an incredible number of subscribers in the beginning. It's wiser for you to offer a free newsletter alongside a "fee" one. The idea is to hook subscribers on something great and then offer them something even better for a little bit of money.

With a free subscription, you'll build subscriber numbers and brand recognition at a more rapid, steady pace. Under this system, you'll presumably fall into an advertising-based model for income.

How will the ads appear? It depends on your mode of publication. While HTML e-mail can accommodate either type of ad (text or graphic), text publishers are obviously stuck with text-only ads. Which style of ad is more effective? Well, advertisers are just starting to discover that text-based ads give them more bang for their advertising buck. You're going to be battling traditional banner-based models for a little while longer, though; not every businessperson is aware of the tremendous power of e-mail quite yet.

Advertising and E-mail: A Great Match

You'll get asked how many "hits" your site receives. Kindly inform the individual that your rates are not based on random hits, but on a number of regular-reading, satisfied subscribers. You can then explain how newsletters are infinitely better than Web sites. But don't be surprised if he doesn't get it. Salespeople are currently in the mind-set that "if it doesn't have a graphic, it isn't an ad." They're dead wrong, and consequently missing out on remarkable opportunities with mailing lists. Is list advertising the way of the future? No—it's the way of *today*.

Some e-mail publishers want advertisers, and all advertisers want high click-thru rates. But most advertising businesses are turning to the wrong venue: the Web. As I explained in earlier chapters, e-mail publication readers digest more of the presented information than do Web page visitors viewing the same material. Trying to convince people of this phenomenon is difficult, but the logic is not that convoluted. You're in a different mind-set when reading e-mail (active) compared to surfing the Web (passive). Now, would you rather have 10,000 subscribers providing you with 1,000 click-thrus or 20,000 Web page visitors providing you with 50 click-thrus? By and large, a list will have a remarkably targeted, receptive, captive audience, whereas a Web page will generally attract random, unqualified, "mindless" visitors. I'm not asking you to believe me, either—see for yourself.

Sponsors would be considerably better off with mailing-list advertising. Whereas graphics take a while to download, need to be aesthetically pleasing, and generally can't get an idea across without trying to be cute, text-based advertisements are much more dynamic. Text ads can be written as the writer sees fit and customized for certain publications or campaigns, and they have the potential for being more descriptive than graphical banners.

The better a writer is, the stronger the advertisement's impact. However, just because you deal with salespeople doesn't mean you're dealing with powerful writers. You should always reserve the right to rewrite submitted ad copies; who knows your audience better than you? If free stuff trips their trigger, make sure that gets mentioned toward the beginning of the ad (if possible). Keep it clean, honest, direct, and intriguing. You'll be happier with the wording, your subscribers will see the advantages of visiting, and your advertisers will be happier with the results.

When Can I Start?

People will pay more for Web advertising than they will for newsletter advertising. I realize this is messed up, but I can't directly control the way businesses think. So, just how large should your subscriber base be before you can start accepting advertisements? Well, that "magic number" is entirely up to you! If you think 2,000 subscribers is enough—it's enough.

Some charge *x* cents per subscriber, and some operate on a flat fee. In a way, the amount depends on what kind of list you're publishing. Discussion group members are typically more active than newsletter readers; this trait should be reflective of their fiscal worth. Advertising in a discussion group with 1,000 members could be considered more valuable than advertising in an e-mail newsletter with 1,000 subscribers. An advertisement's value also hinges on how many businesses are trying to gain placement in the same ad spot.

How much should you charge per ad? That's entirely up to you. Start small, and as advertiser interest grows, increase your rates. It's better to undercharge than it is to overcharge. Your costs are low to begin with; it won't take much for you to turn a profit. A good rule of thumb is to charge well under a thousand per insertion when your mailing list has under 100,000 subscribers. The lowest rates I've seen have been US$2 per thousand, and the highest have gone all the way up to US$30 per thousand. Of course, if your list is smaller (under 1,000 subscribers), but extremely targeted, you may offer US$50 or US$100 per advertisement. Again, these numbers depend a lot on the demand of your list. For example, Lockergnome has 135,000 subscribers receiving the *Text Weekly* edition and a "top" ad placement has run as high as US$2,500 and as low as US$1,000.

Do your best to have your ad spots filled in every issue—something is typically better than nothing. Try throwing together a few pricing packages for each potential advertiser. Everybody likes having options; give people a choice and you'll wind up with greater success. It's much better to hear "no, no, *yes*, no" than simply a "no."

You'll have some advertisers who are just looking to place one advertisement and then move along. In those situations, don't be afraid to charge a higher rate. If the advertiser is not going to be around for long, you might as well get as much from the company as possible. However, as with individuals and/or companies with whom you'd like a future relationship (advertising-centric or not), consider charging less.

Announcing That You're Open for Business

Advertisers can't read minds; *tell them* that you're receptive to sponsorship. Give them the opportunity to talk to you about advertising. Set up a separate Web page for ad-related information, and create a specific e-mail alias for inquiries. Give out your phone number (if possible). If they don't know how to get ahold of you, how do you expect them to do it?

In a similar vein, why not tell your subscribers that advertising opportunities are available? You might even offer special ad discounts for your members—

especially when ad sales are stagnant. It may not be very special for you, but some people are just waiting for the right opportunity to come forth and express an interest in sponsorship.

Having a cool name and an awesome subscriber base often isn't enough to win over a salesperson. You have to promise potential advertisers some value for their money. You don't want them to have to ask: "Why should I advertise in your e-mail publication?" The answer should be obvious, and if it's not, you need to be able to educate them about your value. You'll need to be tactful, knowledgeable, and ready to wheel and deal. And don't feel that you have to accept every offer that comes across your desk; if you don't feel comfortable with a certain company, you don't have to work with that company!

Expanding Your Sales Operations

A few e-publishers have found that a few hundred-dollar ads in a single issue will cover all their costs (and then some). However, you may not be able to close those kinds of ad deals with ease—especially if you're not familiar with ad sales. As multiple companies begin to approach you to advertise, consider hiring a salesperson or outsourcing those responsibilities to a professional firm. Even if *nobody* is approaching you for ad placements, finding someone to represent you could prove advantageous.

Don't give away too much of the pie, though. Depending on the amount of work done, the percentage split might be anywhere from 20/80 to 40/60 (them/you). There is usually more involved in advertising sales than making contact with someone and negotiating a deal. Invoices have to be written, sent, and followed up; URLs may need to be tracked with special ID codes; performance reports and statistics should be released sometime after an advertisement's run. Delegating these tasks to other people is better if you don't function well in a high-pressure environment. But sponsored advertising isn't the only way to make money with your mailing list.

Associate with Affiliate Programs

You can actively seek advertisers, wait for them to come to you, or use that ad space for something other than traditional advertising. Associate—or affiliate— program popularity is skyrocketing at a phenomenal rate. The concept revolves around you getting paid to "associate" with other businesses. In exchange for traffic or purchases, you'll get a commission. Essentially, you become an agent. As an affiliate, instead of charging a fixed amount for an advertisement, you work on a percentage or predetermined fee. Your results will vary from placement to placement, program to program.

Finding an associate program is relatively simple. Most sites that offer products or services will have some kind of a commission-based plan already set up for content providers. Obviously, you'd like for your subscribers to act upon any given advertisement. The closer you can match an affiliate program's offerings with your audience's interests, the more you will earn.

You can start or stop working with an associate program at any time, so you are free to advertise your participation sporadically or not at all. When you don't have a paying sponsor, you might as well use that space for something!

It's important for you to do a little detective work before dealing with companies that offer associate programs. Some are legit, while others are not. What's the quickest way to determine the validity of a program's claims? Ask around; talk to other people you know and trust. Have they worked with this business before? What were their results? Did they see any "red flags?" Don't jump into something if it sounds too good to be true—there's almost always a catch.

> **NOTE**
>
> *While minimum "impressions" aren't typically required to benefit from an associate program, some companies will not cut checks below a certain dollar amount.*

Sponsorship Foibles

I used to eat red licorice by the pound. As a result, I experienced the world's biggest stomachaches. Had I eaten only a few pieces per day, my body wouldn't have minded, but I overdid it. Keep my tummy troubles in mind when you start placing advertisements in your e-mail publication. I've seen far too many mailing lists alienate their users by engaging in "ad overkill." Nobody wins in these situations.

Would you be inclined to watch a television show that was 7 minutes long and had 23 minutes worth of commercials? Probably not. Even if you enjoyed the show, there's no reason to sit through close to a half-hour of sales pitches (unless, of course, you're an infomercial junkie). In time, if your e-mail publication goes overboard with advertisements, your click-thru rates will suffer, as will your subscriber base. Most "Internet Marketing" e-mail publications miss the mark here; not only do they have a lot of duplicated content among them, but they're drowning their readers in ads! Subscribers are looking for substance. If you continue to pelt them with ads, they'll drop you. And where are you without subscribers?

It's also important for you to draw a clear line between advertising and editorial matter. A user should know when you are endorsing a product or service because you like it, as opposed to supporting everything that will bring in a buck. Should substance be indistinguishable from sponsorship, your integrity as an information provider will suffer. You may decide to accept only advertisements to which your readership will be attracted. In that case, the boundaries must be even more apparent. If you don't let subscribers know (visibly) where the content ends and the selling begins, you'll wind up with subscribers who feel used and misled.

Building to Sell

Your mailing list will be worth money from the start, should you decide to sell it. As to the exact amount, that's completely up to you. Some databases will be worth a penny per subscriber, while others will be worth $10 per subscriber.

However, do you really want to sell your list of subscribers to the highest bidder? Yeah, you're making money—but you're doing so at other people's expense (indirectly). When I sign up for a belt buckle mailing list, I expect to receive messages regarding belt buckles. I don't want to have my address bought and sold to companies who just want to sell me stuff without asking me first.

You can do whatever it is you want to do, but remember that subscribers are people—they're (in all honesty) under your control and trust you enough to pass along private bits of personal information—their e-mail addresses. You're selling data, but in essence, you're also selling people. List brokers are profitable, but I've always questioned their motives.

You should also ask yourself how long you plan to work with your e-zine. What do you want to gain from it in the long run? Do you have an exit strategy? What happens to your list when you're tired of running it? Is its success dependent on your involvement, or can it be easily handed to another company or individual? There's nothing wrong with wanting to sell your entire e-mail publication to another party when the time comes—just be sure to deal with honest, trustworthy people. You will

CAUTION

Be very careful when you're dealing with companies and Web sites that deal specifically with the generation of opt-in lists. By working with them, you're potentially misleading your readers in a dreadful way. Many believe they're signing up for newsletters also run by your organization, when, in fact, those "other lists" are being operated by an outside source. It's a legitimate scheme, but too often, the presentation is deceptive.

have built a seemingly valuable resource, possibly around your own name. This list and everything it entails will become a large part of your life; don't throw everything away for a few bucks.

Syndication: Write Once, Read Anywhere

Some 'Net prophets claim that content will be king. I, for one, agree with them. For as many Web pages as are on the Internet, very few worthwhile resources are available. Businesses are constantly struggling with ways to get visitors to return to their sites, but without good reason, most surfers won't come back. I've already covered how e-mail publications take care of this problem, but how can you take this application to the next level? How can you acquire income without working any harder? It's not too good to be true—it's syndication!

Pick up a newspaper. Chances are, it's filled with syndicated features, editorials, and everybody's favorite—comics. These artists and writers don't spend their time writing the same things over and over again. Likewise, you don't have to compose the same content multiple times when you distribute via e-mail. So why not give another content provider the right to run your stuff? Providing you have style and substance worth reading on a regular basis, the benefits for other parties should be obvious: keeping their readers informed without having to hire a knowledgeable person to tackle the subject.

You're out nothing, getting name recognition, and possibly making a few dollars on the side. They're gaining content, keeping their readers happy, and increasing the value of their publication. The most difficult part of this strategy is finding companies willing to work with a syndication model. For that, you're pretty much on your own. Writing agents might be able to assist, but unless you know people on the "inside," this is a tough road to travel—especially for beginners.

The Challenge

I was minding my own business one afternoon, when a Lockergnome subscriber e-mailed me from out of the blue. He felt that my publication was worth more than "free," so he offered to send me one American dollar. On top of this, he issued a "challenge" for all the other subscribers to do the same. I was extremely surprised with the results; while I didn't make a mint from his proposal, I am now the proud owner of a large box filled with envelopes from just about every country on the globe. Each piece of mail arrived with at least a dollar (some included up to $100). But the most impressive—and heartwarming—part of this situation was seeing the handwritten notes or letters thanking me for my services. When people try to tell me that the Internet is a cold, unprofitable place, I show them my challenge box. The Internet exists because people exist—remember that.

If you publish without charging your subscribers, a voluntary donation drive might not be out of the question. I even set up a Web page for Lockergnome Challengers, to give them an incentive to help: http://www.lockergnome.com/challenge.html. They enjoy seeing their name "up in lights," and I enjoy reading their personal letters to me. They let me know that I'm truly making a difference. Good luck and fortune have nothing to do with it. You can't pay for or buy a contented subscriber.

Publishers' Stories

The Importance of the End-User Experience

by John Funk

As the creator of InfoBeat, one of the most successful e-mail products on the Internet, I'm often asked, "What is the key to success for an e-mail publication?" It's human nature to believe there is an easy answer—a magic formula that will transform any lackluster e-publication into a blockbuster. Unfortunately, a company has to do dozens of things right for its electronic publication to succeed. This book touches on most of them, and you will greatly increase your chances for success by taking its lessons to heart.

Nevertheless, one question does have a straightforward answer, "What is the *most* important thing to concentrate on if I want to succeed with my e-mail publication?" Said another way, "What's the one thing I *can't* screw up?" The answer is deceptively simple yet very challenging to execute: *focus on the end-user experience*. An e-mail publication is not about you; it's about the end user. Whether you're trying to make money from the e-mail message itself, drive traffic, drive a transaction, eliminate paper communication—whatever it is, if the end user doesn't have a great experience, your venture is doomed for failure.

Every single one of us is busy; our days are full, our lives are stretched to the limit, and our e-mailboxes are crowded. If your e-zine doesn't effectively substitute for a current, inferior activity, it will be rejected by the end user. This naturally extends to all interactions revolving around the e-mail publication, such as subscribing and unsubscribing, customer service, etc. The eight key elements to ensuring a successful end-user experience are setting expectations, subscription management, content, frequency, length, design/format, predictability/accuracy, and customer service. Understand that four of the eight relate directly to the message that lands in the e-mailbox—content, frequency, length, and design/format. The other four drivers of positive experience relate to how the subscriber interacts with the e-publication and are just as critical as the message itself.

At the end of the day, it all comes back to this simple question: Is the end user's life made more efficient or enjoyable as a result of your mailing? If not, you're wasting your time—your program will fail.

Setting Expectations

When you design an e-mail publication, you have to make sure that you manage your end users' expectations so that they know exactly what will be landing in their e-mailboxes, why they might want it, and when to expect it. As the designer, you become very close to the publication; you understand exactly what you're going to be sending and why. As a consequence, all too often the designer assumes the end user will know what he's signing up for. The end user most often has no clue!

To combat this, show potential subscribers a sample of a message. (Often a prior message works great in this case.) If appropriate, explain the source of the content that will be in the e-mail message and whether to expect advertising in the message. Explain the publishing frequency, explain what you will be doing with subscriber e-mail addresses (keeping them confidential, I hope), and explain how to unsubscribe or manage the subscription.

Subscription Management

Allowing your readers to manage their own subscriptions is critical to maintaining goodwill in the marketplace. Make it easy to subscribe and unsubscribe (both via e-mail and at a Web site). If customer preferences are stored, make it easy for the end user to edit those preferences via a Web interface. Even a wonderful e-mail product can become spam after a while if the customer no longer wants it but can't get off the list. Most list management software supports various forms of subscription management, but if you're building your own system or using e-mail creatively with your online strategy, make it easy for people to get on and get off your list.

Content

An old adage says that "Content Is King." I believe it truly is the single most important element in ensuring a positive end-user experience with your e-mail publication. In order to be invited into the end user's mailbox (and to get the end user to read the message), you have to offer something unique and of value. Perhaps it's timely financial information, perhaps it's information about something important to the end user, or perhaps it's simply highly enjoyable and unique.

An end user seldom wants to hear you beat your chest about new things at your company (unless perhaps the end user is an investor), so make sure you choose content that will excite the user and be interesting. *Never* send out an e-mail message that contains only links. You must provide usable information within the message *and* provide links to a Web site for more details.

Depending on your strategy and the purpose of the publication, you may decide to deliver 99 percent of the information in the e-mail (pay attention to message length, however) and have very few links, or you may decide to deliver 50 percent of the information in an effort to "tease" traffic back to your site. An example of an e-mail publication that would have very few links is an order confirmation message that indicates all relevant information in the message itself. An example of an e-mail publication that would have many links is a "new book release," which highlights e-mail programs that give short summaries of new books, links to deeper reviews, and additional links directly into a purchasing program.

Frequency

The frequency of sending an e-mail message to an end user is directly related to the type of content you are sending. If the content "spoils" quickly (stock prices or sports scores), you'll need to send it quite frequently. Conversely, if it's information about new features on your Web site or promotional messages designed to drive transactions, few end users will tolerate a daily publishing schedule. If possible and appropriate for your e-mail publication, let the end user define the appropriate frequency; offer separate weekly wrap-up editions for highly spoilable content. As a general rule of thumb, news- and information-based content is best in a daily or weekly format, whereas promotional and marketing content is best in a biweekly or monthly format. Your publishing schedule should reflect the availability/creation of new and different content that is of value and desired by the end user.

Design/Format

Most e-mail is not read—it is skimmed (or scanned). This fundamental truth should permeate all your thinking when you are designing your e-mail publication. Focus on strong design elements (use HTML-formatted messages if you can). Recognize that the reader will not read every word, and do not send densely packed complex paragraphs of important information (except, perhaps, in rare instances of receipts or order confirmations).

Space the message out so that it is pleasing to the eye. Design the message so that it can be skimmed. Organize it into sections, avoid excessive use of capital letters (caps are much harder to read than lowercase letters), and to the extent possible, keep your design consistent from one message to the next. With an e-mail publication, you are trying to become a habit with your end user—a habit that takes the shape of the end user anticipating your message, receiving your message, and reading your message. Predictably, time after time. By consistently using the same efficient design, you begin to develop your "look and feel," and the end user becomes comfortable with your publication and becomes more proficient at reading it.

Length

At the risk of repeating myself, e-mail is not read, it is skimmed, and end users do *not* want to skim a treatise or a manuscript. I generally recommend a couple of screens of text as the maximum target length for an e-mail message. End users do not want to be scrolling down through 20 screens of text. There are, of course, exceptions to this rule, but if you keep the message short and sweet, you will generally be much more successful than if you try to cram all sorts of information into a message. Think of e-mail as a "quick hit"—you're in and you're out.

Predictability/Accuracy

As discussed in the Design/Format section, predictability is an important element of success for an e-mail publication. This is especially true when it comes to delivery times. You typically want your end user to expect to receive the e-mail at a certain time each day/week/month. (That's how you know your publication has become important in his life—when he begins to expect it.) Randomly dropping messages into the mailbox does not build a habit and does not build loyalty.

Think of your e-mail publication like you think of your newspaper: If it's not there in the morning, you are justifiably angry. Toward this end, the reliability of your e-mail system is extremely important. The only things worse than not getting a message when you expected it is to never get the message at all, or to get dozens of duplicate copies! It is quite common for homegrown or cheap e-mail systems to fail to deliver messages and/or to get caught in loops where the system delivers more than one copy. This problem is often a result of poor recovery capabilities of the e-mail publishing system when an error occurs during the middle of the mailing. That is to say, if the system fails for whatever reason and needs to be restarted right in the middle of sending, what happens? Weak systems will give you a choice—send the mail again (doubling up mail for some people) or call it quits for the day (leaving some people without their mail). Consequently, choose your delivery system/outsourcing system with care.

Customer Service

The last (but certainly not least) requirement for a strong end-user experience is to have human beings on the end of the e-mail Reply function. E-mail is an interactive medium; clicking the Reply button is not only permitted, but it is a reality of e-mail publishing. Your end users will reply. Guaranteed. You should certainly explore and implement automated rules to process such replies, but you will also have to personally ensure that all inquiries have been addressed. As your publication grows in readership, you may need to hire customer service staff who can respond to inbound mail. Answering e-mail is not optional—if you fail to respond to subscriber inquiries and issues, your e-mail publication will fail.

This is not to say that you will need armies of people. You may be able to handle incoming e-mail yourself, or farm out the job to one person working an hour or two a week or month. But do not let mail go unanswered and unheeded. Perhaps the end user just wants to get off the list, perhaps he has a question about your business, perhaps he wants to buy something. Perhaps he wants to buy your company for hundreds of millions of dollars! If you fail to provide superior customer service, my prediction is that your e-mail efforts will fail miserably.

Measures of Success

Let me close with a brief discussion about how to measure whether you've succeeded in focusing on the end-user experience. For reasons of brevity, I will not delve into the technical "how-to" here, but these techniques are relatively well known, so you should be able to find someone to help you if you don't know how to implement any of these measures.

The first and most accurate measure of success is to understand how many of your e-mail messages are being read. This *open rate* is calculated as a percentage of mail you sent that was read by an end user. One potential culprit that can cause a low open rate is poor subscription management (in which end users can't get off the list, so they just delete all your mail).

You can calculate this rate in one of two ways: by surveying your users or by using an audit server in conjunction with HTML mail. You also could do some interpolated calculations based on click-thru activity if you have enough pieces of data to have a control set and a test set. Recognize, however, that survey data will obviously have a self-select bias. (In other words, the people who respond to the survey are most likely heavily skewed toward the ones who read your e-mail.) If you have phone numbers, doing call-down surveys is much more reliable than e-mail surveys.

Calculating this measure over time is best, as it provides a good indicator of whether your e-mail program is going stale. This measure also does a good job of analyzing the "quality" of each e-mail subscriber, allowing you to better assess the value of each individual subscriber. Web-based mail users are notorious for their infrequent use of their Web-based mail accounts, and as a consequence are regarded as "lower quality" subscribers by many e-mail publishers. This technique can prove quite helpful when you're designing subscriber acquisition programs and determining how much to pay in a "bounty" fee.

Another good measure of success is your *churn rate*, which is the number of subscribers who unsubscribed during a month or a year as a percentage of your total base. The higher the churn rate, the poorer the end-user experience. If your churn rate seems high to you, find comparable publishers to confirm that you have a high churn rate. Then review your technique for setting end-user expectations, and review the four elements relating to the message itself. Something about what you're sending is not sitting well with the end users, and that is causing them to unsubscribe. Needless to say, the best way to find out what's happening is to survey users as they unsubscribe and ask them why.

A final measure of success is your *net growth rate*, which is your net number of new subscribers (new subs minus unsubscribes) during a month as a percentage of your total base. If your growth rate flattens out or goes negative, you either need to revisit your end-user experience strategy or your subscriber acquisition strategy. You can tell which is your problem by calculating your gross growth rate (new subs as a percentage of your base) and comparing it to your net growth. If gross growth is substantially higher than net growth, you have an end-user experience problem. If gross growth is roughly equivalent to net growth, you have a subscriber acquisition problem.

In conclusion, your e-mail publication is a complex set of interrelated issues and challenges. At its core, however, a successful e-mail publication delivers one thing: a fantastic end-user experience. Hopefully, I've been able to share with you an understanding of the elements of success. Now it's up to you to put all the elements together in a way that no one else can duplicate.

John Funk
jfunk@emailknowledge.com
http://www.emailknowledge.com/
John Funk is one of the world's leading experts on e-mail and is the principal and founder of The E-Mail Knowledge Group, a boutique Internet consulting firm that specializes in e-mail strategy. Prior to EKG, Funk founded Mercury Mail (later renamed InfoBeat) and led the company as its CEO and Chairman to become the largest e-mail publisher on the Internet.

This is True

by Randy Cassingham

Randy Cassingham's *This is True* is a rarity among online newsletters: It was not only designed from the start to be delivered by e-mail, but it was planned as a commercial product that would enable the author to quit his regular job and work online full-time. Those plans succeeded: Randy quit his job two years after *True's* launch and now makes more with his online offering than he did working as a software engineer for NASA.

Putting All the Elements Together to Make a Living with Mailing Lists

It is often said that you should "do what you love and the money will follow." In early 1994, I was stuck with "golden handcuffs." The money was good in my 8–5 day job, but I wasn't really doing what I wanted to do. At the time, I was working at NASA's Jet Propulsion Laboratory, which is an awfully cool place to work. However, there was no creative outlet for me. I wanted to work on my own, and work to create what I believe is one of the great "motherlodes" available to the individual: "intellectual property" that grows in value over time. I wanted to do something on the Internet, since I realized what an important tool it would eventually become. Plus, I wanted to move somewhere else; I hated living in Los Angeles. The problem was figuring out how to put all these things together and make a decent living after quitting my fairly high-paying job.

During the summer of 1994, in the middle of one of L.A.'s terrible heat waves, I was lying in bed, tossing and turning because of the heat. The idea hit me like a bolt of lightning. All the elements came together: intellectual property, writing and publishing, the Internet, maybe even fame and fortune, and, like icing on the cake, it would also integrate my hobby of clipping out strange newspaper stories for my office bulletin board. I sat bolt upright (the classic "Aha!" moment), leapt out of bed, booted my computer, and jotted down some notes of how it would all work. (If you have to ask "Why not write it on some paper?" then maybe the online business isn't for you. Besides, I can type four to five times faster than I can hand-write.)

What hit me in that flash of inspiration was, paradoxically, a newspaper column that I knew would be sensational online. This was 1994, and the World Wide Web was starting to take off, but I knew that the Web was the wrong place to publish. I needed to publish by e-mail. My contrarian instincts told me that the WWW venue would lead me to failure, and that low-tech e-mail services would be "the place to be."

I told a couple of friends what I had come up with: an e-mailed newsletter that anyone could subscribe to for free. Timeless, fun stories that would be compiled into books each year to be sold online. If it got popular enough, my electronic publication might also work as a real newspaper column, being syndicated to many different publications. Everybody thought I was crazy; they didn't see how I could make money by giving my column away for free over the Internet. I replied that I ought to be able to quit my day job in about two years, and then went home that night and expanded my notes into a business plan. That plan has remained virtually unchanged and, virtually two years to the day later, I quit my day job, moved to Colorado, and went to work full-time on *This is True*.

Publish via E-mail, Not the Web

Why e-mail and not the Web? My favorite analogy is this: I subscribe to *Newsweek* magazine. Whether I think of it or not, and whether I'm in town or not, it shows up every week in my mailbox. I certainly do not have to call them every week to ask them to send it to me. Web sites want you to "call" every week (or more/less often) by visiting the site.

Like *Newsweek*, *This is True* is available by subscription. Readers subscribe by entering their e-mail addresses on a form on my Web site (or by sending an e-mail command). The column is sent to their Inbox every week; I'm not depending on the subscriber to do anything but read it. Subscribers don't have to remember to visit to my site, since the information they're interested in comes directly to them. *Newsweek* wouldn't make money if people had to call and ask for their issue every week, even if it costs the publisher virtually nothing to take the call. And what a surprise: Virtually every Web-based publishing operation doesn't make money either.

Is the Web a terrible thing, then? Absolutely not! I know I need a Web site. Some people might have heard of *This is True* and want more information before they subscribe, or maybe they simply need to know *how* to subscribe. (I certainly don't want a few thousand people a day e-mailing me for those answers.) Or, they might want to find out if I plan to sell their e-mail addresses to spammers. (The answer is no, and no reputable e-mail publisher would ever give, sell, or transfer e-mail address lists to advertisers, spam-based or not.) They also might want to peruse the *This is True* archives or see what products I have for sale. In my case, what's for sale *is* the archives! The content of my weekly issues are collated into a book each year and sold online; they sell by the thousands.

Autoresponders Supplement the Site

I realized early on that a lot of my readers would be overseas. In fact, *True's* distribution hit 100 countries in less than two years; and achieving that number was a lot harder in 1996 than it is today. Not everyone has a fast modem, a real-time connection, or free telephone service. In most countries, surfing the Web is difficult and expensive, so I set up autoresponders to relay the same basic information (which can be found on my Web site) through e-mail. That service has instant turnaround time, 24 hours a day. Even in 1999, my autoresponders see several hundred hits per month, thus providing information (or a sales message) to my customers who don't have Web access or who don't want to bother firing up their Web browsers. You can't win customers over in any situation by demanding they play by your rules; you need to make it easy for people to play by their *own* rules.

And that philosophy continues in the format I use for my weekly postings: *This is True* is sent as simple (ASCII) text. It allows for reading by virtually any e-mail client—the "lowest common denominator" theory. I want people to be able to read it easily, without having to use any special software. It seems to me that the easier something is to read, the more people will actually want to read it. I don't have an HTML version of *True*. In my opinion, all that does is add overhead; with an HTML version there's more data to send and formatting issues to worry about. While I might end up with a prettier-looking message, it would be at the cost of making it difficult for some users to read. HTML e-mail makes it possible to send sexy, colorful advertising, but that does not serve the reader—it serves the publisher at the readers' expense. If you show you put the readers first, you'll get more of them! And then you will be able to charge more for advertising, if that's how you want to make your income.

Massive Growth

So what is attracting *my* readers? Or, what the heck is *This is True*? The short answer: It's a weekly column that reports bizarre-but-true news items, complete with a short comment at the end of each story. It might be an ironic observation, a smart-mouthed one-liner, or an outraged opinion. In essence, it's a collection of short, weird, funny stories that people love . . . plus a joke or one-liner to make people laugh, nod in agreement, or think about the item in a different way. And (if you haven't figured this out yet) *This is True* is available for free by e-mail subscription only. That, I figured, ought to be a popular draw.

Was it ever: I had 10,000 subscribers within four months. And this was back in 1994!

Starting from the day I announced it, I've had new people subscribe every day—without fail. The word-of-mouth phenomenon was helped greatly by newspapers and magazines, which found the concept to be fun, interesting, and unusual . . . so they wrote about it. *This is True's* first review appeared in another online newsletter, now long gone, called *Net Letter Guide*. It called *True* "a tasty weekly collection," and that endorsement brought in a few hundred new subscribers. Then the *Detroit News*, which was one of the first print publications to list interesting online fare, featured *True*. That mention drew in hundreds more. Then *Newsweek* plugged it in one of their first "Cyberscope" pages, and that sent several thousand subscriptions to me in a single week. The *Washington Post*, *Internet World* (which named *True* one of the "Best in Online Entertainment" six months after I went online), *Playboy*, and the *New York Times* have all written about *True*. But remember, the Internet is an international medium; write-ups came from all over the world, including Japan, Slovenia, and even China. Articles continue to come—and in many languages, even though *True* is currently available only in English.

So what's the point to all of this? If you have a compelling offering, you'll get noticed. That translates directly into more subscribers. If you plan on creating a list that will appeal to a wide audience, prepare to be hit by several thousand people wanting to subscribe on a single day if you get written up by a large publication (online or print). You can run a list through your own e-mail program if it's going to be small, but if you're going for a mass audience, you need to be ready for it right from the beginning.

Making Software Do the Work

I knew a free e-mail newsletter filled with fun stories would be popular. I also knew that I had no desire to do a ton of work to get thousands of e-mails delivered every week. So, before I announced my publication to the world, I set up software to do most of the back-end work for me. I started with a mailing-list manager called Majordomo. The program, which pretty much needs to run on a server that's always connected to the 'Net, receives e-mailed commands from subscribers. "Subscribe" and "Unsubscribe" are obviously the most important ones. Of course, the program's biggest job was to accept a message from me containing the newsletter and redistribute it to everyone else on the list—without my having to do or say anything but "Go."

Majordomo was able to do that, but it had several frustrating shortcomings. First, it slowed down to a snail's pace after the list grew larger than 10,000 subscribers (which, for me, was four months after I started). It would take hours to load the addresses in, even before it started to actually distribute the e-mails. To be fair to Majordomo, this may have been a server setup problem, rather than being Majordomo's fault. Still, I was the one who had to deal with it. Second, the list of subscribers was not secure; anyone could easily get a copy of every e-mail address on my list. Not only could subscribers get it, but spammers could get it, too. The only thing worse for your online reputation other than sending spam yourself is to provide your readers' addresses to spammers. Since the ISP who was hosting my list wouldn't upgrade Majordomo to fix the glaring security problem, I had to take the database offline so it couldn't be downloaded. But once the list was offline, people couldn't unsubscribe anymore! To make matters more difficult, when I was ready to send an issue, the list wasn't on the server, so I couldn't send it out. At that point, I hired a programmer to write some utilities to help automate the same things that Majordomo was supposed to do in the first place, functions I had thwarted in my effort to increase my list's security and protect my readers. The savvy readers, by the way, appreciated that effort very much; most of them are still on my list, many years later. Reader loyalty is important to me, but it has to be earned.

The custom-built utilities made my list functional again, but Majordomo had yet another problem: It couldn't handle bounces (notifications of undeliverable mail). As the list got bigger and bigger, I got more and more bounces. Even if you very aggressively delete bad addresses, as I do, you can still expect to get about one percent returned as undeliverable. A person may have closed down an account without unsubscribing from your list, his provider may bounce a message because that subscriber's mail account is full, or there might be problems with the reader's server, intermediate servers, domain servers, etc.

Note that such problems with a particular address may be temporary. I started using a terrific software package to process those bounces (SmartBounce, from Orion Software, found at http://www.smartbounce.com/), but I was still frustrated. I wanted computers to do all the work. Instead, it seemed like I was wasting hours every week routing several megabytes of bounce messages into a folder so they could be processed. I had apparently exceeded the capability of Majordomo, even with the help of a hard disk full of utilities. Something had to change, but changes aren't always problem-free.

Moving Your List Is a Nightmare

If I wanted my list to grow to the next level (and I did), I had to face the fact that I needed a more capable software solution that would do the work I personally didn't want to do. I found that in Lyris, a commercial list management package. I had no desire to run the list on my own server, so I worked with the folks at Lyris Technologies (http://www.lyris.com/) to move my list onto their servers. At the time, they couldn't handle a list as large as mine: They didn't have enough bandwidth nor the high-capacity hardware necessary to deliver all my messages quickly. Eventually, they worked those issues out, and I could see that the software could not only handle my very large distribution list, but would also be able to handle significant growth. So I picked up the list and moved it.

Let me tell you: Moving your list is awful. I had a taste of that already; originally, I started *This is True* under a different name but then found out that name had just been trademarked by a large corporation. They had lots and lots of lawyers, so I had to change my list's name. Ironically, a week after I made the change, I got a nasty letter from those lawyers: "Cease and Desist" using their name. It was rather fun indeed to tell them, "Oh, that old name? I already changed it." But what about those old articles in *Newsweek* and *Internet World*? They were still out there, and people were using those old instructions to subscribe to the newly named publication. (Four years later, subscription requests under that original name are still coming in.) Even though I moved the list long ago, I'm still paying that old ISP to accept subscriptions from readers, so that instead of getting a "no such list" response, they get information on where to find it in its new location.

Do I really care that much about those few subscriptions? Yes! Though the vast majority of *True's* readers subscribe for free, those free readers are worth something. If you're publishing by e-mail to make a profit, take a year's revenues and divide that by the number of subscribers to learn how much each "free" subscription is worth. It's probably going to be less than a dollar each, but consider you could end up with more than 100,000 subscribers!

I hate that extra expense, but there's nothing worse than having readers who want to subscribe but can't because your list has moved and they can't find it. That's a missed sale. So, moving is a big deal—not a task to be taken lightly. Here's the lesson: Overestimate your needs. If you're comparing Service X and Service Y, and Y costs a few bucks more than X because it offers more features, consider that the extra few bucks might be worth it. Even though I started out with the industry-standard mailing-list software (at least, at the time), it couldn't handle my explosive growth. Even when you do try hard to be ahead of the curve, sometimes growth overtakes you.

Promotional Gimmicks

Word of mouth works great. Having dozens of "large" publications write about you is fantastic. How do you encourage these things? And do you even want to? If your list was built to make money, it follows that the more people who subscribe, the more money you'll make. A list with very wide appeal (such as humor) will obviously pull in a wider group of people than a list with a narrow niche (such as Osborne CP/M computers). The latter may very well be interesting, but it's obviously going to attract a smaller audience.

Buying advertising to find readers can be expensive, especially when you're first starting out. One way to save money on ads, and also to use up some of your own ad space (that is, if you're even planning on selling ad space), is to trade ads with other lists of a similar size. Don't approach the owners of 100,000-subscriber lists and offer to trade them ad space in your 300-member publication—find several 300-member publications to swap ads with! And don't forget your readers—they may well want to advertise, too. So if you have nothing else to put in your ad space, put in an ad for the space! Or, donate the space to a cause you believe in, or to your friends. Having ads tells your readers—especially the potential advertisers in your audience—that you accept ads.

And keep your mind open to other (possibly nontraditional) marketing ideas. Along with every *This is True* book, I include two copies of a bookmark that, in a mere 7 square inches, has the *This is True* title in large, bold print, explains what about *True* might be interesting (it's "Free by e-mail!"), reports what it is ("A weekly syndicated newspaper column featuring bizarre-but-true news stories and headlines by Randy Cassingham"), gives three brief-but-impressive reviews from large publications, and tells you where to go for details by showing both *True's* Web site and autoresponder addresses. People who buy these books are, by definition, enjoying the content, so why not give them an easy way to "spread the word" to their friends about my free online offering? I also hand a bookmark to anyone who asks me where I work. It gives them something to take home and look at when they're logging on to the Internet. Plus, it saves me from having to explain what it is I do for a living. I've even occasionally included a bookmark in the envelope when I pay bills—after all, they stuff advertisements in with the bill, so why shouldn't I do so with my payment? It's amazing how quickly you can reach a lot of people. I give away 2,500 to 3,500 of those bookmarks per year!

But, by far, your most effective promotion will be the product itself: *This is True* is copyrighted, but the copyright notice specifically allows readers to forward issues to friends, as long as they send the issue in its entirety. I do not allow stories to be clipped and sent individually, and if I find out someone has, that person is deleted from my distribution and banned from subscribing again. I also prohibit issues from being sent out on other lists.

Why am I so stringent? First, I want entire issues to be forwarded so that others can get the feel of what they'll get if they subscribe. If someone forwards just one story, say about a stupid criminal, the recipients might get the incorrect impression that *True* is about stupid criminals and nothing else. Second, I want my copyright notice attached to reduce the chance that my stories get posted on Web sites or printed in publications without permission. Third, I want the instructions on how to subscribe to be included; if someone reads it and likes it, I want him to see that he can also subscribe and get such stories every week for free! And last, I don't want *True* posted to other lists—that's not what the other lists are there for. If readers on that list want to read *True*, they should get their own subscriptions. If nothing else, I need to be able to count those readers, since I do sell ads, and the more subscribers I have, the more I can charge my advertisers. It also helps that the advertisers know that I allow forwarding, but that I require their ad be included. It essentially gives them more exposure for no additional cost. I suppose it comes down to a control issue. "Intellectual property" is just that: property. I want to control how my property is used, and it's my right to dictate the terms. In fact, that's exactly what the word "copyright" means: the right to copy. That right lies with the owner of the copyright, so I guard that right carefully.

Ad Sales and Other Sources of Income

Ironically, the mass appeal of *This is True* makes it difficult to sell advertising. Advertisers want to know the demographics of any specific audience—in essence, the specific interests of the readers. "People who like funny stories" is not particularly specific. The best demographic I know of is another newspaper column that has a big online presence: *Ask The Builder*, written by my friend Tim Carter (http://www.askbuild.com/). He writes about home improvement from his perspective as an extremely experienced homebuilder. His demographic is essentially "homeowners who are ready to spend $50,000 on fixing up their house." Can you see why that might be an attractive audience to manufacturers of replacement windows, flooring, cabinets, fireplaces, drywall, and any number of other high-cost construction products? While an ad in a general-interest publication might sell for $5–15 per thousand readers (or "impressions"), an ad in a home improvement newsletter might cost hundreds of dollars per thousand impressions—and be well worth that cost to the advertiser.

Ads aren't the only way to make money with a mailing list. If you sell things on your Web site, you might do well to simply entice your readers to check out those things—and skip over the whole "advertiser" model completely. Or, you might figure out a way to have two mailing lists: one that is free and another for which the user would have to pay in order to receive. The free list should bring in massive numbers. You could then use space in it to tout the benefits of the "pay-for" list—whether it has more information, more timely information, or some other benefit for the subscribers.

This is True uses all of these techniques to bring in income: third-party ads bring in cash to help pay the expenses of the massive free distribution. It periodically reminds readers that the book compilations are available for purchase and gives a URL for details (as well as an autoresponder address). Every week, a short paragraph gives readers a brief summary of what other stories they missed by not having a subscription to the "Premium" (paid) version of *This is True*. And, of course, *True* is also sold to print publications in several countries, fulfilling its "newspaper column" roots. None of these sources of income alone brings in a gigantic amount of money. But combined, the income is now higher than what I would have made had I stayed at my day job.

Since I talk directly to my readers every week, I'm sure not going to let someone else sell them my books! I point buyers to my own Web site. Thus, I not only get the author's royalty, but also the retailer's cut and the distributor's cut. And since I have a background in print publishing, I was also able to do a very professional job publishing the books, so I also own that aspect—and therefore collect the publisher's cut of the sales price. One thing that owning the entire operation allows me to do is offer the Premium subscribers a 20 percent discount on books. That benefit, in turn, helps make the Premium subscriptions a better value, so more people pay for the Premium subscriptions. That approach also sells more books. It's a nice win-win situation, and a positive feedback loop.

I should perhaps make something a bit more clear at this point: I am able to sell *True* to several different markets largely because I have kept ownership of the text and all of its methods of distribution—not just the e-mail portion, but also the newspaper syndication, and the company that publishes the books. Copyright law is very much misunderstood by most people—even some lawyers. I believe every publisher ought to get a couple of textbooks on copyrights and how they're defined. Ownership of timeless intellectual property is a very powerful concept. Can you imagine how much it would be worth to own, say, the copyright on *Star Trek*? Paramount has made more than a billion dollars of profits from *Star Trek* alone—not a bad return from a "failed" 1960s TV show!

If you have a concept from which you might profit, but don't know how to implement it, only then should you consider letting someone else do the work for you. You may have no experience in publishing books, but if your material is excellent, you might try selling your material to a book publisher instead of publishing it yourself. Personally, I believe I'm a terrible salesman; I'm considering turning over the newspaper distribution of *True* to a large, professional syndication company. Since I already have a good track record (and quite a few papers on my roster), I'm likely to get much better contract terms than someone just starting out.

To reiterate, you don't necessarily have to accept ads in your e-publication, sell your content to newspapers, or try to get readers to pay for a special edition of your fare. There are many other ways to make e-mail publishing very profitable for your business.

The E-mail Operation Itself Does Not Have to Make Money

I have a friend who owns a tax preparation business. It took me forever to convince him that he needed to "be online"—if just to have an e-mail address for clients to send him messages. Since he has clients all over the U.S., it's a significant advantage for them to be able to get in touch with him without having to make a phone call. Now that he has (and, more important, *uses*) e-mail, he realizes how important it is to have an online presence; he even advertises his e-mail address to his clients.

He brought me in as a client (before we were friends) years ago because a mutual acquaintance gave me a copy of his client newsletter. I really liked his attitude and philosophy ("make the money first, worry about how to reduce the taxes on it later!"). Now I'm trying to convince him to offer his client newsletter online, by free subscription, to anyone who wants it. Can you imagine how many new clients that could bring in? And best of all, it would be cheaper to send the newsletter by e-mail to 10,000 people than it would to mail it on paper to fewer than 100. That kind of power is astounding.

In case you missed my point, here it is explicitly: Traditional businesses can leverage an online presence into a tremendous new growth of their core service or product. It doesn't have to be a service of an "online business." If you forget about trying to make a profit from the online content itself and think about how to use it simply as a communications tool to promote what your business already offers, you may see its financial viability. You can still make a profit without having to charge for your newsletter or accept paid advertisements.

One major mistake: running too many ads. Face it: People are constantly bombarded by advertisements from all directions. Having a strict limit on the number of ads in any given issue allows you to charge more for the ones you *do* accept. The fewer ads you have, the more likely your subscribers will look at each one of them. As an advertiser, would you rather have one of 50 ad pages in *Newsweek*, or the only one in the entire magazine? Savvy advertisers understand the power of being highlighted, rather than being one of many. Conversely, readers like knowing they won't be hit with more lines of advertising than actual content. A typical *True* story is 7–9 lines long, so I limit ads to 7 lines plus two lines of "border"—and I allow only one ad per issue. This approach makes for a good mix, and gives minimal offense to the readers who don't like ads. Don't try to fool your subscribers into believing that you don't have ads, only "sponsors." They know better. If it talks like an ad, looks like an ad, and smells like an ad, it's an ad. I show respect for my readers by calling my ads just that: ads.

Some Negatives to Consider

E-mail publishers are, indeed, publishers. That implies certain responsibilities. Do you need to have a lawyer on retainer? Don't say "no" too quickly; publishing brings the potential of liability—"defamation of character" if you talk about real people or products, for instance. Do you need a trademark? Even with an attorney, it took me two years to get *This is True* registered as one. Do you need to go after copyright infringements? A magazine swiped six of my stories, but ignored letters from me. They didn't ignore my lawyer; they settled for $2,000 (which just goes to show how valuable content is).

You shouldn't ignore other legal ramifications. For example, if you run a stock tip newsletter and it grows to be influential, trading in the stocks before you mention them could be a big problem . . . enough that it *could* lead to jail time.

To be successful, you need to have a fair understanding of the Internet's culture. The 'Net has a unique culture as much as Japan does. Would you move to Japan after a week of planning, open up a storefront, and expect to make a profit without fail? Do you even know the language? Do you know how *not* to offend your customers? I'm personally offended by the dozens of different individuals and companies who send me "spam" every day. These advertisers think they can make a killing by "getting the word out on the Internet," yet they have no clue as to what the 'Net is all about. They don't understand when 10,000 people call their 800 number and complain about the junk in their mailbox. Someone who I called to complain to happened to be a travel agent. Their lame excuse was "e-mail advertising isn't illegal." Well, it might not be illegal to open up a topless Bible store, either, but I wouldn't expect you to make much of a profit from it if you tried. Think of how ludicrous that is! The best thing spammers can come up with to defend their unsolicited mailings is: "my advertising method is not illegal"? Unbelievable. Junk e-mail is such a vile method of advertising that the States are racing against the Feds, trying to be the first to outlaw it. Don't even think about using spam.

Have you ever noticed that some sites or e-mail lists feel more homey, more relaxed, more comfortable, or even more professional than others? Sometimes you just like one site over another, but you're not really sure *why*. There are many styles and expressions that are unique to the Internet community—that's its culture. If you've noticed that some sites *seem* better than others, you're probably being influenced by the culture, even if you're not consciously aware of it. Ignoring the conventions of that culture (LIKE INSISTING ON TYPING IN ALL CAPS) makes people uncomfortable and drives them away from you.

Lastly, writing quality counts—a lot. People lament over how literacy is declining, but what is the 'Net if not a medium of printed words? Yes, yes—the Web makes use of audio and graphics, but we're talking about e-mail publishing here. Remember that the average "Netizen" is well educated; he wants high-quality content! Give him garbage and he'll go somewhere else. On the 'Net, there's always somewhere else to go.

Randy Cassingham
arcie@thisistrue.com
http://www.thisistrue.com/
©1999 by Randy Cassingham. All Rights Reserved
Randy Cassingham writes This is True, *one of the most popular weekly columns on the Internet. A former paramedic, technical journal editor, and software designer, he quit his job at NASA's Jet Propulsion Laboratory to work full time on his e-mailed publication. He lives in Boulder, Colorado.*

I-Advertising

by Adam Boettiger

Picture the world's largest conference on Internet advertising. Thousands of people—industry professionals from all over the globe—gathering in one location, learning from the experiences of others and sharing information. Now combine this with the valuable, informal networking sessions that take place at the pubs at the end of the conference day and then extend the conference from 3 days to a full 365 days a year. Add to this the convenience of never having to leave the comfort of your home or office to attend the event and not paying for it. The event comes to *you* daily by e-mail.

I-Advertising is the world's largest e-mail discussion forum specific to the online advertising industry. It is currently received by over 10,000 subscribers in 78 countries on 6 continents around the world. I founded I-Advertising in 1996, largely because at the time, there weren't really many quality places where one could go to make industry contacts, share ideas, or solve problems. The Internet, specifically e-mail, is wonderfully suited for virtual communication and community building. It has been for quite some time now.

I started the I-Advertising Discussion List with some very basic but aggressive objectives in mind:

1. I wanted to provide one of the best industry resources online specific to the niche industry of Internet advertising. If someone else were already doing it, I would simply do it better.

2. I wanted what I did to have a profound and positive impact on the industry and those who were deeply immersed in the Internet culture.

3. I wanted to structure it so as not to exclude anyone, neither geographically, academically, nor with regard to experience level. I wanted to produce something that would be useful to those who were brand-new to the online advertising industry (of which there were

many) as well as those who were experienced veterans (of which there were few at the time).

4. I wanted the list to have international appeal. I felt it would have a much wider reach and larger audience if it were not U.S.-centric.

5. I wanted subscriptions to be free, because I felt that the audience would grow far more rapidly that way.

6. Most importantly, when professionals recommended a place to go to learn about the online ad industry and to stay current with industry trends, I wanted I-Advertising to be the first thing that came to their minds.

7. Lastly, I wanted to find some way of generating revenue from the publication, such that I would be able to pay for list-hosting fees, throughput, ISP dial-up fees, my time invested, and other expenses associated with production.

I told you they were "simple" goals!

Back in 1995, I started to prepare for developing the list by learning as much as I could about what an e-mail discussion list was and what features and characteristics I wanted to include. I spent hours online researching what was currently available in the same area that my list would focus on. It was difficult, however, because while there has always been a huge volume of e-mail discussion forums and publications, there has never really been a large amount of material published on running them or moderating them (until this book!). When I found a publication or discussion list that was similar, I quickly identified what I felt was wrong with it and added those traits to my laundry list of "Don'ts." When I saw things I really liked, I incorporated them into the way I was going to run my forum. When I didn't see things I wanted, I developed them and wrote my own rules.

This is a technique that I highly recommend to anyone, not just in the online ad industry but in life itself. As you go through life online or offline, make as many new contacts as you can. Networking is a learned skill—one that will allow you to get a better job, acquire new business, satisfy customer needs better than the competition, and show others that you are a skilled businessperson. You can learn just as much from those who are unsuccessful as you can from those who are successful in the online world. Simply adopt some of the traits of those professionals in your industry who are successful and be sure to stay away from the traits of those whom you don't wish to be like.

At the time I was developing I-Advertising, I had heard through friends that Glenn Fleishman of the I-Marketing list was one of the best list moderators on the Internet. I-Marketing was one of the first quality marketing discussion lists about the industry, and Glenn ran it with an iron hand. By definition, a "moderated" e-mail discussion list is one in which posts submitted are first reviewed by a human being (the moderator) and then either killed or approved. Those posts that are approved are then sent by the moderator to list members through a list management program.

The basic role of a list moderator is to act as a giant filter, keeping out the chaff (bulk unsolicited e-mail ads, off-topic posts, etc.) and allowing the quality content to make it through to list members' Inboxes. Glenn ran a tight ship and despite the fact that at times a handful of his list members thought he was a tyrant, he and his style of moderating were generally very well received by his community of list members. Glenn's list is still spoken highly of today, despite it being "retired" in 1996. One of the traits that I learned early on from Glenn was *organization*.

Literally thousands of e-mail discussion lists are available on the Internet—on topics ranging from the discussion of dogs (I-Dogs) to online advertising to psychology. You name it, and there is most likely a discussion list about it. It was important to me to create something that subscribers would tell their friends about, for as we all know, word of a good thing (or a bad thing) spreads like wildfire on the Internet. As my funding was rather low (nonexistent), free promotions and viral marketing (word of mouth or friends referring friends referring friends) were going to be an important part of growing the list to a critical mass of subscribers.

In order to be a quality e-mail discussion list, a list has to have good layout, it has to be well managed, and it has to have a leader—the list moderator. An online community must also have rules of etiquette, or "netiquette." Many of the discussion lists online are unmoderated, meaning that they don't really have a leader to guide them or that they have open posting. Open posting means that anything a subscriber posts to the discussion list is instantly distributed to its members. I briefly considered making I-Advertising an unmoderated list, largely because I was unsure of how people would feel about having discussions being censored or how it would affect the free flow of discussions.

What I found in my research was that the majority of list members felt that it was far more valuable to have a moderated list than an unmoderated one. Clearly, the major complaint that I have heard from people who subscribe to e-mail discussion lists is that at times they can feel inundated with e-mail. A moderated list reduces this to some degree and keeps out those truly "valuable" messages that everyone wants to get, like "I totally agree with Dave. –Bob"

In launching the list, it became clear to me that I would definitely need to create a Web site associated with the list for several reasons.

First, I wanted a URL to use for promotions, advertising, PR, and referrals. It's far easier to tell radio talk show hosts or newspaper reporters to send people to "internetadvertising.org" than it is to tell them to have people send e-mail to listserv@guava.ease.lsoft.com and in the body of your message, put SUBSCRIBE I-ADVERTISING. Without question, if you are considering publishing a list or e-mail publication, get a good URL and site to go with it. Treat it like a business, because if you are serious about it, it will become far more than a hobby.

Many things that you can do with a Web site can benefit your publication. For example, when users subscribe to I-Advertising, they are taken to a "Thank You" page after they submit their subscription requests. On that page, they are prompted to tell a colleague about the site through a referral form. If you get one referral from even a portion of the new subscribers, it will reduce your advertising costs and really decrease the time it takes to grow your list.

A site can be used to host a Web archive of past discussions. Make it searchable so that new list members can search for topics that may have been previously discussed. Nothing is worse than having to rehash the same discussions month after month.

A site will also allow your list to be indexed in the search engines and directories. Unless your mailing list has a URL, you cannot list it in industry-specific directories, advertiser indexes, and major search engines. They will be a source of new subscribers for you as well as a potential source of advertising revenues when/if you start to accept paying sponsors to help offset the production costs of your list.

Lastly, you'll want to be able to provide additional resources and services to your readers, should the list grow. Having a site associated with your list will allow you to expand it easily. A list is also an excellent tool for driving customers back to your Web site.

Seeding the List

I personally invited 10 industry friends to join the list. I specifically chose those whom I felt were well-networked experts within the online advertising industry, and who could contribute to discussions in a professional, useful manner. What I've found in my experience as a list moderator has been that typically about 90 percent of list subscribers will join a list simply to "lurk" or to read the publication. About 10 percent will actively participate in discussions, for whatever reason. Knowing that, it really benefits e-mail publications just starting out to have good content from the very first day.

Looking back over the years, I've spent very little on promotions for the forum, yet it has grown quite rapidly through media coverage and word of mouth. I probably could have grown the list quite a bit faster if I had had a monthly promotional budget to invest into I-Advertising, but I'm not in a hurry and it will come with time.

In 1998 I had the I-Advertising Web site redesigned professionally for a new look and started building up the site as a resource for the I-Advertising list members. One of the main reasons that the I-Marketing list went by the wayside after a couple of years was the cyclical nature of forum discussions. With the growth of the Internet, many new users go online each week. Discussion lists get many new subscribers each week. New members who have little industry experience may have questions on topics that have been previously discussed.

I formed a Question & Answer section on the site where anyone may visit and ask a question about Internet advertising—no matter how basic. I formed the I-Advertising Panel, which hosts over 30 industry experts who receive the questions by e-mail and help with solutions. Slowly, I am building an industry Frequently Asked Questions on the Web site. This will allow me to keep the discussions on the e-mail forum advanced and of interest to all, but also allow those who are new the opportunity to catch up. It is also likely to be a place others will link to and refer their friends to. The better the quality of your forum, and the more useful it is, the more your readers will tell others about it. I-Advertising is now required reading in many advertising and marketing programs of universities across the U.S. I am told that it is one of the first publications that all new online advertising and marketing employees are required to sign up for when they start work. That means a lot to me, considering it was something that grew out of a home-based project in my spare time.

A Few Words of Advice

It is not your job—as a list moderator—to be liked. It *is* your job to keep the get-rich-quick ads from making it into your subscribers' mailboxes. It is your job to keep the content quality level of your publication high and the noise level low. It is your job to end off-topic discussions before they bloom. It is your job to maintain order in your forum and to make it a valuable experience for all your readers. It is your job to do this day in and day out without fail—rain, shine, family emergency, vacation, etc. Fortunately, laptops and nationwide ISPs can accommodate this need. I have published my forum from Maui while on vacation, from Sweden while speaking at a conference there, from Austria and a number of other locations.

Being a list moderator is not a popularity contest. You will have days when you really wonder why you ever decided to start a discussion list in the first place. Through it all, you must remember your objectives and remain focused. A truly good, effective list moderator is one who focuses on doing a job well and who does not concern himself with trying to please all the people all the time. You'll find that no matter what you do, there will always be people who don't like what you are doing or the way that you are running your list.

For such instances, paste the following note on the wall by your computer:

This is my forum. I own it. I do my best to run it the way I see fit, for the benefit of the forum community as a whole. If there are individuals on the list who do not like the way I run it, they know how to unsubscribe and may do so at any time.

In addition to posting this note, you'll also find it beneficial if you save the nice comments that you receive about what you do. Saving them in a folder or mailbox on your e-mail program is easier than pasting them all over your office wall. Most people write to complain but remain silent if they are happy. A handful will take the time to write to you and tell you that they appreciate what you do. Save those messages and read through them when you need an emotional boost.

In your discussion forum, as in life, there will always be pants-pullers. A pants-puller is someone who just can't stand to see another person in the spotlight or succeeding. As you run by on your way to bigger and better things, they will try to pull your shorts down to embarrass you or keep you from succeeding. Pay no attention to the pants-pullers online and in life. The bottom line is doing what you feel is right, making the decision and then sticking with it.

Good luck in your online endeavors !

Adam Boettiger
ab@internetadvertising.org
http://www.internetadvertising.org/
Adam Boettiger is Editor/Publisher & List Moderator for I-Advertising (http://www.internetadvertising.org/). *He has been involved with the online advertising industry since 1995 and has served as Vice President of Business Development for eyescream interactive, inc.—an Internet advertising agency based in Portland, Oregon—since 1997. For a free subscription and additional information on the I-Advertising Discussion List, visit* http://www.internetadvertising.org/.

The Accidental Publisher

by Fred Langa

Let me start by telling you the *end* of the story: I now have a healthy e-mail-based newsletter. It's running smoothly with about 50,000 readers (as of spring 1999) and is growing by about 500–1,000 new subscribers per week. It seems to be a hit with its readers; almost three people sign onto the mailing list for every one who leaves. The newsletter is currently noncommercial, but it clearly has commercial prospects. I have no idea how large my mailing list can get; it's showing no signs of slowing down.

But I'm telling you the story backwards, with the happy ending first, because I didn't plan to have a large—or even modest—mailing list. It just sort of happened (and I'll tell you how in a moment). My lack of an up-front plan caused me to run down just about every blind alley there is and to make just about every mistake a person can when it comes to publishing via e-mail.

In fact, getting to the point of having a working, growing, healthy e-mail newsletter has been as convoluted and indirect as any project I've ever been involved with. If I were to do it over, I'd do almost *everything* differently: The ending may be happy, but getting to that point was—well, let's just call it a learning experience.

And that painful experience may be able to help you avoid some of the same errors. So pull your chair a little closer, and I'll reveal all the sordid details of how *The LangaList* came to be—and all the dark, ugly secrets of its error-strewn, chaotic birth!

Quarter-Baked Ideas

You've heard the expression "half baked"? Well, my initial ideas for an e-mail newsletter weren't even that far along. Call them "quarter baked."

You see, after a 20+ year stint in the publishing industry, I'd decided to get back to my first professional love, which was writing. I resigned from my job as

Vice President and Editorial Director at CMP Media, moved my family out of New York and back to our native New England, and began writing again as a freelancer.

Having been on the editor's side of the desk, I knew how precarious the freelance life was. I had several contracts for columns and online work, but still, it was a leap going from the security of a biweekly paycheck to—who knew? So the first piece of the online/e-mail-publishing puzzle started to fall into place: I had a hazy idea of starting some kind of self-publication effort so I could communicate directly with readers, rather than being totally dependent on traditional publishing processes.

I also knew that if my contract columns and online work got substantial traffic, the publications paying me for them would be happy: They'd have lots of "eyeballs" visiting their sites and reading their pages, which in turn would allow them to make money selling ads. With my work bringing in ad dollars, they'd be more likely to continue my contracts. So a second piece emerged: I needed a way to self-publicize my work so people would know about it and read it, and keep my publishers happy.

There also was a third element—and I know it sounds corny. But I'd been in publishing for a long time and had made a good living running a variety of magazines and online sites. The last fuzzy piece was the idea of somehow "giving back" to the readers and to the computing community in some way.

There was no "Eureka" moment—I didn't run naked through the streets of my hometown—but eventually the ideas firmed up enough so that I figured I'd send a weekly e-mail message to interested readers. The e-mails would contain useful tips, tricks, and other information about using computer hardware and software, and also would contain pointers to the for-pay columns and Web sites I was doing.

The e-mails wouldn't be just a tease: I wanted them to contain enough "meat" to be useful and worth reading in their own right. And I wanted them to be rich with pointers to other sources of information, only some of which would be my own work. I didn't want the e-mails just to be a giant ad.

I also wanted the e-mails to have a personal tone, more like a letter from a friend than some kind of corporate-speak publication or generic-voiced magazine article. The weekly e-mail letter was going to be from *me*, personally, and written in the first person.

And I wanted it to be free: no subscription hassles, no ad banners, no sponsorship messages. Just a clean, free, friendly, and (hopefully) helpful e-mail from me to interested readers, once a week.

And because my paying jobs fully occupied my time—to the tune of 50–60 hours a week—I wanted the e-mail newsletter to be a mostly background operation I could do in a few hours on the weekend.

Sounds simple, right? Well, at first, I thought so, too.

First Steps

I already had a Web site of my own at http://www.langa.com/; that site provided me with numerous e-mailboxes. I named one of them subscribe@langa.com and started including that address in the signatures in my outbound e-mail. (I get hundreds of e-mails a day.) I also put the "subscribe" address on my Web site, in the little author bios that followed the articles I write, and so on.

I didn't buy any mailing lists or do any prospecting for subscribers; this was a low-level thing, intended mostly as a background operation. I wasn't out beating the bushes to sign people up. And hey! On their own, people started signing up for what I then called *The LangaLetter*.

At first, the names came in a few at a time—a few dozen per week. I use Eudora for e-mail (Eudora is an e-mail client with powerful mail-filtering and handling capabilities), so I simply added each name to a Eudora "alias." Then, each week, I'd write and send out a new *LangaLetter*. I'd address the e-mail to an imaginary subscriber called langaletter-subscriber@langa.com and put the Eudora alias in as a "blind carbon copy." This way, each reader would get a copy of the e-mail seemingly addressed to langaletter-subscriber@langa.com, and nobody would see any of the other subscribers' names.

This approach worked fine for a while. But then troubles started.

For one thing, Eudora lets you store only about 1,500 names per address book alias, so as soon as I reached my 1,501st subscriber, I had to split the subscriber list across two aliases. That worked for a while.

But then, in an effort to counter the growing flood of spam, more and more ISPs—including mine—started limiting outbound e-mails to 100 names at a time to prevent bulk e-mailers from blasting out e-mail with tens of thousands or even millions of names attached. That meant that any mailing list sent via standard mail would now have to be split into separate aliases, each containing fewer than 100 names. Even a 1,500-name mailing would have to be sent out as at least 15 separate e-mails. What a pain.

And by now, my subscriber list was actually several thousand names, and growing at about 1,000 names a week. Managing the list was becoming a burden. It wasn't so hard to add new names—that was basically just appending them to an existing mail alias. But *removing* names was a major hassle: Someone would ask to unsubscribe, and I'd have to wade into the aliases manually to find and delete his name.

Over a thousand manual transactions a week? Something had to give.

Early Automation

My list was getting too large for manual maintenance, but it also was too small to justify a full-blown mailing-list software application such as Majordomo or LISTSERV. Both are very capable packages and reasonably priced when you amortize the cost over hundreds of thousands or millions of names. But for more modest, noncommercial lists like mine, they are quite pricey.

Also, setting up a traditional mailing list requires privileged access to a mail server—dial-up accounts usually don't work. And the software can be cranky and rough-edged. Starting a Majordomo or LISTSERV list was hard enough and pricey enough that it usually made sense only if you needed to pump out *very* large numbers of e-mail messages, or if you were running a serious list as a business venture. At this point, my little mailing list was a small, free sideline. I didn't want the hassle or expense of moving to a commercial mailing-list solution.

You know the saying, "When all you have is a hammer, all your problems look like nails"? Well, I had some very, very limited experience as a programmer, so I had the brilliant (not!) idea of writing my own little list management program.

It worked, sort of, because Eudora's mail folders are really just a type of plain text file. My little program would open the subscribe@langa.com mail file and read in each line. When it found a line starting with the word "From:" it would save the rest of that line—which was presumably the e-mail address of the person wanting to subscribe—in a new text file. This way, I could gather new subscriber names automatically and simply cut and paste them to the growing subscriber list. What used to take minutes now took seconds. I was cookin'! (Or so I thought.)

But more and more people were signing up for the list. Even with the name-grabber program, I was still spending too much time working on the mailing list instead of creating content. I created a new mailbox for *un*subscribe requests and set up a Eudora "mail filter" to place all inbound unsubscribe e-mail in that folder. I then wrote a second little program to extract the unsubscribe addresses.

I'd import the subscribe and unsubscribe lists into Microsoft Word and use Word's alphabetic sort function. With both lists in alphabetic order, I could much more easily locate and delete the names of people wanting to unsubscribe.

But the list kept growing, and even that got to be very time-consuming. So I then wrote a *third* little program to automatically search through the alphabetized subscriber list and auto-delete any matching names found on the alphabetized *un*subscribe list, and that worked for a while.

But meanwhile, I was still having to manually split the subscriber list to stay below the arbitrary 100-name anti-spam limit, and that was getting to be a major hassle. I then found a mail server I could use that did not have the 100-name limit. (The people running the server knew me and knew I wasn't sending spam.) This eliminated the 100-addressee limit, but put me back at Eudora's own 1,500-name alias limit.

I then wrote a *fourth* program to split the final subscriber list into alphabetic chunks on the theory that it was unlikely that I'd anytime soon have more than 1,500 names starting with any one letter of the alphabet: This program dumped all the As into one file, all the Bs into another, and so on, creating 27 files of names each week. (The 27th group was for numeric e-mail addresses, such as CompuServe's.) Each week, I'd write the newsletter, create 27 different e-mails, BCCing one group of alphabetized names in each, and send them off.

It worked but was getting to be a crazy hodge-podge of separate pieces and procedures. (Can you say "Rube Goldberg"?) Before long, it wasn't even close; I was spending far, far more time maintaining the mailing list than actually writing the newsletter!

And, of course, all I'd really done was delay the inevitable. Soon, I ended up with individual alphabetic groups that exceeded Eudora's 1,500-name limit, forcing me to split them manually again (A1, A2, A3, B1, B2, B3, etc.). This wasn't getting me anywhere! But, busy with other work, I let things limp along in increasing complexity (the process's) and confusion (my own).

The Mini Meltdown

One of the banes of mailing lists is "looping." This happens when a bad address somewhere in the list causes a copy of an outbound message or newsletter to be returned to the server in such a way that the server interprets it as a new, authorized message that should be sent out to the full list. This causes a second copy of the message to be sent to everyone on the list.

Of course, the bad address is still there. When the second message arrives, the bad address again returns the message in such a way that the server sends it to the entire subscriber list again, a third time. That triggers a *fourth* duplicate message. And then a *fifth* . . .

Eventually, in the worst cases, a human has to shut down the server and manually flush the e-mail queues to stop the loop.

Most industrial-strength mailing-list software can detect and quash a loop very early on, sometimes before the second loop ever starts. But, remember, I wasn't yet using mailing-list software. I was using Eudora and ordinary e-mail.

Many e-mail servers also will detect loops on their own, but usually they're configured with high loop thresholds—sometimes as high as 30 or so loops. Until that loop count is exceeded, the server just sits there, happily grinding out duplicate messages one after another.

And yes, this happened to my Rube Goldberg mailing-list setup. Sometimes the loops would self-destruct, and people got only a few copies. Other times, the loops ground on for hours, undetected, before one of the server technicians would notice that, gee, the server seemed awfully busy, and figuratively pulled the plug.

In one memorable week, over 10,000 readers each got up to 14 separate copies of *The LangaLetter*! When these loops happened, readers would unsubscribe, thinking that would stop the flood of duplicate messages. But it didn't, because the duplicates were one old message, endlessly recycling itself over and over. Because the duplicates were not being generated afresh from the subscriber list, unsubscribing had no effect.

Well, that's not true. It had *one* effect: I lost subscribers in droves. My mailing list actually began to shrink. After a couple of horrendous weeks of duplicate e-mails, I'd lost *half my readers*. I felt ill.

Salvation?

I decided to move my mailing list to a commercial mailing-list server hosted by a local ISP. This server prided itself, they said, in tech support and getting mailing lists to work perfectly. Although I was now spending money out of pocket on a newsletter I was giving away for free, I figured I had no choice.

It worked, sort of, for a couple of months, except that loops still would occur from time to time, to the annoyance of my readers and to my own embarrassment. The number of subscribers stagnated as unhappy, loop-beleaguered readers bailed out as fast as new readers signed up. I started looking for alternatives.

Around that time, several free "list hosts" started up. They are (usually) advertising-based services that allow anyone to publish an e-mail-based newsletter or discussion group. The hosting company appends small ads at the bottom of each message to pay the bills and make a little money. As the list owner, you don't need any special hardware or software; all you need is a Web browser and a list of people you want to contact.

There are two basic kinds of free lists, which more or less mirror the kinds of lists you can run with full-blown list software such as Majordomo or LISTSERV.

First, there's a one-to-many version called an "announcement list." It's a one-way mechanism by which the list owner broadcasts messages to everyone on the subscriber list. If any recipients choose to reply, the replies come back by private e-mail and are seen by no one but the list owner.

There's also a many-to-many option called a "discussion list," an interactive post-and-reply mechanism. Any member of the list can send an e-mail to the list software, and the software then automatically disseminates the e-mail to everyone else on the list.

Both types of lists are available, for free or at low cost, on the Web, and they're incredibly easy to set up and use. Usually, you visit the Web site of your chosen list host and fill out a few forms. For legal reasons and to prevent spammers from using the list services, you have to provide a valid, personal e-mail address. Next, you give your new list a name, enter a description, and—in some cases—choose a category in which you want your new list to be placed on the site. You click "Done" and in about five minutes, your list is up and ready to use.

Most list hosts provide a Web-based list management interface. From inside your Web browser, you have all the control you'd have with a traditional list server application, but with far fewer hassles.

Once your list is set up and you've entered the names and addresses of the first subscribers, you can begin sending out messages. From then on, you can either add and delete subscribers yourself, or allow your subscribers to do it themselves: All the list host services I've seen will allow your subscribers to subscribe or unsubscribe at will. Three of the largest free list-hosts are http://www.egroups.com/, http://www.onelist.com/, and http://www.listbot.com/. (You can find many more with your favorite Web search engine.)

I decided to try one and signed up with eGroups because I liked its interface, and it had an easy way to keep a local copy of your subscriber list. (I didn't want to entrust all my thousands of hard-won names to a free service I knew little about.)

So, I poured my names into the eGroups interface and started using it to send out *The LangaLetter*.

The Full-Blown Meltdown

But if my previous problems were my own private Three-Mile Island, I now faced a Chernobyl: There still was a bogus address from the old system buried in the address list when I moved the remaining names across to the new server.

I sent out the first issue of *The LangaLetter* on the eGroups server and went to bed that night thinking that—at last—everything was fine. But when I logged on at 7 a.m. the next day, I found some 2,000 messages in my mailbox, the leading edge of what would be a tidal wave of e-mail.

Once I restarted my heart, I was able to track down what had happened. The eGroups list seemed to be working perfectly, but that one bad address from the old system had inadvertently accessed and activated the *old* server, which was merrily sending my newsletter to itself, and thus to everyone on the mailing list, over and over and over.

I manually deactivated the old list server as best I could from afar and purged the mailing list. But even with the old list dead, the flood of duplicate messages continued.

At 8 a.m., I contacted tech support at my former list host and said (in part), "Please pull the plug on my list—kill it, wipe it out, and delete anything in the mail queue." I also contacted billing and canceled my old account outright so there'd be nothing active at all on the old site. But the flood of messages continued.

At 8:41 a.m., tech support answered my mail and reassured me the problem was being taken care of and that the e-mail queue was "frozen."

But the duplicate messages still came. And came. And came. Thousands and thousands and *thousands* of them, some from the berserk mailing list itself, others from readers who found that duplicates were cluttering up their mailboxes and wrote to alert me to the problem.

Finally, at almost 5 p.m. and only after getting further urgent e-mail from me, tech support actually got around to killing the wayward e-mail processes and flushing the mail queue as I had requested at 8 that morning. Some *nine hours* had passed since my first call for help. I have no idea how many duplicate messages were needlessly spewed out in those nine long hours, but it's a lot.

It caused a huge mess. Readers who looked at the duplicate mail headers saw what was going on and correctly identified the source of the problem as a berserk mail list from my old list host. But others blamed me, thinking I was deliberately spamming them or sitting at my desk and personally sending them a duplicate message every so often. (Sigh.)

Still others thought the *new* list host was at fault because the duplicate text had originated there. In reality, the new system worked *perfectly*, sending out just one copy. All the duplication was done by the old system, which inappropriately took that one good message and cloned it a huge number of times. But to a casual eye, it looked like the new system was fouled up, and some people tried to get the new (blameless) list shut down as a spammer.

It was a nightmare.

When the smoke cleared, I had wiped out months of work attracting readers, and my subscriber list had shrunk yet again.

Size Matters

I started rebuilding, and eGroups worked great for a while. I actually began to pick up new subscribers and started to regrow the list to its former size. After several months, I recrossed the 10,000-name mark, but this time in a positive (growing) way. The 15,000 mark came and went. Then 20,000, and 25,000 . . . I started to relax.

That was a mistake.

Most eGroups lists were much smaller than mine, and although the service was theoretically able to handle very large lists, the service had little practical experience doing so. Plus, the service as a whole was growing extremely quickly, which caused its own set of teething problems.

One common trouble was that the service would seem to hang for no reason. I'd try to send out my weekly newsletter, and nothing would seem to happen. Was the server hung? Was the list actually being processed? If I re-sent the message, would everyone on the list then get two separate copies? Some weeks, I tried to wait out the hangs; those weeks, none of my readers got their copies. Other times, I did resend, causing everyone to get two copies, and reawakening fears of looping again. Talking to tech support there was like talking to a wall. Arghhhhh!

My list was now approaching 30,000 subscribers, and once again, I felt the familiar sensation of my wheels spinning. The free service just wasn't working for a list this size.

Starting Over

By that time, Chris Pirillo and others had suggested to me that I try the Lyris list software, as hosted by Dundee Internet. Lyris offered aggressive pricing, great tech support (although I'd heard *that* one before), and reliable service.

So I moved the list from eGroups to Dundee—and haven't looked back. The Lyris package offers a good interface and the tools necessary to control membership, access, and critical things like loop prevention.

The folks at Dundee also have been great at providing support the few times I've needed it. And all in all, the service has worked exactly as promised.

Which brings us back more or less where we started: I now have a healthy e-mail-based newsletter that's running smoothly with about 50,000 readers (as of spring 1999) and is growing by 500–1,000 new subscribers per week. I still don't know how large the list might eventually end up, or if I'll try to make it a commercial offering, but I don't worry about it because the infrastructure is now there to handle just about whatever I eventually decide to do.

As is, the newsletter does its job and fulfills the four fuzzy goals I had in mind when I started. I am "giving back." Although the Dundee setup costs me a modest amount of money each month, it's not bad, and I feel that I am providing a useful service for my readers. I can and do successfully direct literally tens of thousands of readers each week to my for-pay columns and Web sites. That keeps my publishers happy—and, because the information there is good, it keeps the readers coming back for more, too. I do have a modest, but growing self-publication effort that could, if necessary, be turned into some kind of commercial operation if or when I need an alternative to the traditional publishing process. I can produce the weekly newsletter in a few hours on Sunday, leaving me free to pursue for-pay work through the week.

So, after many false starts and blind alleys, I'm more or less where I wanted to be.

Lessons Learned

At the end of it all, I've come away with five major lessons:

- Have a plan. Don't drift into e-mail-based publishing, or if you already have, stop and figure out where you want to be. Short-term solutions and Band-Aid approaches will only hurt you in the long run.
- You get what you pay for. Free services can be fine for small mailing lists and early trial runs, but if you're serious, hook up with a commercial list host. The modest investment will pay for itself many times over in fewer headaches and better service for your subscribers.
- Don't reinvent the wheel. You can waste an incredible amount of time trying to solve problems others already have completely resolved. Unless there's a clear and compelling reason why an existing solution is no good for you, stick with the proven approaches.
- Don't make e-mail clients do things for which they were never designed. E-mail clients (Eudora, Outlook, etc.) are fine for lists of dozens to hundreds of names, but clearly are not meant for heavy-duty mailing-list work. Trying to make them serve that way will only cause trouble.
- Decide where you want your energy to go. I wasted far too much time dealing with infrastructure issues when I should have been creating content. If you're in the content game—and anyone who runs a mailing list, newsletter, or discussion group is—use tools that let you focus on content: *That's* where you'll make your mark.

Fred Langa
fred@langa.com
http://www.langa.com/

Fred Langa is a freelance computer/Web author, editor, analyst, and consultant. His current primary work now reaches an audience of over two million readers per month. He writes the Explorer *column for* Windows Magazine *and is on the* WinMag *masthead as Senior Consulting Editor; the* LangaLetter *column for* CMP's Information Week Online; The Monitor *monthly column for* BYTE Online; *a weekly online column for* Windows Magazine's Dialog Box; *and also manages three popular Web sites. Fred's free weekly newsletter is available via* subscribe@langa.com.

Poor Richard's Web Site News

by Peter Kent

Late in 1997 I prepared to publish a book called *Poor Richard's Web Site: Geek-Free, Commonsense Advice on Building a Low-Cost Web Site*, the first book in this *Poor Richard's* series. (*Poor Richard's E-mail Publishing* is the third.) For a few months I'd been slowly promoting the book. I had set up a Web site about the book, and I had started offering to give away copies of the book in drawings. For instance, Budgetweb (http://www.budgetweb.com/), a directory of low-cost hosting companies, talked about the upcoming book and invited visitors to enter to win one of several copies I was giving away.

Budgetweb linked back to an entry form at my Web site (http://PoorRichard.com/). The form asked for the entrant's name and e-mail address, and one other thing; it asked if the entrant would like to receive a newsletter containing information about setting up a low-cost Web site.

Almost all of the entrants checked the Yes option button, and so my list of subscribers grew. By the time I began publishing my newsletter—on February 13th, 1998—I had a little over 1,000 subscribers. And the list grew quickly from there; I ended the year with over 18,000 subscribers.

My list is not that large when compared to some of the newsletters owned by the other publishers writing in this book, but its size—which will be around 30,000 subscribers by the time this book is in print—puts it well into the "pretty good size" league, and well above average. And building a specialized list up from 1,000 subscribers to 30,000 in a year and a half is still quite good. So one of the most common questions people ask me about my newsletter is "How did you find so many subscribers?" Well, I'll explain that in a minute. But I think there's a more important question that should be dealt with first. *Why do I publish this newsletter?*

There's More Than One Reason to Publish

To begin with, I saw the newsletter as a way to promote my books. I would dispense advice, and if my readers felt that the advice was worth reading, I hoped they would go out and buy the book. Was I right? Does the newsletter sell books? Yes, it does, though it never quite pushed people into buying books in numbers I expected. In the early days sales were disappointing, but now I'll see a flurry of orders after each newsletter goes out. (I always devote a little space to my books in each newsletter, but not enough space to make the newsletter appear to be nothing more than a giant ad for my books. As I'll explain in a moment, you have to provide real meat in your newsletter, or people won't read it.) In the few days after the newsletter is published, I'll gross perhaps $1,500 in Web-site sales. (I publish every two weeks). Undoubtedly there are other sales I can't measure, though. If the newsletter encourages people to buy from me, it must also be sending some of them to other bookstores, both online and offline. I spend around $40 to mail to 30,000 people, so you can see that these mailings certainly make more than they cost me.

But there are also other reasons to publish a newsletter. There is advertising revenue to be made, of course. But don't think all you need to do is publish to a few thousand people and the money will start flooding in. It doesn't seem to work that way. The newsletter publishers I know who do well out of advertising work hard at it. They have a "system," and spend a lot of time and effort finding advertisers. I have too many irons in the fire, perhaps, and simply haven't found the time to go out and sell advertising, so my ad sales have been pretty low. I do make a little money from ad sales (just recently one advertiser paid me $2,000 to run his ad six times), but I think the newsletter has the potential to make much more . . . if I can find someone to help me sell advertising space.

Another reason to publish a newsletter is to forge a connection between yourself and a group of people. Right now I have a channel of communication open to around 30,000 people who are interested in setting up Web sites and carrying out online marketing and promotion campaigns. How can I use that connection?

Well, here's an example. At the front of each *Poor Richard's* series book you'll find five pages of testimonials or reviews. When the book is first published, those pages contain nice things that ordinary readers have said about the book. Later, as press reviews come out, those testimonials are replaced by nice things members of the press have said.

While this book was being edited, I made an offer to readers of the newsletter. The first 200 respondents who agreed to provide feedback within three weeks would get *Poor Richard's E-mail Publishing* in electronic format—in word-processing files. I clearly stated that I expected them to tell me what they thought of the book, good or bad. I sent out the newsletter containing that offer 8:00 a.m. one Saturday morning, received the first 200 responses in around ten hours, and ended the day with around 350 responses. (Responses to these kinds of offers tend to continue strongly for several days, then dribble in for weeks afterwards!) On another occasion, I needed beta testers for some programs created by my software development company, BizBlast.com. An announcement in the newsletter brought in hundreds of volunteers.

I can also use the list as a form of research. For example, I've decided I need a graphics program that will help me manipulate the .gif and .jpg files I use on my Web site. I plan to ask my readers what programs they recommend. With that many people, I know I'll get dozens of responses, and probably find one or two excellent programs.

Of course I'll publish the list of recommended software in my newsletter. If this information is useful to me, it's bound to be useful to others. In effect I'm getting my readers to help me build the content. Many readers are quite happy to do this anyway; I get several messages each week from people recommending products and services, and often mention those recommendations in the newsletter. Many on the Internet have long recognized that discussion groups— whether they are mailing lists, newsgroups, or Web forums—are a way to get others to provide content for you. But you shouldn't underestimate the power of a newsletter to generate content, too, by way of reader feedback to the editor.

Here's yet another reason for publishing a newsletter. It's a good "background" promotional tool. If you write a good newsletter about a particular subject, you'll eventually find that writers interested in the subject start to subscribe. Journalists and freelance magazine writers will sign up, and eventually they'll begin to mention you here and there. You'll become a source of information on that subject, worth quoting and consulting. You can even target these people directly; I occasionally use the newsletter to ask for reviewers to contact me.

So overall, there's no single reason for me to publish *Poor Richard's Web Site News*. I'm making a little money on advertising, but not a lot. It sells a few books, perhaps enough alone to make it worthwhile, but not the flood I'd hoped for. It provides a connection to readers that's useful sometimes, but perhaps not useful enough to give me reason enough to publish my newsletter . . . but add all these things together, and then I have good reason to keep *Poor Richard's Web Site News* "in print."

Building the List

So back to the question most people ask. How did I build the subscriber list so large? To start with, it was a by-product of promoting my book, *Poor Richard's*

Web Site. I had a very active "guerrilla" promotional campaign that brought many people to my Web site. *Poor Richard's Web Site* became probably the most widely reviewed title in computer book history, and those reviews led to a lot of traffic to my Web site. Anything that pushes people to your site is also pushing potential subscribers to your site, so lots of traffic means lots of new subscribers. I have always encouraged every book reviewer to mention the Web site in their reviews. (Readers can find the table of contents and sample chapters there, so many reviewers regard giving out the URL as a service.) I also worked with an "advertorial" company, placing an article I wrote in scores of newspapers across the country. In that article I mentioned my newsletter, and offered a couple of free "reports." When someone e-mailed me, an autoresponder would send out these reports automatically, the e-mail address being saved in a text file so it could be added to the subscriber list later. (If you'd like to know more about the grassroots promotional techniques you can use to bring people to a Web site, or promote pretty much any product, service, or belief—or e-mail newsletter—on the Internet, see *Poor Richard's Internet Marketing and Promotions*, which I cowrote with Tara Calishain.)

In the early days I (foolishly) kept the subscription form for the newsletter in the newsletter section of my Web site—and I probably lost many subscribers because people never saw the form. Eventually I moved the subscription form to the main page of the Web site, and to many other pages as well. Many people publishing newsletters try to lead people several steps into the site to a subscription form, as I used to. But if you put the form right there on the first page your visitors see, you'll get more subscribers.

You should also make everyone with whom you come into contact on the Internet a potential subscriber. For instance, when people buy books at my site, they'll see a question: "Would you like to receive a free e-mail newsletter, *Poor Richard's Web Site News?*" There are two option buttons, Yes and No, and by default the Yes button is selected. The buyer can always switch to No if he wants, but I've found that 95% of buyers will leave it set to Yes.

Another technique I used was to join in a partnership with several other newsletter publishers with newsletters more or less the same size as mine (at least at that time). If you come to my Web site and subscribe to my newsletter using one of my Web forms, the confirmation page that appears after you've submitted the form recommends three other newsletters, *The Naked PC, Neat Net Tricks*, and *The LangaList*. And when people subscribe to one of *those* newsletters, they see a page recommending *my* newsletter. The great thing about this promotion is that we share our successes. When one of us is mentioned in the press, or perhaps in another e-mail newsletter (Chris Pirillo has mentioned some of us in

Lockergnome, for instance), and a flood of traffic hits his Web site, then the other three newsletters share in the "fallout." Most subscribers act on the recommendation and subscribe to the other newsletters. This system has brought in many, many subscribers for all of us.

Where's the Meat?

But there's another thing to remember—something that it's easy to forget in all the talk of subscriber-hunting techniques. You have to write something worth reading. There are literally thousands of electronic newsletters, and to be honest most of them are *not* worth reading. Too many newsletter publishers think they can publish any kind of garbage, use the newsletter to promote their products, and rake in the profits. Or, perhaps more commonly, many newsletter publishers don't really know what people want; their newsletters lack the "meat" that makes them worth reading. The newsletters are often poorly written too. It's clear that little effort goes into these newsletters, or perhaps enough effort but little talent. The result is a plethora of newsletters that few people want to read.

For the last couple of years I've been explaining, in books and in my newsletter, how to create Web sites and how to bring people to those sites. I've written that there are two secrets to a successful Web site. First, you have to create a site that's worth visiting. Then you have to tell people about it. It's the same for electronic newsletters. You have to create something worth reading, and then do all you can to tell people about it.

This basic principle is so simple that one might think it goes without saying. But it's clear that many people do *not* understand this concept. Many companies have created Web sites that seem to be based on the idea, "Hey, we're selling stuff, come and buy from us." And many newsletters are nothing more than an excuse to carry ads for the newsletter publisher's products.

Long term, such a strategy won't work. Create that sort of newsletter and you may be lucky enough to get people to read it once, and perhaps to get some of them to buy a product or two. But they won't read it again. The worst examples are newsletters that are stacked full of classified ads—scores of five- to seven-line ads. Mixed in with the ads are little pieces of "editorial" material. These newsletters really annoy me—they're garbage. They're not designed to be read; they're designed to earn money from advertisers who don't know any better.

But there are plenty of other newsletters that are just plain weak. So how do you provide the meat that people want? Well, first of all you have to find a "voice." I don't think you can *create* a voice, and I don't know really how you find it. A writing voice is something that develops over time. And if you're lucky, it's a voice people like listening to. (If not, well, get out of the business.)

However, you can't develop a strong voice if you're constantly worried about offending people, or trying to create a voice by copying someone else's style. It's a sort of "Zen" thing; you have to just let go and let it flow, and your voice, good or bad, will come out.

I've had subscribers thank me for "telling it like it is" and not pulling punches. I tend to say what I want, and in the way I want to say it. Randy Cassingham, who is the publisher of *This is True* and also a friend who lives just a few miles away, tells me that he gets criticized by both Democrats and Republicans. He seems to offend people on both the left and the right, so he figures he must be doing something right. You've got to write what you feel, without worrying about political correctness or upsetting people. You also have to accept that some people won't like your voice. The most popular newsletter writers have very distinctive voices. In many cases they have a very loyal readership that hangs on their words, but there will always be some people who hate the way they write. That's okay; you can't please all of the people all of the time. You may also find, though, that even though people will disagree with you, you will earn their respect if you're up-front and say what you feel. I recently received e-mail from someone about an article I'd written. He said "I wouldn't have said it like that" (I think he felt I was being *way* too blunt), "but you may well be right."

But how about the meat? Read what you've written. Are you stating the obvious? Are you saying things that every other writer in your area is saying? If you were a reader, would you find the content useful? Are you talking in general terms, or explaining things in nuts-and-bolts terms? Can your readers use the information you've provided? Or have you educated your readers in such a way that they now understand an important concept better than they did? It's really not hard to tell whether your writing has any meat in it. You know it when you read other people's work, after all. If you finish an article and feel as if you've taken nothing away with you—you haven't learned anything of any great importance, you don't have any real information you can do something with—then there's no meat. You have to learn to assess your own work in the same way, to measure just how worthwhile what you're saying really is.

Ups and Downs

E-mail newsletter publishing can be very rewarding. I'll admit, if there weren't tangible benefits to writing *Poor Richard's Web Site News*, I wouldn't do it. (I work way too many hours on other things as it is.) Nonetheless, I do enjoy writing it. In particular I enjoy getting to write something *my* way, without any outside interference—interference from editors and publishers, for instance. And I do enjoy passing on to my readers the interesting things that I've learned during my work online. The Internet is an exciting new medium, one which allows publishers to start with a *very* low initial cost. Even school kids can start in this business. Talented writers and publishers can build large subscriber lists and turn their newsletters into something really valuable, perhaps even a way to make a good living. I believe over the next few years we'll see a number of large and very profitable newsletters run by publishers who began their newsletters as a hobby while still at school.

But publishing a newsletter is not all wonderful. There are times that it can be very frustrating. For example, when you write something that upsets a lot of people and you get stacks of mail telling you you're wrong. Or when you say something that upsets nobody but still leads to tons of e-mail that you simply can't manage to respond to. (You'll have to find a way to deal with the floods of e-mail if you want to be in this business.) You may find that you end up spending far more time putting together the material than you originally estimated. And even if you get the best mailing-list software available, you may still end up fooling around with subscriber addresses, unsubscribing or changing them. The most annoying factor for me, though, is the spam backlash. Even if you don't spam, you're going to be accused of it. You may even be banned from some domains, after someone tells their system administrator that you sent out spam. The Internet community has reached a stage at which an accusation of spamming is almost the same as a conviction for spamming in many people's minds. Many administrators will block your newsletter at the first bleatings of an upset recipient.

How does this happen? If you send out only to people who have subscribed, how can you be accused of spamming? Well, here's an example. I once received an irate e-mail from someone saying "Please remove our name from your garbage e-mails. We do not want to keep deleting them." (*Garbage!* . . . that annoyed me, I can tell you.) I took that person off the list, but I published the message in my newsletter under the heading *No, I'm Not a Spammer!—A Plea for Civility.* The next day I received e-mail from someone apologizing. It had been his wife, he said, who sent the rude message. They share an e-mail account. He had subscribed to the newsletter, but when his wife saw it she just assumed it was spam. Shared e-mail accounts and subscribers who quite simply forget that they have subscribed are the source of most accusations of spamming. It's simply part of the territory, an occupational hazard of being in the e-mail publishing business.

Overall, though, the benefits can far outweigh the headaches. So go ahead, try it. "Build it and they will come" doesn't work in the newsletter business, just as it doesn't work on the World Wide Web. But "Build something really good and then spend a great deal of time and effort telling people about it" really *does* work, as Chris Pirillo and the other writers in this book have proven. E-mail publishing is an amazing new technology, bringing the cost of reaching huge numbers of people down to the levels at which it's available to almost everyone. Some large e-mail lists, run by ordinary people working in a spare bedroom or basement, are sending out tens of millions of messages a year. I'll probably send out around a million individual e-mail messages this year, for around $1,200. If getting the word out to people is what you're trying to do, the economics of e-mail publishing are pretty hard to beat!

Peter Kent
PKent@TopFloor.com
http://TopFloor.com/

Peter Kent is the author of around 40 computer and business books, including the best-selling Complete Idiot's Guide to the Internet (Que). *He's also the founder of Top Floor Publishing, and the author of the first in the Poor Richard's series,* Poor Richard's Web Site: Geek-Free, Commonsense Advice on Building a Low-Cost Web Site.

The Naked PC Newsletter

by T. J. Lee

[The Naked PC is] not Bill Mahr exposing himself, but great information about your computer.—Netscape NetCenter What's New

The Naked PC newsletter (*TNPC*) is about computers and the love/hate relationship we all have with them. Mechanically, *TNPC's* format is plain ASCII text, 66 characters per line, and we try to bring in each issue between 600 and 700 lines. Content consists of several short articles (some recurring themes have developed, more on this shortly), regular "Recommended" items, and a number of current newsworthy blurbs with links to more information.

The Naked PC newsletter's mission is to provide solid information about your computer, your software, and how to use them to be more productive. It's a free opt-in newsletter, which means anyone who's willing can enter his or her e-mail address and click on "subscribe."

TNPC started in July of 1998 and as of the time of this writing we've sent out 22 biweekly issues. Our subscriber list has grown from a standing start with no subscribers to over 22,000 in the 10 months we've been publishing the newsletter. That works out to 2,200 new subscribers per month or 1,100 per issue. To say we've done this on a shoestring budget would be an understatement.

We don't have a magic formula on how to guarantee a successful newsletter, but in this article we'll try to give you an overview of how *TNPC* came about and the things you might want to consider when creating your own newsletter.

Wanted: A Visionary

The Naked PC is great. I get at least one meaty little tip from each issue, and not just one that I would have to get a Ph.D. from MIT to use.—F. C.

217

Back in June of 1993, T. J. Lee and Lee Hudspeth were having their lunch usuals at the Koffee Kart in Manhattan Beach, CA, ruminating over the marketing strategy of their computer consulting company. T. J. said, "Hey, buddy, we need to get information about us to our clients in a form other than printed brochure. After all, we're a technology company, let's gather their e-mail addresses and push electronic content their way. As new prospects filter in, we'll e-mail them, too."

We kicked the idea around for several weeks and actually did several issues of an in-house newsletter for our consulting clients. We couldn't come up with a format we liked, trying first a hard copy printed newsletter and then several electronic issues using the Windows Help file format[1]. (This was long before *HTML* was a household term.) But we never hit on a formula for content and distribution that we felt was workable. (A lot of companies didn't even have e-mail back in those days.) Finally, T. J. got his wish some years later as several factors converged to conceive *TNPC*, and therein lies the story. . . .

TNPC is a group effort to be sure, but every newsletter needs a visionary to drive the effort, especially in the early days, because getting a newsletter off the ground is no easy feat. For a free newsletter, this is doubly so given there is no short-range income or even feedback from your subscriber base until you reach a critical mass (which for *TNPC* was about 5,000 subscribers). It's a real Catch-22 at the outset.

TNPC's visionary is Lee Hudspeth. Lee is a former financial analyst (Unocal Corporation) who became a computer consultant and author when, in an epiphany worthy of Scott Adams, he "got tired of being the blunt end of his department manager's pencil" and went out and started his own successful consulting company.

Lee managed to get his partner T. J. Lee, their business associate and good friend Dan Butler, and several other interested parties excited about *TNPC* to the point where it became a reality. Not as easy as it sounds since those involved frequently asked each other, "Tell me again why we're going to go to all this effort and then give it away *for free?*" The keys to the launch were (1) forging a consensus about the newsletter's mission, and (2) writing a polished first draft of Issue 1 for everyone to review and catalyze the gang's thinking.

Lee's initial contribution was to write a mini business plan for "a list," as *TNPC* was fondly known in its infancy. This informal document's sections included Potential Titles, Keywords, Potential Topics, First Issue Topics, Contributors/Participants, Infrastructure, Style and Content, Launch Announcements, Sources, and Miscellaneous To Do Items and Ideas. Together,

---

[1]You can download these early newsletters in Help file formats at http://www.PRIMEConsulting.com/freeware/#PINF01/.

Dan, Lee, and T. J. spent many a phone conference hour and endless e-mail threads coming up with their vision of *TNPC:* a biweekly newsletter that talks about computer productivity issues in a straightforward manner with a target audience ranging from beginner to advanced techno-guru. Based on the gang's consensus, Lee wrote the *TNPC* mission statement in part as follows:

> *Here at TNPC we vow to help make your daily PC experience a more productive one. There are plenty of good books, newsletters, and e-zines out there (we should know—we write and contribute to them), but we bring you content with a spin you won't find elsewhere. Like the **good neighbor who's also a computer consultant**, we offer you—for free—our latest thinking and advice on what you need to know about your PC. It will be as though we're sitting right there at your office or home, talking with you in person about the issues at hand. **Friendly, accurate, to the point, no-nonsense advice from people you can trust**.*

The theme of "good neighbor who's also a computer consultant" was very important, and brilliantly so, to Dan. Together we came up with the notion of "people you can trust" as a corollary to the good neighbor theme. Also notice how the mission statement's first sentence provides the essence of what it's all about.

Lee sat down and wrote the first draft, and the next thing we knew we were in the Internet publishing business. The actual Issue 1 as published wasn't much different from the first draft, since we all knew each other so well and Lee had already chosen approved topics that he knew from our lengthy discussions would "fit" into our own voices and interests. That's not to say that Dan and T. J. didn't contribute to Issue 1. On the contrary, they had plenty of candle-burning editing sessions. But the overall drafting process was a good omen, and the vibe was right.

There's a moral to this group effort story. Lee cranked out the first draft, but also honored his co-workers' interests and themes, thereby giving them all a tangible document to work on together and further stimulating their individual interests. The point is that if you're working in a group environment, some things are best done by one person, and other things are best done by committee. When you undertake a task that affects the group, take special care to recognize each member's special interests: It forges consensus and camaraderie.

If you're going to create a newsletter, *you've got to have a mission statement* against which you can measure your production and performance. While it's well and good to stray occasionally into side topics, you want to keep on the course you've set for your newsletter overall. Without a clear mission statement that defines content and audience, it can wind up so eclectic that it meanders all over the topic map, and you'll have trouble finding—and keeping—a solid subscriber base.

This is not to say that you can't make changes as you find out what works and what doesn't (based on reader feedback), but you can't try a new direction every issue. Have an idea of what you are trying to accomplish and stay on target until you have a reason to conclude that it's not working. Then take it back to the drawing board and come up with a new vision if need be.

Who Are Those Naked Guys?

Seriously, this is a truly top-end, award-winning newsletter, written by a large bunch of intelligent contributors . . . —ANDOVER.net

The group that became the nucleus of *TNPC's* writing staff has among them some very credible experience writing on computer topics, which has contributed enormously to the success of *TNPC*. While each of the players wears different hats in getting the newsletter out each issue, we all write and generate content, which is the backbone of any publication.

If you are going to make your newsletter a group effort, be sure everyone involved is capable of writing good content and willing to put the time in each issue (we call this "the grind"). If you're publishing a newsletter all by your lonesome, you'll have to wear all the hats yourself, but keep in mind that sometimes you have to think like the publisher, sometimes like the editor, sometimes like an author/contributor. If you get lost in just cranking out words, you run the risk of losing the focus of the newsletter, and your subscriber base may erode or fail to increase as quickly as it otherwise might.

Also consider keeping two or three issues ahead of your publication cycle so you can wear some of these other hats. If you are always behind schedule on generating content, you'll get bogged down and won't have the time you need to think strategically about marketing your newsletter.

Published By

Lee Hudspeth and T. J. Lee are the publishers of *TNPC* in addition to their day jobs running PRIME Consulting Group, Inc., a computer consulting, training, and development firm they cofounded.

The publisher's role in *TNPC* is to keep the e-zine true to its mission statement and to evaluate the subscriber feedback and make sure the newsletter is addressing the needs of its readers.

Writing about computers is nothing new for Lee and T. J., as they are frequent contributors to *PC/Computing* magazine[2] and have written numerous books about Microsoft Office and personal computers.

Starting back with *The Underground Guide to Microsoft Office, OLE, and VBA* and *The Underground Guide to Excel 5.0 for Windows* (Addison-Wesley) in 1994 through their current *Office Annoyances* series[3] (O'Reilly & Associates), Lee and T. J. have applied their training philosophy to all their writing projects—namely that computer users simply need someone to demystify the computer techno-jargon and explain how to use the technology to get real work done.

It's amazing how often we've heard from consulting clients that the computer training they took did not return the benefits they expected. No wonder when you consider that most training consists of teaching the feature set of a given computer application but leaves it up to the end user to figure out how to apply that feature set to their actual jobs.

Showing users how to actually accomplish real work was well received. This skill led to Lee and T. J. joining with their oft-times coauthor and becoming the Editors-in-Chief of a paper newsletter, *Woody's Underground Office* newsletter (*WUON*). *WUON* published its first issue in January 1996[4]. As editors and contributors, they cranked out one 12-page issue per month and put together one of the finest stables of article authors in the business, ultimately winning the Computer Press Association's 1997 Best Overall Newsletter award. Eventually, *WUON* was sold to Ziff-Davis and became *PC/Computing's Undocumented Office* published by the Cobb Group.

Editor-in-Chief

Dan Butler is the Editor-in-Chief of *TNPC* as well as the Internet marketing genius who has contributed greatly to *TNPC's* astounding subscriber growth curve. The editor has to focus on such mundane things as subscriber metrics and the mechanics of running the list. Is it easy for users to subscribe? When you get a flurry of new subscriptions, someone needs to find out where they're coming from in case you can capitalize on a mention or review somewhere. Then there are the mechanics of actually getting the issues out on time (or as close to it as possible). The editor's life is not a simple one.

---

[2] See http://www.PRIMEConsulting.com/articles/pccmagazine.html for links to the articles that Lee and T. J. have penned for *PC/Computing* magazine.

[3] *Excel 97 Annoyances, Office 97 Annoyances, Word 97 Annoyances,* and *Outlook Annoyances* coauthored with Woody Leonhard. See http://www.PRIMEConsulting.com/annoyances/ for more information on these titles.

[4] The first issue of *WUON* and other selected articles can be viewed online at http://www.PRIMEConsulting.com/articles/wuonarticles.html.

A regular contributor to *WUON*, Dan worked with Lee and T. J. on numerous pre-*TNPC* writing projects, and his extensive knowledge of the Internet and World Wide Web made him a tremendous resource for a successful newsletter project. Dan is a Webmaster by trade and the sites he manages receive 1,000,000+ hits per month. His site at http://www.dbutler.com/ is a collection of resources for people getting on the 'Net and those looking to maximize the resources they already have.

Contributing Editor

Al Gordon has been our contributing editor since Issue 4. Al is also an alumnus of *WUON* and runs Gordon Communications, a Boston-area wordsmithing company. He's also a principal in the strategic consulting firm Mary Fifield Associates.

Having worked with the crazy crew of PRIME Consulting Group, Inc. as a beta tester of their productivity add-on software[5] and having acted as Technical Editor for *Outlook Annoyances*, he was very interested in the gang's vision for *TNPC*. Because he is a professional journalist and expert in advising small-office and home computer users in system setup and applications use, the idea of a venue where he could talk about the issues he and his clients were experiencing and get instant feedback from others intrigued him.

A Free Newsletter?

> *Just wanted to say congrats—you guys are keeping the quality up, and it shows!—Woody Leonhard*

Let's try to answer the question raised earlier, "Tell me again why we're going to go to all this effort and then give it away *for free?*"

You definitely need a reason to go to all the work and headaches associated with managing an electronic newsletter. A *very* good reason. Advertising revenue is most likely not going to be it. It's tough to make a bundle solely from a free newsletter. What that reason ultimately is will depend on what you are trying to do with your newsletter.

If your e-mail list is to grow to a respectable number, you're going to have to put together a newsletter that people want to read and continue to receive. Just because you're giving it away for free doesn't mean you can turn out schlock and

---

[5]PRIME Consulting Group, Inc. develops award-winning Microsoft Office add-ons such as PRIME for Excel 97, PRIME for Word 97, PRIME for Excel 2000, and PRIME for Word 2000. See http://PRIMEConsulting.com/software/ for more information.

expect to have subscribers sign up in droves. "Hey, whaddya expect for free?" does not enter into the equation.

Sure, you'll have good issues and better issues, but you can't put too many bad issues back to back and still make a go of it. That means work and focus. You have to stay focused on your goal and how best to attain it.

Defined Goals

*Terrific content. In fact, getting TNPC free almost makes one feel guilty. —
Rachel H.*

For *TNPC* the goal is fairly straightforward, and if you've slogged through this chapter to this point, we'll bet you've already figured out what's first and foremost on our minds. Self-promotion.

All of the principals involved with *TNPC* are writers and/or have technical expertise to sell. We also all have client lists, and it's nice to have a newsletter you can recommend to your clients (remember that fateful Koffee Kart luncheon story?). A newsletter to keep your name in front of your clients (keeping you on their radar screen so to speak). A newsletter for which you have total control over the content so that you don't have to worry about misinformation about the latest bug or virus going out and causing a panic among your clients, friends, and associates for nothing.

Promotion Is Not Necessarily Hype

I LOVE The Naked PC! You guys are the best! I trust the information you put forth and am constantly sharing it with my co-workers and IS department. Thanks for keeping us ahead of the rest.—Kathy M.

All four of us are book writers, and having umpteen thousand regular readers of our newsletter is a good thing when we have a new title coming out. The computer book buying public is tired of getting bamboozled into shelling out hard-earned samolians for books that don't help them make their computers do useful work. Since that is what our books are all about, we decided that a free newsletter would contribute to establishing a sense of trust with book purchasers (existing and prospective) and consulting clients (again, existing and prospective). We could use the newsletter to dispense our advice, discuss current events and newsworthy topics, show readers where to find interesting and useful software, and even reprint book excerpts as enticements.

We take this trust thing very seriously, by the way. We strive to pack as much real value into every "free" issue of *TNPC* we give away. We shoot for substance in each article. We don't bash for the sake of bashing or scream *the sky is falling* every time a bug is found in some application or a virus gets loose.

One of the statements in our early *TNPC* business plan was not to be a "bug rag." This is our term for a bulletin that exaggerates, distorts, and otherwise uses fear-mongering tactics to trick its readers into thinking Bug X is the ultimate bug/malware demon—when in fact the rag's publisher is simply using the public's fear of software bugs to try and clamber above the noise level. We even went so far as to consider excising the term "bug" from our style guide vocabulary, but have since recognized the untenable nature of that position (after all, the truth is simply the truth). When there's a serious bug to report, we report on it factually and objectively and then move on. We take our inspiration on bug reporting from the quintessential virus/malware oracle of truth, Rob Rosenberger[6].

TNPC presents the facts as we see them and tries to come up with practical solutions for the things that affect real users in the real world. When Melissa and Happy 99 were raging, we came up with some practical solutions for minimizing exposure. Our mission statement (discussed earlier) helps keep us from getting too far afield from this philosophy. Sure, sometimes we do better than others, but we always swing for the fence. Yes, we sell ads in *TNPC* to help defray the costs related to putting out the newsletter, and we participate in a number of affiliate programs, but those revenues are not the goal. When we recommend something, we mean it.

Why Naked?

> THE NAKED PC NEWSLETTER *is one heck of a "Made you look!" name, isn't it?*—ANDOVER.net

A common question we get is, "Why did you name your newsletter *The Naked PC*?" The primary reason is the obvious, to get you to look, to set it apart from the plethora of corporate newsletters that are floating around in cyberspace. We also recognized that the adjective "naked" goes to the heart and essence of the noun you attach it to, as in the expression "the naked truth." Our company, PRIME Consulting Group, has a trademark on the term *Truth by the gleaming merciless truckload*™ that was spawned when we were writing in the *Underground*

---

[6]Everyone should bookmark Rob's Computer Virus Myths home page at http://kumite.com/myths/.

book series for Addison-Wesley. The bridge from *Truth by the gleaming merciless truckload*™ to *The Naked PC*™ was a natural one. Now you know.

The Naked PC defines the way we look at computing. Strip away all the garbage, the useless help files, the poorly written documentation, the posturing and breast-beating, and at the naked core of it all is . . . a human being hunkered down in front of a computer trying to get some work done so he can turn the bloody thing off and go home to the real world. That's the bottom line, and that's where *TNPC* tries to deliver value.

If the newsletter doesn't have real value, you'll never be able to build up a substantial subscriber base.

It's An E-mail Newsletter, So What's with the Web Site?

If you do an e-mail newsletter, don't discount the benefit of having a Web site to complement it. *TNPC's* Editor-in-Chief, Dan Butler, and co-Publisher, T. J. Lee, are both Webmasters and made sure that in doing an e-mail newsletter we did not neglect the Web-based *alter ego* of *TNPC*[7].

Each issue of *TNPC* has its key content highlighted on the main page of the *TNPC* Web site. A current or back-issue article is featured on this page, and all back issues are available on the site (and fully searchable) as HTML pages, or can be requested as e-mails via our *TNPC* mailbot. This translates into added work every two weeks when a new issue comes out, but we strongly feel it has contributed to the success of *TNPC*. We get a substantial number of subscribers from the *TNPC* site (along with a fair number of positive comments on the site itself), and it makes it easy to steer people to a place to subscribe. Instead of getting people to send in an e-mail to opt in to our list server, they can go to the *TNPC* site, type their e-mail address into a form, and click on the Subscribe button. Being easy to subscribe is a good thing, so be sure to put a sign-up form on every page.

Dan correctly pointed out early on that a number of readers would prefer to peruse each issue in their browser rather than their mail reader. Based on the reader feedback we received, he was entirely correct. That's not the same thing as saying that readers would prefer the newsletter in HTML format in their Inboxes. There is still not enough acceptance of HTML messages to make that worthwhile, and the added work involved in running both a text-based and HTML-based version ruled out that possibility. Of all the text/HTML dual-availability newsletters we've seen, only *Lockergnome* does a credible job of providing both formats on a regular basis.

---

[7]Check out *TNPC's* home on the Web at http://www.TheNakedPC.com/.

A Free Newsletter Is Free Only to Subscribers

Face it, no matter how cost-conscious you are, an e-mail newsletter—even a free newsletter—is not free when it comes to putting it together and getting it published each cycle. One area where we'd recommend you spend a few bucks from the outset is getting set up on a real list server. Trying to send out large amounts of e-mail through your ISP will only cause you grief, and many ISPs restrict the amount of mail you can send at any one time.

This is not to say you have to spend big bucks for a list server either. We publish *TNPC* on the freeware Majordomo running on the open-source Linux operating system. It's all managed by Blue Horizon Enterprises,[8] a Web host and ISP located in Texas. We e-mail a copy of our newsletter to their server, and distribution is handled automatically.

Get the Word Out

> *Thanks for a useful publication that rises from the mire of junk e-mail.* — *Mark W.*

If you write it, they will come. Not! You can crank out the best newsletter around, but if people with even a passing interest in your content don't know about it, you'll not get any subscribers. You have to get the word out.

Newsgroups and Message Boards

Lots of things you can try; posting messages on targeted newsgroups and message boards is one. This can generate a flurry of subscribers (and more than a few flames). It helps if you're a regular poster and have some credibility with your chosen subject matter. PRIME Consulting Group, Inc. hosts the Annoyance Board where people post computer- and Office software–related questions, and we get a fair number of subscribers from this board because we always include a link to *TNPC's* Web site when we post messages answering questions here.

Cross Marketing

Finding related, but not competing, newsletters and cross marketing is something that has been very successful for *TNPC* in attracting new subscribers. When you're starting out, you'll probably have to pay for ads you run in other

---

[8]Blue Horizon Enterprises is one of the last "Mom and Pop" operations left on the Web. They specialize in virtual Web hosting, Web development, mail services, including mailing lists, and everything else that can enhance your presence on the Internet.

newsletters. Once you have some subscriber base, you can contact other list owners and propose an advertising swap. You run an ad for them in your newsletter, and they can run one for you in theirs. If there's a gross inequity in subscriber numbers—say you have 5,000 and the list you want to swap with has 10,000—you can offer to do a 2-for-1 or 3-for-1 swap. For one running of your ad, you can run theirs two or three times over a number of issues.

Another low-cost way to promote your newsletter is by writing articles in other newsletters. Newsletters are generally hungry for good-quality content, and if you write something that fits their market, you might be able to work out a deal where your newsletter is plugged in your byline.

Get Others to Mention *You* By Mentioning *Them*

Another low-cost way to get others to advertise for you is to let everyone you've mentioned in your newsletter know about it as soon as your issue goes out. People like to have their products and Web sites mentioned, and they'll use your coverage of their service or product in their own marketing and often mention your newsletter in the process. We do this by using friendly form-letter e-mails that tell the recipients exactly in what issue, article, and context (including if they're on the *TNPC* home page) they or their product/service was mentioned.

Referrer Logs

Monitor the referrer log on your newsletter's Web site. This log shows you where visitors to your site are coming from. If you are getting a significant number of visitors from a particular address, you need to go there and see what is directing people to your site. Often you'll find a review or link you were unaware of. Consider contacting the site Webmaster and discussing doing cross marketing.

T. J. Lee
tnpc@PRIMEConsulting.com
http://www.The NakedPC.com/

T. J. Lee and Lee Hudspeth, the publishers of The Naked PC *newsletter, have an extensive background in computer publications having won the Computer Press Association's 1997 Best Overall Newsletter award for* Woody's Underground Office *newsletter and the prestigious National Magazine Award for their work appearing in* PC/Computing *magazine. They coauthored* The Unofficial Guide to PCs (QUE) *with* TNPC *editor Dan Butler, and authored the best-selling* Office Annoyances *series of books (O'Reilly).*

In the Trenches with The Kleinman Report

by Geoffrey Kleinman

The Kleinman Report (http://www.Kleinman.com/) was started in 1995 by Geoffrey Kleinman to help people get more out of the Internet. It has catalogued the growth of the Internet and the emergence of Internet titans Yahoo!, Netscape, AOL, and Amazon.com, and discovered new and emerging sites before they became known (including InfoBeat, Mapquest, Ask Jeeves, ProLaunch, The Internet Movie Database, and Call Wave). In early 1999 Geoffrey launched DVD Talk, which quickly rocketed to the position of top DVD community site on the Internet.

Solve a Problem

The first thing I think about when starting a new venture is "What problem am I solving?" Before you do anything else, answer this question. You don't want to have a great idea that you work very hard on, and then have to take your "solution" and go hunting for the problem it solves. Creating a newsletter is tough stuff, so it's better to know that all your hard efforts are the answer to someone's problems. If you're lucky, it'll be the solution to a *lot* of people's problems.

It's important to understand that when you launch your newsletter, you'll be in direct competition with many other newsletters, e-mail, Web pages, magazines, television shows, and countless other demands for your readers' time. The first thing any prospective reader is going to ask about your newsletter is "WIIFM?" (or "What's in it for me?"). The most compelling answers you can give are: It will save you time, save you money, make you money, or make you happy. If your newsletter addresses more than one of these, you'll find yourself quickly on the road to success.

I created *The Kleinman Report* when I was working at one of the first Web design firms in Portland, Oregon. I saw that people didn't have time to find all the useful sites on the Internet, and even if they did, they often missed some of the best parts. The great thing about this problem is that almost everyone on the Internet has it! Our solution was to create an e-mail newsletter that saved them time looking for the good stuff on the 'Net. I owe a great deal of our success to the simple fact that we continue to help solve people's Internet problems.

You might not know it, but somewhere out there is a problem that *you* are uniquely able to solve. Discover this problem by taking a close look at the things you are most interested in, as well as the things you know best. Newsletters require a lot of content, so it's best to pick something you are very interested in or something you know very well. Think of the things you could talk about to people for hours, and they wouldn't doze off to sleep. Finding the right subject for your newsletter might take some time, but be patient and continue to ask yourself what problem your idea solves.

Once you think you've come up with a compelling solution to a widely held problem, check it out with your family and friends. Ask them if they have the problem you're going to try to solve. Don't be discouraged if the answer is no. It's better to find out now that you're on the wrong path, rather than further down the line. After a while you'll find a problem that a lot of people have, and when you begin to tell them about your solution, their eyes will light up. These people will be your first newsletter subscribers.

Have a Blurb

After choosing your problem/solution, take that solution and turn it into a *blurb*. A blurb is one or two simple statements about the problem you're going to solve and your solution. This blurb should be easily understandable by your audience and should quickly communicate to them what your newsletter is about. The blurb for *The Kleinman Report* sums it all up:

> *A free monthly e-mail newsletter that will change the way you use the Internet. Featuring important Web sites, valuable information, and a unique perspective on technology and the Internet.*

Once you're happy with your blurb, print it out and show it around. Do people understand what you're trying to say? Once you've fine-tuned your blurb to the point that people "get it," print it out and keep it close by. It will be the driving force of your newsletter and will be a constant reminder of what your newsletter is all about.

Get Read!

Once you've decided what problem you're going to solve and you've formulated a blurb, your number one goal is to get read. It doesn't matter how many subscribers you have, who you have as an advertiser, or how much money you're going to make. Your number one, myopic, never-ending goal is going to be to get as many people as possible to read your newsletter from start to finish every time you send it. Unless you get people to read your newsletter, you'll start down the slippery slide from topic of interest to e-mailbox clutter. If your subscribers aren't reading your newsletter, it's only a matter of time until you become among the dozens of e-mails per day that people delete without even opening them!

Last year over 3 trillion e-mails were sent over the Internet. How many do you think went straight from the Inbox to the trash without ever being opened? Quite a few. When you're publishing your newsletter, focus on getting it opened and read. Work so people look forward to receiving your newsletter, and miss it when you don't send it out. Some of my favorite e-mails come when I am delayed in sending out my newsletter, and people ask eagerly when it's going to be sent.

Secrets of Getting Read

Getting read is actually much easier than it sounds. When people sign up for your newsletter, they are interested in reading it. (Otherwise, they wouldn't sign up.) With each new subscriber you start with a clean slate and a lot of enthusiastic interest. It's yours to lose.

Have a Consistent Personality

One of the secrets of getting your newsletter read is giving it personality. When people read e-mail, there is the perception that it is actually *from* someone. Attention spans are short, and if people can't connect with what you're saying, they won't read it, so make your newsletter *from someone*. Give it a consistent, unifying voice that people can connect with every time they read it. It doesn't matter if you are the only writer or if you're an editor bringing together content from a number of sources; you need one singular, common narrative that runs throughout your newsletter.

When I created *The Kleinman Report*, I decided to model its personality after my own personality. When I sit down to write my newsletter, I always try to keep the same tone and structure I use when I send an e-mail to a friend. This approach has been wildly successful. I've met readers for the first time who tell me how much they like what I do, and how much they feel like they know me. I get tons of personal e-mail from people who want to share what's going on in their life with me. People say that my newsletter is like getting an e-mail from a good friend!

Be Readable

It sounds like a truism: The best way to get read is be readable. When you write your newsletter, you're going to need to do several drafts. The first draft should get you to the point where you feel good about what you've written. Get to that point, and then go over everything you've done and trim it down—*way* down. It's easy to use too many words to say something very simple. When I write my newsletter, it's not uncommon for me to trim down paragraphs into sentences and sentences into words.

Keep a critical eye when revising your first draft. Ask yourself why you wrote something, and if it isn't helping your readers, lose it! People can spot BS a mile away, so don't try it. It's amazingly important to be straight-up with people in your newsletter. The second they think you are trying to work an angle or put a spin on something, you're dead. Be straightforward, honest, and humble.

After you've revised and trimmed down your newsletter, read it out loud to someone. It'll feel funny the first time you do it, but there's no more effective way of making something more readable than actually reading it out loud. You will be amazed at how much you can catch when you read it to someone. Don't be surprised if you constantly have to stop reading in order fix things that just don't sound right. Statements that make perfect sense when you write them can often sound odd or awkward when you read them out loud.

So you've done your first draft, revised it, and read it out loud. Now it's time to really get it reviewed. Have someone else look over your newsletter before you send it out. Make it someone who is great with spelling, grammar, and details. Be sure it's someone who will freely give you constructive feedback and who isn't afraid to tell you something you don't want to hear. Put your ego aside and focus on your readers. Do everything you can to make your newsletter easy for people to read. Every newsletter I ever send is always read by at least one other person first. I can't tell you how many little things have gotten caught this way.

Make Subscription Management Easy

People can't read your newsletter unless you give them every opportunity to get signed up. Far too many great newsletters out there are next-to-impossible to sign up for, so don't be one of them. Make your subscription form the first thing people see when they visit your Web site. Put an option to subscribe on every form and in any area where people are asked for any sort of information.

Don't make your subscription form overly complex. If you ask too many questions, it will prevent people from signing up. On all of my sites, the first thing people see is that I have a newsletter to subscribe to, and they can easily sign up with one click.

One of the great pitfalls many people fall into with subscriptions is making unsubscribing too difficult. Many of your potential subscribers will look to see that it is easy to unsubscribe *before* they subscribe. If they can't easily find this information, you stand a real chance of losing them. Always make it very clear how to unsubscribe. Don't fear "unsubscribes," as they are a natural part of running an e-mail newsletter.

Make People Feel Good about Reading

If you don't make people feel good about subscribing and reading your newsletter, they'll stop doing so. Don't panic, though. Making people feel good is a lot easier than it sounds.

If your newsletter is free, you've got an easy place to start. When you ask people to subscribe to your newsletter, be sure to tell them that it's free. People like to think they've stumbled on a great deal, so *be* a great deal. If you're giving away lots of great information or solving their problems for free, tell them! There's no better way to get someone to sign up than to tell them you've got the solution they've been looking for, and it doesn't cost them a single dime.

Thank them over and over and over again. When they subscribe, send them a confirming e-mail that thanks them for subscribing. Tell them that you appreciate them taking the time out to sign up and read your newsletter. In every issue be sure to thank people for being loyal subscribers and for supporting your newsletter. Thank them for taking the time out to read it, and if you ever get great feedback, be sure to graciously thank the sender publicly for helping make your newsletter even better. The key here is be gracious to a fault.

When you've discovered something really interesting to share with your readers, it's important to present it not as something that you've discovered but something that *they've* unearthed. Share your enthusiasm and excitement when you're writing about something exciting. You won't believe how infectious enthusiasm can be.

Most importantly, *never* think you are smarter than your readers are. They'll pick up on that attitude and show you that you *aren't* by unsubscribing. Never forget that people want to be made to feel like they are special, and it's your task to make that happen.

Look Good

It's not enough to just have great content in your newsletter; you must present it in a way that is clearly organized and easy to read. One of the great stumbling blocks that great newsletters often have is clutter. Look over your newsletter and make sure it doesn't look cluttered. Break up and clearly label different subjects by numbering them and having an index at the top. Chop up long paragraphs into smaller, shorter paragraphs. If you can turn a number of long sentences into short bullets, do it! People like to get their information quickly, and bulleted points make people think your newsletter is short and efficient.

It's All about Relationships

It's really important to remember that newsletters are all about relationships. When your readers start reading your newsletter, they will start to connect to it. In time, the basic publisher-subscriber relationship will change as your readers begin to trust you. Your readers' trust is the greatest currency and responsibility you'll have with your newsletter.

If people trust you, then when you say they should visit a Web site or read something specific, they will. It sounds unbelievable, but it happens. I was talking to a VP of Marketing at one of the sites I mentioned in *The Kleinman Report*, and he said his company had had more people visit their site and sign up with their service than when they were featured in *Business Week*. His exact words to me were "Your readers really trust what you have to say."

As fantastic as your readers' trust is, with it comes an immense amount of responsibility, and there is no quicker way to lose subscribers than by violating that trust. When people trust what you say, it is vitally important that you be trustworthy. There's no tap dancing you can do with this one; it's a black-and-white issue. Either you'll be able to maintain that trust or you won't. This is where your success or failure is squarely in your hands.

Who Owns It?

If you think you own your newsletter, you're wrong!

You are going to work very hard on your newsletter—very hard coming up with the idea, very hard launching it, very hard getting people to sign up, and even harder getting every issue out the door. At the end of the day, you are going to feel very tired but very good about "your" newsletter. Well, I hate to burst your bubble, but you don't own your newsletter. Nope, not even after all that hard work you've done on it. You are merely a servant, a facilitator, a conduit to meet the wants and needs of your subscribers. That's right—*they* own it, *they* are in control, and *they* will determine your success or failure. And you should never forget it.

Be Responsive

Once you realize that your subscribers control your newsletter's fate, responding to their e-mails becomes a whole lot more important. The simple fact is that you are going to get way more e-mail than you can respond to. It will be really important that you look past this fact and do whatever you can to respond to every piece of e-mail that comes into your e-mailbox from your subscribers. Remember that you are continually asking your subscribers to read your newsletter. It's a two-way street, and they expect *you* to read theirs. (Remember, this is now a relationship.)

In general, your subscribers will understand that you are swamped. After all, you publish a great newsletter, and it takes a lot of time to create a masterpiece. Sometimes all that people are looking for is a simple indication that you've read their e-mail. It can be a couple of lines in response and a thank you for writing.

After a short time you'll begin to see a pattern in the questions people send you, and an equal pattern in your responses. Once you've got the hang of responding, you can create canned messages that you can quickly use to respond to a question you commonly get. On the occasions when you get a question or comment that you've not answered, take a few moments and dash off a response. The time you spend interacting with your subscribers is the time you invest in truly building your newsletter.

Live for Feedback

I have a saying: "I don't appreciate feedback, I *live* for it." If you're not asking your subscribers at least once a month what you could do better, you are missing the boat. In no other medium do you have such a great opportunity to find out what your customers need. Getting into the brains of your customers is not rocket science. All you have to do is ask. Some of the best things about *The Kleinman Report* came out of feedback from my readers. If you are starved for an "attaboy," ask your subscribers what they think of your newsletter. When you ask them, they'll tell you, and you'll be amazed at how many happy customers you have out there.

Of course, not all of the responses will be praise. You might have 100,000 subscribers, but sometimes all it takes is one angry person to ruin your day. I've found that in general you hear the most from the people who are the most unhappy. Think about it—when was the last time you called or e-mailed a company, asked to talk to a supervisor, and told them how happy you are with their company or service? Not too often. Now run that scenario again, now with something wrong. It is inevitable that at some point in time, you will make someone disgruntled enough to send you an e-mail detailing how awful everything you do is.

You need to take these people with a grain of salt. Do the math. What percentage of your subscribers do the vocal minority represent? If the answer is more than 1 or 2 percent, then you have a problem. If it is less, you just have someone who will probably unsubscribe.

When you do get angry e-mail from subscribers, politely respond and thank them for their feedback. Remind your subscribers how much you appreciate what they have to say and how important their feedback is to you. Never argue with subscribers! It will suck more time from your life, make you feel really rotten, and will never lead to a positive resolution. You will never win an argument with subscribers, so it's better to simply thank them and shuffle them on their way. If they continue to berate you, kindly suggest that they are free to unsubscribe if they wish and send them clear directions on how to do so.

You Don't Have to Make Money

Believe it or not, I have never made one penny directly from *The Kleinman Report*. Not one cent in the over four years I've been doing it. Shocked? Don't be. There are other reasons to do a newsletter than to cash in.

Every year I ask my subscribers to take whatever money they think *The Kleinman Report* is worth and send it to Hospice of Contra Costa (Hospice of Contra Costa, 2051 Harrison St., Concord, CA 94520). Why do I do that? Because the Hospice needs that money more than I do. The Hospice takes that money and pays people who take care of terminally ill people. Let me tell you, I can't put a price tag on what it means to have people I've never met send money to a place that really needs it simply because I asked them to. Why that specific charity? It was there for my father when he was dying, and it never asked for one penny from us. His care was paid completely by donations.

So why do I toil countless hours a week making a report that doesn't make me money? Because it has helped make me a great life. My report has connected me to more interesting people in more areas of the world than anything I could imagine. After working at that little Web design company, I got hired to work at Intel Corporation. How did Intel hear about me? Many people there read my newsletter.

With *The Kleinman Report* I have helped show thousands of people how to get more out of using the Internet. I have helped great Internet companies get attention and visibility at a time when it really made a difference, and most importantly, I have reached out from my little computer, from my home in Portland, Oregon, and touched people. I have affected their lives. That's powerful stuff.

A year or so ago I added a section to my report called "What's on My Nightstand" in which I gave a review of the books I was reading and a link to a related Web site. I wanted to help people look at the Internet as a resource for all kinds of things, even getting more from the books they read. After I added the section, I asked my readers what they thought. As a whole I got a great response, but what I never expected was the e-mail I got from a woman named Karen:

I like your newsletter and look forward to receiving it. I am disabled with a chronic illness so I don't get out much. Your new section at the end of your newsletter makes me feel like I am still in touch with the real world, just a little bit. I vote for keeping it.

Newsletters are powerful stuff; they reach out and touch people. It's not easy work, and it's easy to get discouraged, but after an e-mail like Karen's, it's somehow all worthwhile.

Geoffrey Kleinman
http://www.Kleinman.com/
©1999 by Geoffrey Kleinman. All Rights Reserved
Geoffrey   Kleinman   is   the   Editor   of The   Kleinman   Report (http://www.Kleinman.com/), *a monthly look at how to get the most out of the Internet. During his tenure at Intel Corporation, Geoffrey was significantly involved with marketing the Pentium II and Pentium III processors online as well as managing many of Intel's newsletter publications. He is considered an expert in the field of digital communications and has been involved with Internet communications since 1988. Recently he launched* DVD Talk (http://www.DVDTalk.com/), *which has quickly become the top DVD community site on the Internet.*

APPENDICES

Service Providers

You've written your first issue, but who's going to help you distribute it? Your ISP might have mailing-list software already installed, but it might not be what you're looking for. Sometimes it's cost-effective to go through your dial-up or Web host, but remember that not all list software is created equal. Check out the resources in this section. You can always change providers if a service doesn't impress you. Just be sure to get something *in writing* that promises that your database will not be compromised, used for purposes other than mailing your newsletter, or sold to list brokers.

Best Internet Communications

http://www.best.com/faq/bestserv/

bestserv@best.com

Phone: 650.940.7835
List Software: BestServ
My Notes: The mailing-list service is free, but you'll need to have a best.com account first.
Their Blurb: "Unlike Majordomo, which is written in Perl, BestServ is written in C. BestServ is configured totally by e-mail . . . the owner of the list never needs to telnet into a UNIX account. BestServ does not allow anyone other than the list owner access to the subscriber list."

BIGLIST, Inc.

http://www.biglist.com/

info@biglist.com

Phone: 212.686.2140
List Software: Majordomo (and integrated packages)

My Notes: Prices are above average, but they seem intent on delivering high-quality service.

Their Blurb: "BIGLIST, Inc. manages electronic mailing lists. We provide comprehensive services to create, maintain, and administer e-mailing lists of any size for anyone: your sales force, your customers, or your suppliers. Your customers are already connected to the Internet. Cut your costs and improve your service by distributing information via e-mail."

CanTec Communications

http://www.cantec.com/

dbigham@cantec.com

Phone: 330.478.9263

List Software: NTMail/NTList, Majordomo

My Notes: Documentation is sparse, but they offer to help you start up your list.

Their Blurb: "We will show you how to set up your business or organization with this efficient, low-cost advertising tool. For those who need assistance, CanTec can write your newsletter for an additional charge."

Carnell Information Systems

http://www.carnell-engineering.com/is/caml/

caml@carnell-engineering.com

Phone: 608.249.9936

List Software: cAML

My Notes: The software is relatively simplistic, but the prices are extremely low.

Their Blurb: "Carnell maintains the cAML system through our own resources, so there's no need to install any software. You simply place a small form on your Web pages wherever you wish to advertise your list. There's nothing you otherwise need to do to facilitate subscription."

Coollist

http://www.coollist.com/

sales@coollist.com

Phone: None listed on site

List Software: Coollist (Proprietary)

My Notes: Yes, it's free—but a small advertisement will appear at the bottom of each newsletter mailing.

Their Blurb: "Coollist is a Web-based system that allows users to create free mailing lists on the Coollist server. No matter where you are in the world, or whether you are an individual or a big corporation, you are free to use our service."

Crosslink Internet Services
http://www.crosslink.com/html/maillist.html

support@crosslink.net

Phone: 703.642.1120

List Software: Majordomo

My Notes: They have a few pricing schemes available, depending on your total monthly volume.

Their Blurb: "You can select the unmoderated list feature and let visitors to your Web site subscribe themselves, or if you prefer, you can moderate your list and screen new list additions generated from your Web site. You can even enter e-mail addresses obtained from other sources."

Cuenet Systems
http://www.cuenet.com/

support@cuenet.com

Phone: 408.246.3388

List Software: Proprietary

My Notes: Different plans are available, though they seem to be geared toward smaller list owners. The highest price listed is for databases with up to 5,000 subscribers.

Their Blurb: "Cuenet list servers are modern, full-service Internet e-mail list servers that include standard and advanced features. They can also be configured as 'One Way' mailing lists allowing only the list owner or authorized individuals to post messages to the mailing list."

Dundee Internet Services, Inc.
http://www.dundee.net/isp/email.htm

pat@dundee.net

Phone: 888.222.8485

List Software: Lyris

My Notes: Writing from personal experience with this company, I have found Dundee's support and pricing to be quite exemplary.

Their Blurb: "Dundee Internet Services was the first ISP on the planet to purchase the Lyris List Server. . . . We've been commercially hosting Lyris lists longer than anyone else. We can run lists of any size."

eGroups
http://www.egroups.com/

info@egroups.com

Phone: None listed on site
List Software: Proprietary
My Notes: A few list administrators have run into performance problems with eGroups when their database contained over 10,000 subscribers. These difficulties most likely stemmed from software limitations.
Their Blurb: "Anyone can easily create a group in a few minutes. In addition, users can manage their subscriptions to all the groups they participate in through a simple Web interface (including subscriptions to lists not hosted by eGroups.com). eGroups.com offers a unique combination of features that makes electronically participating in groups much simpler and more interesting for everyone."

Esosoft Corporation
http://www.esosoft.com/mailinglist/

sales@esosoft.com

Phone: 909.985.0372
List Software: Majordomo (with proprietary enhancements)
My Notes: Free 10-day trial period, up to 2,500 subscribers for $5 per month, commercial use allowed.
Their Blurb: "We use the newest version of Majordomo to auto-manage mailing lists. For a complete description of the Majordomo improvements that are featured only at Esosoft, send an e-mail to: newfeatures@esosoft.com."

Euphline
http://www.euphline.com/lists/

lists@euphline.com

Phone: None listed on site
List Software: PowerPlus or Majordomo
My Notes: Documentation is sparse, as are service options. Their prices seem reasonable.

Their Blurb: "You maintain the list yourself—a text file with up to 1,000 addresses."

Fat City Network Services

http://www.fatcity.com/

ListMaster@fatcity.com

Phone: 619.538.5051

List Software: ListGuru (coded in-house)

My Notes: They deal with both mailing-list services and mailing-list software (ListGuru).

Their Blurb: "ListGuru is an Internet Mailing-List Manager (MLM) program designed for maximum flexibility and ease of use. Depending on your role in association with a mailing list, ListGuru appears differently to each person. This makes ListGuru both simple and yet still powerful at the same time. As your needs change, ListGuru changes with you."

Harte & Lyne Limited

http://www.halisp.net/halisp/mailprice.html

consult@halisp.net

Phone: 905.561.1241

List Software: Majordomo

My Notes: While they do provide list service, their support and documentation aren't very extensive.

Their Blurb: "Our software allows your list subscribers to manage their own participation on the discussion list. Individuals can add or remove themselves at will but are prevented from interfering with other list members. Standard help and information files are provided to the list owner for customization."

Institute for Global Communications

http://www.igc.org/igc/services/majordomo.html

support@igc.apc.org

Phone: 415.561.6100

List Software: Majordomo

My Notes: Their prices are moderate . . . their mission is worthy.

Their Blurb: "IGC provides this service to organizations and individuals whose work is consistent with our mission, which is to serve, expand, and inspire movements for peace, economic and social justice, human rights, and environmental sustainability around the world. As a general rule, IGC sets up mailing lists for nonprofits working in progressive movements. For-profit businesses can also use this service, but only if their use of the mailing list supports IGC's mission."

ISFA (Internet Soccer Fans Association)

http://www.isfa.com/isfa/lists/own-list.html

questra@isfa.com

Phone: None listed on site

List Software: LISTSERV

My Notes: If you're publishing a soccer-related e-mail newsletter, this is probably the place for you.

Their Blurb: "You pick out the team or soccer subject and we'll set your mailing list complete with automated subscription, autoresponders, automatic copies of subscribers sent to you, digest edition if needed, etc."

ListBot

http://www.listbot.com/

(Run by LinkExchange.com)

Phone: None listed on site

List Software: Proprietary

My Notes: It's a great service for those who want to drive traffic back to a small (not-heavily-traveled) Web site. Give someone else the headaches!

Their Blurb: "ListBot provides you with a FREE home page for your list from which your members can manage their subscriptions or view the list archive. It sends e-mail to all your visitors with just one click, gives you demographics such as age, occupation, etc., manages your mailing lists for you, and conveniently stores your messages for reuse."

Listbox.com

http://www.listbox.com/

support@listbox.com

Phone: None listed on site

List Software: Webdomo (Majordomo-based)

My Notes: Their customized administrative functions are nice to see.

Their Blurb: "Since 1995, Listbox has been providing mailing lists using Majordomo. List owners from beginners to experts enjoy using Webdomo,

Listbox's free proprietary Web-based interface to the Majordomo mailing-list manager. Webdomo makes administrating your list a snap."

ListHost.net

http://www.listhost.net/list/highlights.htm

support@listhost.net

Phone: 613.933.5133

List Software: Post.Office, Lyris

My Notes: Their pricing plans seem reasonable, though documentation is a bit spread out. They also have an e-mail newsletter covering . . . well, e-mail newsletters.

Their Blurb: "At ListHost.net, our specialty is everything related to mailing lists. Whether you are planning on starting a new list or are looking for a new provider, we can help make life easier for you."

ListServe.Com (Whole Systems Design, Inc.)

http://www.listserve.com/

sales@listserve.com

Phone: 703.550.7565

List Software: ListSTAR, LetterRip

My Notes: While this company's name sounds similar to the "LISTSERV" product, this site is not affiliated with L-Soft International, Inc.

Their Blurb: "Whole Systems Design, Inc. can create and host these powerful e-mail tools for you. We configure the list server to fit your needs."

ListService.com (CyberCorp, Inc.)

http://www.listservice.com/

listmaster@listservice.com

Phone: None listed on site

List Software: NTList, Post.Office, Proprietary (all of which are run on Windows NT)

My Notes: The documentation isn't very extensive, but the Listmaster seems friendly.

Their Blurb: "With our service, the entire process of joining, posting, and leaving a list can be done via a Web page. All the commands that you need to administer your list can be set up on a password-protected Web site."

L-Soft International, Inc.

http://www.lsoft.com/ease-head.html

sales@lsoft.com

Phone: 301.731.0440

List Software: LISTSERV

My Notes: Prices are a little high, but you're dealing with a rock-solid company that uses a well-known product. Business, Bulk, and Home packages are available.

Their Blurb: "L-Soft is the company that develops and licenses LISTSERV, the product that introduced the concept of computer-assisted mailing-list management in 1986 and that has led the development of mailing list technology since then. With EASE you are assured of always having the latest version of the software with the latest bug fixes."

Lyris.Net

http://www.lyris.net/

info@lyris.com

Phone: 510.597.0647

List Software: Lyris

My Notes: This is the same company that codes the Lyris software package. It's pricey, but extremely robust.

Their Blurb: "Because we control the software and the Internet connection, and use high-end servers, we can guarantee an exceptional level of service, making your list run fast and fuss-free. If you don't have the technology or resources to run Lyris yourself, we'll do it for you here at Lyris.Net!"

The Mailinglist.net

http://www.themailinglist.net/

support@themailist.net

Phone: None listed on site

List Software: Majordomo

My Notes: This host is located in the U.K. They can handle small- to moderate-sized lists.

Their Blurb: "Normal e-mail is a fantastic way to run discussions or debates, but when more than 10 people want to hear what the others have to say, you need a list management system to ensure that all runs smoothly. We can provide you with a mailing list to meet your needs; we set it up and then give you full management—allowing you to run it however you want."

MailingLists.Org

http://www.mailinglists.org/

abc@mailinglists.org

Phone: None listed on site

List Software: MajorCool (Majordomo-based)

My Notes: These guys and gals aim to make e-zine distribution a brain-dead operation; that's a good thing.

Their Blurb: "MajorCool allows administration of your mailing list from any browser. Password protection keeps others from modifying your mailing lists. Settings available to the list maintainer keep your members' e-mail addresses private."

mail-list.com

http://www.mail-list.com/

info@mail-list.com

Phone: 713.627.9600

List Software: Customized SmartList / Procmail

My Notes: Their service appears simplistic, but that can be an asset for those who want the least amount of administration headaches.

Their Blurb: "A regular mailing list can easily cost you time, aggravation, and ill will, but our custom software provides an easy-to-use system for both you and your subscribers."

Milepost 1

http://www.milepost1.com/

listmaster@milepost1.com

Phone: 253.850.0787

List Software: AutoShare and LISTSERVE

My Notes: All they do is "mail stuff."

Their Blurb: "We are able to host and administer mailing lists for you, your company, or your organization. We will also supply you with the e-mail accounts needed for your list. Discussion lists have an unlimited amount of usage. Announcement lists have a limit of two postings per week. We do not charge more just because you are a business."

The Nerve Internet Service

http://www.thenerve.com/services/

questions@thenerve.com

Phone: 905.465.0342

List Software: Majordomo or SmartList

My Notes: They offer a flat fee for all their list services, but you'll need to have a Web account with them.

Their Blurb: "We've been in business for nearly three years and we have close to 1,000 customers. We're not going away."

North Star Technical Services

http://www.mystery.com/ml.html

sales@mystery.com

Phone: None listed on site

List Software: Majordomo

My Notes: There are a handful of lists here, but not much in the way of service documentation; prices are okay.

Their Blurb: "North Star Technical Services has been offering public access computer services to Royal Oak, Michigan, and neighboring communities since 1988. Since the beginning, we have included basic e-mail service free of charge."

OakNet Publishing

http://www.oaknetpub.com/

editor@oaknetpub.com

Phone: 352.376.5822

List Software: ListSTAR

My Notes: You have the opportunity to make money from referrals, as well as look into advertising in their already-hosted e-publications.

Their Blurb: "Earn $50 for every new customer you refer to us. If you are able to bring us one new customer every other month, the commissions we pay you will offset the cost of your account with us. Once your readership exceeds approximately 3,000 we may be able to sell newsletter advertising for you."

ONElist E-mail Communities

http://www.onelist.com/

comments@onelist.com

Phone: None listed on site

List Software: Proprietary

My Notes: If you want to leave small list management in someone else's hands, consider using ONElist.

Their Blurb: "ONElist is a full-featured mailing-list system. Through the ONElist Web site, it is easy to search for mailing lists, view archives, subscribe to mailing lists, and create new mailing lists. List messages are delivered to subscribers within seconds of being sent by the author."

Petidomo

http://www.petidomo.com/hosting.html

info@petidomo.com

Phone: None listed on site

List Software: Petidomo

My Notes: You can either buy the software to run on your own machine, or use them as a list host.

Their Blurb: "Petidomo is very fast and efficient. Processing mailing lists with more than 100,000 subscribers is not a problem at all on the average computer. The software is constantly enhanced and developed by CyberSolutions GmbH; it is not a freeware package, but Petidomo is completely free for noncommercial usage, and scientific or educational purposes."

Postbox Mail Services

http://www.silverquick.com/

sales@silverquick.com

Phone: None listed on site

List Software: NTList

My Notes: They offer all the basics; customization is the key concept here.

Their Blurb: "We will custom-build a service to include any mixture of autoresponders, mailing-list management, document-on-demand servers, and electronic newsletters in a combination to suit your needs and integrate into your Web pages—plus, manage it for you."

Revnet Systems

http://www.revnetexpress.net/html/service.html

info@revnet.com

Phone: 256.519.4000

List Software: GroupMaster

My Notes: They offer a Web-based interface, bounce handling, and (most importantly) trackable URLs.

Their Blurb: "Revnet Express starts where other e-mail list-hosting services end. With Express, you get a full range of e-mail management and delivery functions as part of our fundamental functionality. Plus, you have advanced options allowing you to target demographic or interest groups, personalize your messages, track click-thru behavior, or deliver e-mail campaigns."

Rivertown.Net

http://www.rivertown.net/listserv.html

support@rivertown.net

Phone: 914.478.2885

List Software: Ezmlm

My Notes: This provider would be best for those with databases smaller than 15,000 subscribers.

Their Blurb: "Rivertown.Net is one of the few Internet service providers that actually encourages the creation of mailing lists. We do not view mailing lists as an annoyance we must endure for our existing customers, but as an activity to be encouraged as an additional way for people to trade information and expertise or even to rave about their favorite rock group or stamp collection."

SKYLIST.net

http://www.skylist.net/hosting/sales.html

sales@skylist.net

Phone: 412.422.4004

List Software: Lyris

My Notes: They call themselves a *community of communities*; friendliness goes a long way online.

Their Blurb: "There are so many variables involved with mailing lists that no one pricing scheme can efficiently cover them all. When we discuss your list options in person, we will determine whether your specific requirements involve any discounts or additional fees."

SPAM (Rajeev Surati & Philip Greenspun)

http://www.greenspun.com/spam/

spam@greenspun.com

Phone: None listed on site

List Software: SPAM RDBMS (Relational Database Backed Announcement Mailing List System)
My Notes: No, this isn't the junk mail that everyone keeps talking about. It's basic stuff, but it works.
Their Blurb: "Webmasters at popular sites get a tremendous amount of e-mail from people requesting that they add them to their mailing list. This can be very time-consuming, particularly if one does not have a mailing list. SPAM allows you, the Web publisher, to have a mailing list where people add and subtract themselves automatically."

SparkLIST (SparkNET)
http://www.sparklist.com/
sales@sparklist.com
Phone: 920.490.5908
List Software: Majordomo (with modifications)
My Notes: There are loads of options here, and even a few performance guarantees.
Their Blurb: "At SparkNET, we take your list seriously, with dedicated sales reps, dedicated Majordomo technical experts, dedicated servers, dedicated T1s, dedicated toll free phone number, multiple backups, and redundancy in place to make sure your list is a success."

Spunge.org
http://www.spunge.org/services.html
shell@spunge.org
Phone: None listed on site
List Software: Majordomo (with MajorCool)
My Notes: All you need is a shell account here to use their mailing list services.
Their Blurb: "No huge lists. No very active lists (because of bandwidth limitations)."

Talklist
http://www.talklist.com/
sales@talklist.com
Phone: 609.652.7221
List Software: LetterRip Pro
My Notes: Prices look good; they'll quote a price for larger lists.

Their Blurb: "Our many years of experience with list servers enables us to make the price very attractive. We strive to have the best support in the industry. The customer is our number one concern. We are happy to assist with any problem we possibly can."

Topica
http://www.topica.com/

support@topica.com

Phone: None listed on site

List Software: Mailshield & Lyris

My Notes: Here's the newest kid on the "e-mail publishing service" block. They're using the "right" type of software for both large and small lists. If you're between novice and pro, Topica should meet your needs. You should also be able to get your e-publication listed in their database.

Their Blurb: "Built by and for the most demanding list owners, Topica has also tackled the numerous problems associated with owning and moderating an e-mail list. Topica offers owners free list hosting, message archiving and promotion services, and usage statistics graphs, and has developed state-of-the-art management tools including flexible list settings, error and bounce handling, user privacy controls, and more."

VP Mail
http://www.list.to/

adam@sparks.to

Phone: None listed on site

List Software: Proprietary

My Notes: This service is based in Australia (and there's nothing wrong with that). There's a cost calculator here so you can figure out your pricing scale with VP Mail immediately. "Free" service is available, too.

Their Blurb: "VP Mail is easy to use and you can create regular mailing lists with a basic range of features. For advanced users, VP Mail will be supporting a huge range of features and functions to allow moderation, e-mail commands, multilingual, digests, archives, encryption and security, payment options, and private lists."

Web Site Post Office

http://www.websitepostoffice.com/

gigi@websitepostoffice.com

Phone: 408.733.2319

List Software: Proprietary

My Notes: Free and commercial packages are available.

Their Blurb: "Web Site Post Office gives you all the tools necessary to set up a sign-up box on the home page and ask subscribers demographic questions. You can even have an area for comments, so people can enter questions or suggestions that will help you get back to them with answers."

WebWrite Productions

http://www.varcode.com/

sales@webwrite.com

Phone: 919.549.0214

List Software: Procmail & SmartList

My Notes: The mailing-list services are complimentary when you have a Web account with them.

Their Blurb: "For the end user in both the public and private sector, WebWrite Productions provides a range of Internet products and services, including award-winning server hosting, Internet access, prepackaged and custom software, outsourcing, education, and consulting services."

World Data Network, Inc.

http://www.wdn.com/maillist.html

support@wdn.com

Phone: 703.648.0808

List Software: Majordomo

My Notes: Documentation is sparse, and prices vary. They're more of an ISP than a dedicated list service.

Their Blurb: "We use the Majordomo program to manage our customers' mailing lists. This provides an ideal way of connecting a group of people who share a common interest and want to carry on a discussion of relevant topics. Mailing lists provide immediate access to messages and can be used to quickly provide information to mail list members."

Mailing-List Software

Each software package is different. Who's to say which one is the best? I have a favorite, and I'm sure you will, too. But remember that smaller list owners are going to have different needs than larger list owners. Evaluate how much you want to spend and what each mailing-list software package has to offer in return. It has been my experience that you get what you pay for. If you don't have any headaches at the end of the day and your subscribers are happy, you'll know you made the right choice. Keep in mind, too, that you don't need to purchase this software if you can find a provider that is already running it on its server (see Appendix A).

Arrow Mailing List Manager

http://www.jadebox.com/arrow/

arrow@jadebox.com

System Requirements: Windows 9x/NT

Their Blurb: "Arrow features an Explorer-like interface for browsing lists, folders, and messages. You can even create your own folders for storing and organizing messages. ArrowMailer allows Arrow to send messages directly to each recipient's SMTP server, taking much of the burden off your ISP's mail server."

Atrium MERCUR

http://www.atrium-software.com/mercur/mercur_e.html

info@atrium-software.com

System Requirements: Windows 9x/NT

Their Blurb: "The new user manager was designed in the Windows Explorer style. This allows easy administration of user accounts, mailing lists, autoresponders, executables, remote mail accounts, and static routes in a multidomain environment. The immediate collaboration with our customers helped us create a mail server that supports many helpful and easy-to-use features."

Aureate Group Mail

http://www.group-mail.com/

info@aureate.com

System Requirements: Windows 9x/NT

Their Blurb: "Mailing Management features allow you to review complete mail logs to see who has received messages and recover from errors without sending duplicate messages. Group Management lets you keep up to 32,000 different groups with an unlimited number of recipients in each. MX Inspector allows you to verify e-mail addresses before you send your messages by checking with the recipient's ISP for a valid e-mail host."

AutoShare

http://www.dnai.com/~meh/autoshare/

meh@dnai.com

System Requirements: Macintosh

Their Blurb: "AutoShare is robust, speedy and requires little memory. The 68K and PowerPC native server applications, tested with Mac OS 8.5.1, are fully scriptable and may be configured using the AutoShare Admin, an administration tool with balloon help. Lists in the hundreds and subscribers in the thousands per list are supported, as are subscription, open, moderated, announcement, and private list types."

Cerberus Mailer

http://www.abiogenesis.com/cerberus/

cerberus@abiogenesis.com

System Requirements: UNIX

Their Blurb: "Cerberus Mailer is a software product written in Perl. When you purchase Cerberus Mailer, you get the source code, so you can configure it even beyond the capabilities already built into the software. You need a semitechnical knowledge of computers to configure Cerberus Mailer for your needs. Once it is installed and running, it requires less technical knowledge to maintain, but still requires basic working knowledge of the UNIX shell and file installation and removal."

CREN ListProc

http://www.cren.net/listproc/

cren@cren.net

System Requirements: UNIX (Windows 9x/NT version in development)

Their Blurb: "List subscribers and administrators can interact with ListProc in three ways: through the new Web interface, through ListProc's interactive clients, or with simple e-mail commands. ListProc is highly efficient, allowing sites to conveniently maintain thousands of lists and hundreds of thousands of subscribers all on the same server."

DOLIST

http://www.povlab.org/dolist/

support@povlab.org

System Requirements: Windows NT

Their Blurb: "DOLIST uses the EMWAC Internet Mail Server for Windows NT; system error built for NT application event viewer . . . does not write anything to the Registry . . . very small executable (~100k) . . . auto-stopping options to prevent data loss and crashes . . . command line console mode for debugging."

Eudora Worldmail Server

http://www.eudora.com/worldmail/features.html

eudora-custserv@qualcomm.com

System Requirements: Windows NT

Their Blurb: "Automated mailing lists using the List Management Agent allow users to subscribe and unsubscribe themselves from mailing lists through simple e-mail messages to the mail system. The List Management Agent provides a range of automation and security options for your mailing lists."

IMail Server

http://www.ipswitch.com/Products/Imail_Server/listserver.html

sales@ipswitch.com

System Requirements: Windows NT

Their Blurb: "Users can subscribe and unsubscribe themselves from mailing lists with a simple e-mail message. You can add 'header' and 'trailer' text to all messages in the list and add text to the subject line, Private Lists let you choose who can subscribe, Moderated Lists allow list owner and/or password approval of all postings before they go to the subscribers, LIST Command Security prevents outsiders from requesting a list of all subscribers to your lists, and Digest Mode allows users to request that list messages be combined into a periodic summary message."

LetterRip

http://www.fogcity.com/letterrip.html

sales@fogcity.com

System Requirements: Macintosh

Their Blurb: "LetterRip Pro contains a powerful SMTP mail server for sending messages and is highly optimized for mailing-list sending. The performance of the computer is rarely much of a factor in performance of the list. The server is optimized to send e-mail to 100s, 1000s, or even 10s of thousands of recipients with ease."

LightningMail

http://www.digibel.org/~mwvdlee/lightningmail.html

mwvdlee@open.net

System Requirements: Windows 9x/NT

Their Blurb: "Easy-to-use interface . . . attach any type of file . . . over 30,000 recipients possible . . . uses SMTP protocol for sending . . . interruptible sending . . . easy inclusion of date, time, symbols and more . . . ability to send to multiple separate lists or parts of lists . . . simulation mode for testing."

ListCaster

http://www.mustang.com/products/we/ListCaster/

sales@mustang.com

System Requirements: Windows 9x/NT

Their Blurb: "ListCaster takes advantage of Active Server Pages in Microsoft IIS for easy setup and administration. But don't let 'easy setup' fool you—it is a high-performance e-mail server product through and through. Unlimited number of subscribers per list, high-performance SMTP/POP3 server included, one-time purchase fee, unlimited number of lists."

ListGuru

http://www.fatcity.com/

ListMaster@fatcity.com

System Requirements: Windows 9x/NT

Their Blurb: "ListGuru provides features that are unavailable in other MLM programs. [It has] enhanced archive sections . . . cross-referenced topical threads . . . anonymous postings . . . user-biography features, allowing your users to create a sense of family . . . the ability of the user to directly place files into the list archives . . . anti-spam filters to keep the fluff out of your list . . . anti-responder filters to avoid those vacation headaches when someone's e-mail autoresponder runs amok . . . creation of policy files for your list that leave the enforcement of things like response-to-quote ratios, large files, binary attachments, and off-topic postings to ListGuru, not you, the owner."

LISTSERV

http://www.lsoft.com/ease-head.html

sales@lsoft.com

System Requirements: VM, VMS, UNIX, Windows 9x/NT

Their Blurb: "LISTSERV provides a number of advanced functions to list moderators and list subscribers. These include: a 'single-server' view to the end user, no matter where or on what operating system the lists are located, automated digests and indexes, flexible security, access control and moderation, subscription options customizable on a per-subscriber basis, junk e-mail detector shielding LISTSERV lists from unsolicited advertisements, 'hands free' bounce processing, and more."

Listar

http://www.listar.org/

loki@maison-otaku.net / jtraub@dragoncat.net

System Requirements: Linux, SunOS, FreeBSD, BSDI

Their Blurb: "Much of Listar's inspiration was drawn from L-Soft LISTSERV, which Jeremy 'Loki' Blackman had administered mailing lists under. He wanted something with LISTSERV's power, but that wasn't quite as complex. Listar's versioning system remains 'alpha' for two reasons: historical (Jeremy once joked that Listar would never actually be 'released,' back when he set up the first lists), and as an indication that though the code may reach release stability, the authors consider it a perpetual alpha. There's always something more that can be done!"

ListSTAR

http://www.starnine.com/liststar/liststar.html

sales@starnine.com

System Requirements: Macintosh

Their Blurb: "ListSTAR can also be used as an automated response system similar to fax-on-demand. Users are sent a menu of available choices, and can request specific messages (including enclosures) just by sending a message using the keywords. You can publish anything from a class schedule to a price list, including Adobe Acrobat PDF documents. ListSTAR comes with easy setup templates; it's highly customizable and one copy supports unlimited lists."

Lyris

http://www.lyris.com/

info@lyris.com

System Requirements: Windows 9x/NT, Solaris for Sparc, Solaris for Intel (Digital UNIX, Linux, and BSDI versions in development)

Their Blurb: "Lyris was the first e-mail list server to offer a Web interface for list administrators and members. Users and administrators can do everything from their Web browser (and/or via e-mail). One of the unique features that sets Lyris apart from other list servers is failsafe unsubscribing. With its built-in mail engine, it is one of the fastest list servers around. Lyris is highly scalable, offers multiple levels of security on the Web and through e-mail, has automatic error mail handling, and handles message scheduling with ease."

Macjordomo

http://leuca.med.cornell.edu/Macjordomo/

mfuortes@med.cornell.edu

System Requirements: Macintosh

Their Blurb: "Macjordomo is NOT a port of the famous UNIX program; there is no relationship whatsoever between the two, except that their names sound similar. The software is very easy to set up, has a nice Mac-like interface for list management, supports all the basic features of a list server (with logging), imports and exports subscriber databases, and is freeware."

MadGoat MX

http://www.madgoat.com/mx.html

webmaster@madgoat.com

System Requirements: OpenVMS

Their Blurb: "MX includes a mailing-list processor and support for mail-based file servers, with automated handling of administrative requests and access controls on lists and file servers. L-Soft's LISTSERV mailing-list processor for OpenVMS is also supported. Most MadGoat packages are freeware; that is, they may be used for no charge but are copyrighted and not in the public domain. Licensing terms are available if you wish to incorporate one of the MadGoat packages into your commercial product; please contact our sales department for more information."

MailKing

http://www.mailking.com/

support@mailking.com

System Requirements: Windows 9x/NT

My Notes: Download a 30-day demo to see if it "works" for you.

Their Blurb: "[This] is a stand-alone product that allows you to store names, e-mail addresses, and other information about people in a built-in database, and then create personalized messages ('mail merge') to selected people in the database . . . MailKing, as a low-cost client-side application, does not handle subscribe/unsubscribe [requests] automatically."

Mailman

http://www.list.org/

viega@list.org

System Requirements: UNIX (pre-GNU)

Their Blurb: "Mailman is software to help manage e-mail discussion lists, much like Majordomo and Smartmail. Unlike similar products, Mailman gives each mailing list a Web page, and allows users and administrators to perform tasks over the Web. It also integrates most things people want to do with mailing lists, including archiving, mail-to-news gateways, and so on."

Mailtraq

http://www.fastraq.co.uk/

sales@fastraq.co.uk

System Requirements: Windows 9x/NT

Their Blurb: "Mailtraq provides very comprehensive mailing list facilities, equal to most dedicated expensive list-processing software. The mailing-list facilities support both open (anyone can post) and closed (only members can post) lists, ideal for discussion forums, announcement lists, and work groups. Message pooling (where each message is delivered to only one subscriber) is also supported, ideal for handling facilities such as technical support groups."

Majordomo

http://www.greatcircle.com/majordomo/

brent@greatcircle.com

System Requirements: UNIX

Their Blurb: "Commands are sent to Majordomo via e-mail to handle all aspects of list maintenance. Once a list is set up, virtually all operations can be performed remotely, requiring no intervention by the postmaster of the list site. Majordomo was developed under UNIX-based systems but will probably work on others. If you can get Perl to compile and run cleanly on your system and can send Internet mail by piping or calling an external program (and that external program reads its list of recipients from a plain text file), you can probably get Majordomo to work on a wide variety of UNIX-based and non-UNIX-based systems."

MDaemon

http://www.mdaemon.com/

sales@mdaemon.com

System Requirements: Windows 9x/NT

Their Blurb: "This is the kind of e-mail server software typically required to send e-mail to users on a LAN and also to the Internet. MDaemon allows an organization to implement an inexpensive but powerful e-mail system that will allow users to e-mail one another without the need for expensive gateways, routers, or dedicated Internet circuits. What makes MDaemon unique is its ability to route e-mail to and from an entire network of users through one Internet connection and mailbox from an ISP."

Minordomo

http://www.speakeasy.org/~cgires/minordomo/

smorton@pobox.com

System Requirements: UNIX

Their Blurb: "Minordomo is a Perl5 script that takes an e-mail message (on STDIN), and remails it to a list of subscribers. You receive mail in the regular way and read it in your mail reader. When someone sends a message to you for distribution to the list, you 'pipe' that message to the script. Minordomo reformats the mail headers (so it looks like a list) and mails it individually to the subscribers. It can optionally archive all list traffic to your Web pages, using hypermail. There are also switches to easily add or remove people from your list of subscribers."

MReply

http://hpux.u-aizu.ac.jp/hppd/hpux/Networking/Mail/MReply-1.0/

tor@netcom.com

System Requirements: UNIX

Their Blurb: "A mail server for incoming messages. MReply responds to commands given to it, typically in incoming mail messages. Possible actions include adding or removing the mailer's address to or from a given list, sending the mailer a file in plain text or uuencoded form, or forwarding the message to another user, a pipe, or a mailbox."

NTList

http://www.ntmail.co.uk/list/index.htm

sales@ntmail.co.uk

System Requirements: Windows NT (duh)

Their Blurb: "The software allows list members to use natural language commands to add and remove their address without the need for human intervention, leading to very low total cost of ownership. Lists may be archived with product keywords that will be found by Internet search engines; unique Magazine List facilities allow you to automate list membership depending upon payment; [and you have the] option to rotate advertisements at the head or foot of each message processed with impression count."

Pegasus E-mail Client

http://www.pegasus.usa.com/

support@pmail.gen.nz

System Requirements: Windows 3.x/9x/NT, Macintosh

My Notes: If you can't afford a mailing-list host, have fewer than 2,000 subscribers, and aren't too concerned with subscription database management, I'd suggest downloading this client. I used it when I first started distributing Lockergnome. It's perfect for newbies, as everything is managed on your personal computer (not directly on the server). However, keep in mind that adding and removing subscribers will become a tiresome, manual task. Start with this and then move on to bigger packages. Note, too, that this is mainly known for being a regular e-mail client.

SLMail

http://www.seattlelab.com/

sales@seattlelab.com

System Requirements: Windows 9x/NT

Their Blurb: "SLmail's powerful list server allows you to choose whether lists are public or private, moderated or open. Using the clear, intuitive interface, you will find SLmail's mailing lists easy to manage, even if you have never hosted a mailing list before."

SmartBounce

http://www.smartbounce.com/

support@smartbounce.com

System Requirements: Macintosh, UNIX, Windows

Their Blurb: "If you're tired of wading through piles of mail bounces and sorting them by hand, then you have come to the right place. SmartBounce will process, classify, and sort your bounces for you, and will create a preformatted file of defunct addresses that you simply send to your list server for removal. . . . It does not matter what platform your mailing list is hosted on, since SmartBounce is designed to be run offline, not on the list server."

SmartList / Procmail

http://www.procmail.org/

guenther@gac.edu

System Requirements: UNIX

My Notes: This software can be customized to your liking; the source code is freely available.

Their Blurb: "The SmartList mailing-list package has been built on top of the Procmail mail-processing package. In order to install it you'll need the source of the Procmail package as well."

SockMail

http://www.sockem.com/

info@sockem.com

System Requirements: Computer with Java Virtual Machine v1.02 (or later)

My Notes: C'mon, did you really think I could write a book without mentioning Java at least once?

Their Blurb: "A simple way to manage small- to medium-size e-mail lists and integrate them into your Web site. Features include multitasking list management from a 100% Java administrative applet and 100% Java e-mail list database server. SockMail Pro is also available; it comes with list manager accounts, a Web server, a bounced mail handler, large list handling (>50,000 addresses), an HTML form manager, etc."

SVList

http://www.softventures.com/htm/SVListblue.htm

sales@softventures.com

System Requirements: Windows 9x/NT

Their Blurb: "SVList is a light-duty mailing-list server. It is intended for home or small-business use and is not recommended for lists of more than 1000–2000 members. SVList has no hard limits on member counts; it just gets kind of slow to open the maintenance screens on real large lists. Usability also depends on traffic."

Tristero

http://ccmail.jconsult.com/cctri43.html

dale@jconsult.com

System Requirements: cc:Mail

Their Blurb: "Tristero is a replacement for our Public cc:Mail mailing lists. It offers features to administrators and cc:Mail clients that are unavailable via cc:Mail lists. Tristero is a complex, responsive system that is easy to implement and administer."

Appendix C

Online Electronic Publishing Resources

A Beginner's Guide to Effective E-mail

http://www.webfoot.com/advice/email.top.html

Their Blurb: "This is not a document on the mechanics of sending e-mail (which buttons to push or how to attach a photograph). I, instead, focus on the content of an e-mail message: how to say what you need to say. This is not dogma . . . if there were only one right answer, there wouldn't be a need to write this guide. Hopefully, this guide will make you examine your assumptions about e-mail and thus help you maximize your e-mail effectiveness. Then you can write to reflect your own personality and choice."

Best Ezines.com

http://www.bestezines.com/

My Notes: Here's one of the newer e-zine review sites around. The publisher recently started to cover non-e-zine topics, so I'm not sure how focused this site will be in the future. At this time, there are only a handful of e-zines listed here; it seems geared more toward marketing resources.

The Book of Zines

http://www.zinebook.com/

My Notes: Chip Rowe is another important e-publishing figurehead, and his site is very extensive. Anything (and possibly everything) you wanted to know about e-zines can be found here. The posted articles were written by people with a considerable amount of experience with electronic publishing. Get a big mug of coffee before you visit—you're going to be here for a while.

Cancel-It!

http://www.cancel-it.com/

My Notes: The services here may be more for your subscribers, but if you're having difficulties with subscription management, it may be worth a look.

Their Blurb: "Cancel-It! features a universal, easy to fill out, onscreen form. This process enables anyone to quickly and efficiently cancel online subscriptions and services. Upon receiving consumer cancellation requests, F8's innovative database software sorts and forwards all submissions to appropriate e-mail addresses for final processing. The consumer is then notified by e-mail that their subscription or service has been stopped."

CataList

http://www.lsoft.com/lists/listref.html

My Notes: This page is operated by the people who also code the LISTSERV package.

Their Blurb: "CataList is the catalog of LISTSERV lists. From this page, you can browse any of the 23,482 public LISTSERV lists on the Internet, search for mailing lists of interest, and get information about LISTSERV host sites. This information is generated automatically from LISTSERV's LISTS database and is always up-to-date."

CONTENTIOUS

http://www.contentious.com/

My Notes: Amy Gahran has got one heckuva zine here; this is a tremendous resource for both novice and experienced e-publishers.

Their Blurb: "CONTENTIOUS is a monthly webzine primarily intended for professional writers and editors who create content for the Web and other online media. Beyond this primary audience, CONTENTIOUS also contains a fair amount of information of interest and value to all kinds of online publishers—from e-zines to organizational Web sites, and more."

Directory of Electronic Journals, Newsletters & Academic Discussion Lists

http://www.arl.org/scomm/edir/

Their Blurb: "The mission of the Association of Research Libraries is to shape and influence forces affecting the future of research libraries in the process of scholarly communication. ARL programs and services promote equitable access to, and effective use of, recorded knowledge in support of teaching, research, scholarship, and community service."

The Directory of Ezines

http://www.lifestylespub.com/

My Notes: This is not free, but it's worth checking out.

Their Blurb: "We offer a unique service that gives you all the information you will need to start, maintain, and track a highly effective Internet newsletter (e-zine) advertising campaign. The Directory of Ezines gives you a total overview of publication times, ad rates, ad deadlines, subscriber counts, and everything else you need to know to advertise in a great number of Internet newsletters."

Disobey (Low Bandwidth)

http://www.disobey.com/low/

Their Blurb: "People look for the best content, the greatest news, and the quickest downloads to satisfy their needs and wants. Corporate and misdirected visionaries have missed the point entirely. What they don't seem to understand is that the greatest 'push' has been underneath their noses since the Internet began . . . they've failed to realize it. Welcome to Low Bandwidth . . . a database of e-zines, newsletters, and journals, all delivered to your mailbox with nary a finger lifted on your part. This is what 'push' was meant to be."

E-Journal List

http://www.edoc.com/ejournal/

My Notes: Here's a small site that provides links to both electronic and regular publications; you can add your own info without having to wade through a hundred questions. Traditional journal publishers looking to make the leap online might want to visit the main page and look into Cadmus's services.

Electronic Journal Access

http://www.coalliance.org/ejournal/

Their Blurb: "This Web page provides a series of indexes to provide easy access to different electronic serials. There has been no attempt in this product to provide any evaluation of the titles in terms of content or quality. However, a unit record for each title must be viewed before launching to a title of interest, which will provide some information about scope and content. New titles are added as they are discovered."

E-mail Address Directory

http://www.emailaddresses.com/

Their Blurb: "There are hundreds of free e-mail services out there . . . so which one to choose? This site taps into the combined experience of hundreds of users to bring you the pros and cons of different free e-mail providers. As well as providing the #1 roundup of free e-mail services, our information center offers e-mail-related tips and assistance."

E-mail-Related Newsgroups

comp.mail.list-admin.software

comp.mail.misc

My Notes: Here are a couple of decent newsgroups to check out when you want to get the lowdown on e-mail software- and server-related issues. Expect most of the regular members to be knowledgeable experts.

The ETEXT Archives

http://www.etext.org/

Their Blurb: "The project was started in response to the lack of organized archiving of political documents, periodicals, and discussions disseminated via Usenet on newsgroups . . . . Not long thereafter, e-zines began their rapid proliferation on the Internet, and it was clear that these materials suffered from the same lack of coordinated collection and preservation . . . . One thing led to another, and e-zines of all kinds—many on various cultural topics unrelated to politics—invaded the archives in significant volume."

E-Zine AdSource

http://www.ezineadsource.com/

My Notes: Whether you're looking to advertise in an e-zine or wanting to accept advertising in your own e-zine, these guys and gals might provide you with the right leads.

Their Blurb: "Our directory has hundreds of listings and is continuously growing. It's constantly updated with the top e-zines that accept advertising. We've collected all the vital information from these publishers and put it into an easy-to-read format."

E-zine Advertising.com

http://www.ezineadvertising.com/

Their Blurb: "Until now, it has been very difficult to search through thousands of e-zines trying to find the ones appropriate for your business. Even worse, when you do find a publication . . . the important circulation and contact information that advertisers need is not available. We make this tedious and time-consuming research a breeze for you by providing a comprehensive database of only those e-zines that accept advertising. Each search shows you complete information about the publication."

E-Zine FAQ

ftp://ftp.etext.org/pub/Zines/WhateverRamblings/publish.txt

My Notes: It's been a few years since this FAQ has been updated, but it still deserves to be recognized. The concepts are still very applicable, and the compiler (Alex Swain) has a great sense of humor. You just might learn something new by reading it. If nothing else, then at least you can see how far e-zines have come since this FAQ was compiled.

e.zine movement

http://www.asphyxia.com/ezm/

Their Blurb: "What we offer is a network of dedicated e-zine publishers who want the best for their e-zine. So instead of just offering up a list of e-zines on the Web, we place a simple graphic or text link on each e-zine that is a member of the e-zine movement. This allows the reader of one e-zine to find some others to read as well. It also offers a starting point for people beginning a new e-zine."

eZINESearch

http://www.ezinesearch.com/

My Notes: Just as the title suggests, you can search through the extensive database of e-zines here. If yours isn't listed, then add it.

EzineSeek

http://www.ezineseek.com/

My Notes: This is a very Yahoo!-ish directory, but visitors also have the ability to rate listed e-zines. You can find links to e-zine publishing articles, and you can sign up for the "EzineSeek Informer" (for e-zine-related information) or join the

EPUB Email Publishers discussion list to meet other electronic publishers. Also notable is the link to InfoBot.net: "a collection of articles available for free reprint in your e-mail newsletter and/or on your Web site."

E-Zines Today

http://www.ezine-news.com/

My Notes: Another place to get your e-publication listed; it isn't very heavily traveled, but every link counts. They also have a decent-sized listing of e-zines here and offer reciprocal links.

E-ZineZ

http://www.e-zinez.com/

My Notes: Kate Schultz has put together a fantastic site that you shouldn't miss. She offers her own e-zine about e-zines, an online e-zine advice column called "Ask Dr. E-zine," an e-zine search engine, and an online handbook for e-publishers. But the most notable part of E-ZineZ is "The E-zine Builder." After entering a little bit of content and information, you can format your own e-zine on-the-fly!

Factsheet 5

http://www.factsheet5.com/

My Notes: These people have been around since the beginning of the e-zine scene. They review both print zines and e-zines, as well as provide links to other related articles, tutorials, and zine sites. If there were a place for "underground" zine stuff, I'd say this is it.

Good Documents

http://www.gooddocuments.com/Techniques/

My Notes: Put down this book and visit this site immediately.

Their Blurb: "Writing everyday documents that are destined to be read onscreen and not printed out means different words and organization than the same ideas written to be printed out on paper. You can't take what you wrote for paper, paste it into an HTML editor, mark it up with a few tags, and call it an onscreen document. You need to write specifically for the screen if you want to take best advantage of the medium. This site gives ideas on how to write and organize when your main target is linked pages to be read onscreen."

IdeaMarketers

http://www.ideamarketers.com/

My Notes: They recently added a service whereby companies can submit press releases and news items, as well as submit products that they'd like the media to review. Now *that's* a good idea.

Their Blurb: "Whether you're an author trying to get published, a company with a hot new product you'd like to get the media to review, or a publisher looking for more subscribers and advertisers, you'll find what you need here."

Infojump

http://www.infojump.com/

My Notes: This is one of my all-time favorite places to look for new and old e-publications. The index is growing by the day, and you can submit peer reviews and vote for your favorite zines. Otis Gospodnetic (the front man of this operation) also has a discussion list set up specifically for e-publishers (ZINE-TALK). He's very friendly, organized, and knowledgeable.

Inklings: Inkspot's Newsletter for Writers

http://www.inkspot.com/inklings/

Their Blurb: "Inklings is a free, biweekly electronic newsletter for writers, and is part of Inkspot, a Web resource for writers. Issue content includes up-to-date market news, writing-related resources, how-to tips, interviews, articles, and advice by industry professionals."

The Internet Scout Project

http://scout.cs.wisc.edu/scout/

My Notes: Here is a well-respected resource, driven by professional librarians, educators, and content specialists. *The Scout Report* is a weekly newsletter that highlights "the best" of the Internet, and *Net-happenings* is a daily guide for Internet-related announcements. *NEW-LIST* is something you should definitely check out—you can post subscription information for your e-zine here for free, and (depending on your subject matter) it should send a few hundred new subscribers your way.

ISSN for Electronic Serials

http://lcweb.loc.gov/issn/e-serials.html

My Notes: ISSN stands for "International Standard Serial Number" and I'd encourage you to apply for one as soon as you choose a title for your electronic publication. It adds legitimacy to your creation and shows your readers that you're around for the long haul.

Their Blurb: "The same criteria for determining if a serial is eligible for an ISSN apply to electronic and print publications: an intention to continue publishing indefinitely and being issued in designated parts. In the case of electronic serials—especially those available online—the most significant criterion is that the publication must be divided into parts or issues that carry unique, numerical designations by which the individual issues may be identified, checked in, etc."

John Labovitz's E-zine List

http://www.meer.net/~johnl/e-zine-list/

My Notes: Don't let the URL fool you; this site has been around forever in Internet terms (1993). Get your e-zine listed here. "Everybody" knows John.

Their Blurb: "This is a list of electronic zines from around the world, accessible via the Web, FTP, e-mail, and other services. The list is updated approximately monthly; it contains over 3579 zines."

The List of Lists

http://www.catalog.com/vivian/interest-group-search.html

My Notes: Not only can you look for lists, but you can add your own to the database. Vivian Neou is another e-zine advocate who has been on the scene for a while; she has amassed quite a collection of electronic publishing resources. This site has not been updated in a while but is still worth checking out (especially for the small article "The Natural Life Cycle of Mailing Lists").

ListQuest

http://www.listquest.com/

My Notes: They provide free mailing-list archiving for list owners; if you're managing a moderated discussion list, this is an excellent service.

Their Blurb: "By providing a fast and convenient interface to these archives, we hope to reduce the amount of repetition on mailing lists. ListQuest is provided free of charge to both mailing-list owners and people wishing to search the archives."

ListsNet Directory

http://www.listsnet.com/

Their Blurb: "This is a freely available, searchable directory of list channels. [They also offer] an integrated software application, the ListsNet Tuner, which steps you through subscribing and unsubscribing from lists and routes incoming messages through your Inbox into organized folders. . . . When you use the ListsNet Directory and Tuner together, you have the best solution for the most common mailing-list questions."

listTool.com

http://www.listtool.com/

Their Blurb: "listTool.com is a revolutionary free tool that makes the process of subscribing, unsubscribing, and sending commands to 729 mailing and discussion lists easy. You no longer have to remember which command you need to send to some obscure e-mail address to subscribe or unsubscribe from a discussion/mailing list. Mailing-list owners (using LISTSERV, ListProc, or Majordomo) can submit their information and they will be added to the system after review."

Liszt

http://www.liszt.com/

My Notes: They've got over 90,095 mailing lists indexed here; if it exists, you can find it here.

Their Blurb: "A gigantic directory of Internet discussion groups: mailing lists, newsgroups, and IRC chat channels. It's a way to find groups of people on the 'Net discussing whatever it is you really care about."

Mailing-List Software FAQ

ftp://ftp.uu.net/usenet/news.answers/mail/list-admin/software-faq

My Notes: This document should answer your general mailing-list inquiries, provide insight if you're shopping for a list provider or list software, and enlighten you with descriptions of a few popular software packages available today. It is not a comprehensive resource and doesn't appear to have been updated for a few years.

mailto URL scheme

ftp://ftp.isi.edu/in-notes/rfc2368.txt

My Notes: Here's a comprehensive (and official) resource demonstrating how to insert header information within a mailto (HTML) tag. Or, as they put it, "For greater functionality, because interaction with some resources may require message headers or message bodies to be specified as well as the mail address, the mailto URL scheme is extended to allow setting mail header fields and the message body." In other words, within a mailto HTML tag, you are able to insert subject, CC, or body information. This is perfect for those of you who post (or plan on posting) subscription e-mail addresses on your Web site. You can have those common fields automatically filled in. Note, though, that not all e-mail programs will work with these extended tags.

MediaPeak!

http://www.mediapeak.com/

Their Blurb: "MediaPeak! publishes a family of e-zines for every interest. In addition, we maintain a free directory of e-zine advertising rates, as well as a directory of e-zine publishers interested in swapping ads with other e-zines. Finally, we run AdSwap, a free advertising exchange program for e-zine publishers."

NewJour Electronic Journals & Newsletters

http://gort.ucsd.edu/newjour/

Their Blurb: "NewJour is the place to announce your own (or to forward information about others') newly planned, newly issued, or revised electronic networked journal or newsletter. It is specially dedicated for those who wish to share information in the planning, gleam-in-the-eye stage or at a more mature stage of publication development and availability. It is also the place to announce availability of paper journals and newsletters as they become available on—and move into—electronic networks. Scholarly discussion lists that regularly and continuously maintain supporting files of substantive articles or preprints may also be reported, for those journal-like sections."

New-List.com

http://new-list.com/

Their Blurb: "New-List is a series of mailing lists segmented by category that provide the Internet community with notification of the creation of new e-mail lists on any topic. This free service is a great way to get the word out to grow your list, and because we deliver the new-list announcements by category, you can sign up to receive all new-list announcements or just the announcements of the specific categories of your special interests!"

Newsletter Access

http://www.newsletteraccess.com/

My Notes: This site also has links to other newsletter-related resources and sites.

Their Blurb: "Browse or search our directory of over 5,000 newsletters (derived from Hudson's well-known Subscription Newsletter Directory). If you publish a newsletter, start by getting listed in the top Web directory for newsletters."

PENN Media (Pulse E-mail Newsletter Network)

http://www.pennmedia.com/

My Notes: The more subscribers you have, the more money you will earn from a PENN Media ad placement. When you don't want to hassle with advertising-related issues, PENN will become a valuable partner.

Their Blurb: "If you are a newsletter publisher, we know how much effort you put into publishing your daily newsletter. Also, it is increasingly difficult to reach national advertisers with only your subscriber base. . . . Let PENN, the largest e-mail newsletter network, bring you advertising revenues from national advertisers. PENN will find a way to sell your advertising inventory."

Propagandist.com

http://propagandist.com/

My Notes: Todd Kuipers is not only a cool guy to know, but he's also a distinguished e-zine proponent. Every week, he reviews an electronic publication at the Sideroad (http://www.sideroad.com/). While he doesn't publish a zine himself, gaining his respect is something golden; he represents the e-publishing industry in a positive light. If you're looking for top-quality e-zine reviews, turn to Todd first.

Publicly Accessible Mailing Lists

http://www.neosoft.com/internet/paml/

My Notes: Here's another one of those sites that every e-publisher knows about. You can either search through their database or browse through the included titles. Part of PAML's charm stems from its maintainers, Stephanie and Peter da Silva. I've always respected (and appreciated) the personal approach; it reminds me that the Internet is run by "real people."

Published.com

http://www.published.com/

Their Blurb: "Published.com is a free directory. It is designed to help promote the work of self-published writers, zine publishers, those who are publishing exclusively online, or anyone else who uses the Internet to promote their own independent, creative work. Listings are free and keyword searchable, with links directly to the artist's Web site or e-mail address."

Response-O-Matic

http://www.response-o-matic.com/

My Notes: This is a great, free service for those of you not wanting to use a mailto form, but not having access to a working CGI script for subscription automation.

Their Blurb: "There was a time when you had to be a programmer to add forms to your Web pages. Not anymore. Thanks to modern technology, all you need to do now is just create your forms in standard HTML. Then have your form call Response-O-Matic. There's no coding, no hassles. The information your visitors enter in your forms will be automatically e-mailed to you."

Sparky's List-Tips

http://www.list-tips.com/

Their Blurb: "Are you an e-mail list owner, or plan to be one soon? If so, Sparky's 'List-Tips' Daily E-zine will deliver about 5 tips a week, dedicated to helping list owners with issues such as: Increasing Your List Member Base, Marketing Your List, How to Do Sponsorship Swaps for Your List, E-mail List Promotion Basics, Finding Paying Sponsors for Your List, Handling Beginner and Advanced List-Owner Duties, How to Build a List from The Ground Up, etc."

TILE.NET/LISTS

http://tile.net/lists/

My Notes: Not sure if there's a list already covering your topic? Tap into their database. You can search for discussion lists, newsgroups, computer vendors, Internet service companies, and FTP sites, or browse through the indexed lists by name, description, or domain; it will provide subscription information for any listed e-publication.

Writers Write

http://www.writerswrite.com/

Their Blurb: "From finding out where and how to submit their work to tracking their submissions, writers can find it all at Writers Write. Editors, publishers, and agents can use the site to add their publication to the listings, find employees with the free job-listing service, and keep up with the latest news in the writing world."

Zine-Related Newsgroups

alt.ezines

alt.zine

alt.zines

alt.etext

My Notes: Usenet newsgroups are a great place to find "everyday people." For the most part, these particular groups are inhabited by hard-core users who have been around for a while and know what they're doing. It would behoove you to "lurk" there for a while before posting anything; this way, you'll be less likely to be viewed as a spammer. This is (potentially) a great place to solicit honest feedback from other e-publishers. If your ISP doesn't carry newsgroups, consider heading over to http://www.remarq.com/ or http://www.deja.com/.

'Zinew0rld

http://www.oblivion.net/zineworld/

My Notes: There aren't many links here (at this time), but you can change that. New subscribers are new subscribers . . . no matter how they subscribed.

ZineZone

http://www.zinezone.com/

My Notes: You can build your own e-zine in a matter of minutes once you've signed up for their service. The site is very busy, but offers a plentitude of content.

Their Blurb: "ZineZone's technology dynamically searches all the links in a given zine and brings back the up-to-date content you want, organized in a table of contents."

Appendix D

Semirandom List of Electronic Publications

The e-zine scene is not-so-mean (and not-so-lean), so if you're keen on checking up on what other electronic publishers are doing, here are a few real-world examples. This list is not even close to being comprehensive, and I have no specific affiliation with or interest in any of these e-publications. If you have a publication to add to the list, e-mail me at book@lockergnome.com and who' knows—when this book is revised, your e-publication might show up here.

American Newspeak
http://www.scn.org/news/newspeak/

Their Blurb: "A biweekly satirical e-zine celebrating cutting-edge advances in the Doublethink of the '90s, ever so carefully scavenged from the back pages of our finer newspapers."

My Notes: While the content is posted on his Web site, Wayne Grytting recommends you subscribe to the mailing list to avoid looking at his photo. He's not *that* ugly.

Associate Programs
http://www.associateprograms.com/

Their Blurb: "You can add revenue streams to your site by becoming an associate or affiliate of another company. To earn commissions, or bounties, you place a graphic on your Web page, or a link in an article or in your newsletter. This site [and newsletter] aims to help you find the best associate programs and market them successfully."

My Notes: This is one of the very few marketing-related e-publications I actually trust. You have to be careful when dealing with different "affiliate programs." I'd suggest signing up only for programs that are related to your e-zine's content; otherwise, you're going to lose credibility in the eyes of your readers.

BEERWeek

http://www.beerweek.com/

Their Blurb: "BEERWeek is your weekly e-mail source for up-to-date brew news, views, rumors and innuendo."

My Notes: I'm not suggesting that you run out and get drunk before trying to write your first issue, but I am recommending that you read a couple of their past issues to get an idea about how comprehensive an e-publication can be. They go way beyond providing the news; they list openings and closings of breweries, as well as beer-related events and festivals. They even have a beer quote of the week.

BetaNet

http://www.betabeta.com/

Their Blurb: "The Beta Report, published five days a week, is a review of a new software program, often in beta [stages]."

My Notes: When a program is "in beta," that simply means it's not a finished product yet. These guys cut to the chase and don't fill your screen with advertisements. Their point of view is refreshing and their reviews (I believe) are honest.

Bizy Moms

http://www.bizymoms.com/

Their Blurb: "If you're a mom searching for a way to work at home, you have come to the right place. If working for yourself is your goal, don't let anyone or anything stand in your way. All you need is a great idea, persistence, and oh a little bit more persistence, and a lot of patience."

My Notes: This quote, of course, applies to everyone—but this site and newsletter were specifically designed for the work-at-home mom.

The Cameron Column

http://www.wbrucecameron.com/

Their Blurb: "[This] went electronic in the fall of 1995. Four of the original six subscribers were relatives of Bruce who felt pretty much obligated to accept the thing, even if they had no idea what it was all about. It's probably fair to say that

Bruce had no idea what it was all about, either. He just knew that the standard rejection notice from book publishers, "Your novel is amusing but you are too ugly to put on a book jacket," led him to believe that perhaps an Internet-based newsletter would be successful."

My Notes: He's funny, he's regular, he's really got something to say; Bruce has been labeled as "the Internet's Dave Barry."

Canine Times

http://www.cfnaonline.com/caninetimes/

Their Blurb: "Each issue includes: Surfer Dog's summary of great reading sniffed out on the Web, health news you should know, what's up in science, pointers to great dog Web sites, articles that help correct behavior problems, stories on dogs helping people, news headlines, occasional touches of humor or heart-moving stories, and pet products galore from our advertisers and sponsors."

My Notes: Even if you don't like dogs, you have to appreciate this site's (and list's) features: autoresponder for the most recent issue, archives of past issues, a listing of all books that have been featured, a reciprocal links page, an easy-to-use subscribe/unsubscribe form . . . they even accept dog-related press releases.

Cheerleader Mailing List

http://www.cheerlist.net/

Their Blurb: "The Cheerleader Mailing List is an interactive, e-mail-based discussion list established to give everyone interested in cheerleading a forum to talk, ask questions, give advice, share experiences, and communicate about any cheer-related topic."

Community Music Mailing List

http://www.io.com/~rboerger/community.html

Their Blurb: "Although there are many outlets for the discussion of professional music problems, little attention has been paid to the backbone of "classical" music . . . the community band and community orchestra. . . . The community music e-mail list has been established to address these problems, and to further the spread of community music throughout the world."

My Notes: This is a great example of what a list's Web page might have on it: links to resources, archives, rules for the list, an FAQ, and so on.

Cyber Age Adventures
http://welcome.to/TheCyberAge/

Their Blurb: "The genre here is superheroes, NOT simply heroism . . . Cyber Age Adventures is not simply a comic book without art. It is a different medium altogether. There are narrative possibilities in prose that you could never pull off in pictures. By exploring the differences in this medium, we can all make a magazine worth reading, full of stories that would not, or simply could not, appear in a comic book."

My Notes: This is a "weekly magazine of superhero fiction" that accepts submissions.

DargonZine
http://www.dargonzine.org/

Their Blurb: "The Dargon Project is a 'shared world' project, where many authors write in a common milieu, sharing settings and characters. The setting is a fantasy world that is predominantly human, at a late medieval technology level, and where magic is relatively rare. . . . DargonZine is an electronic magazine that prints original amateur fantasy fiction by Internet writers. It only prints Dargon-related stories. DargonZine is the successor of FSFnet, which was the Dargon Project's original e-mag. Between FSFnet and DargonZine, it is the longest-running electronic magazine on the Internet."

DarkEcho
http://www.darkecho.com/

Their Blurb: "The DarkEcho newsletter is an electronically mailed gathering of market, genre, online, and publishing news as well as reviews and information for horror writers and avid fans of dark fiction. Published weekly . . . often providing the earliest possible notice of a new market or other horror news."

The Diary List
http://www.diarist.net/list/

Their Blurb: "DIARY-L—founded in association with Open Pages—is one of the most active mailing lists dedicated to the discussion of online journals and diaries."

My Notes: You've read all about it; now write all about it.

The Dollar Stretcher

http://www.stretcher.com/

My Notes: This e-zine is delivered on a weekly basis and is filled with reader comments, articles, tips, and tricks that could save you money. It focuses on "spending less" for a variety of products and services. The publisher will also print off copies and mail them to subscribers for a small fee.

EvangeList

http://www.evangelist.macaddict.com/

Their Blurb: "EvangeList [is] the mailing list of good news about Apple, Macintosh, and third-party developers, plus links to other useful Web sites. EvangeList started as a list server [for] official and unofficial, paid and unpaid evangelists of Macintosh, Pippin, Newton, and Apple Computers."

My Notes: Guy Kawasaki is another one of those "old e-ziners" whom you have no choice but to respect; although he has recently retired from this e-publication, his legacy and following remains strong.

Free Pint

http://www.freepint.co.uk/

Their Blurb: "[This] is a free e-mail newsletter written by information professionals in the U.K. It gives you tips, tricks and articles on how and where to find reliable Web sites and search more effectively. Free Pint is all about helping people find information on the Web that will help them with their work . . . we're saving people a lot of time and trouble and providing information that's genuinely useful in their day-to-day working life."

My Notes: It doesn't matter what country you live in—good information is good information.

Ghost Sites

http://www.disobey.com/ghostsites/

My Notes: Web sites come and go, but nobody seems to care. Well, I suppose Steve Baldwin does. Every day, he'll tell you about the latest cyber-disappearances . . . either on the Web or through e-mail. It's a great example of how you can marry your site with an e-mail newsletter.

Inscriptions

http://come.to/Inscriptions/

Their Blurb: "Inscriptions, the weekly e-zine for professional writers. Each jam-packed issue features writing and publishing-related articles, job opportunities, writing contests, paying markets, book reviews, and links. Earn money for your stories. Find your next job opportunity. Or, enter our monthly writing contest. Enjoy Inscriptions on the Web or subscribe for free."

My Notes: If you're going to be writing, you're going to love the tips and tricks.

Internet Tourbus

http://www.tourbus.com/

Their Blurb: "Tourbus is a virtual tour of the best of the Internet, delivered by e-mail. . . . [Novices and pros] will find this a valuable refresher course in what's hot, what's cool, and what's plain fun in cyberspace. Patrick Douglas Crispen and Bob Rankin [are] your tour guides, serving up a new issue every Tuesday and Thursday with their own informative and humorous commentaries."

Kleinman Report

http://www.Kleinman.com/

Their Blurb: "A free monthly e-mail newsletter that will change the way you use the Internet. Featuring: important Web sites, valuable information, and a unique perspective on technology and the Internet."

My Notes: Geoffrey Kleinman is another one of those "cool guys" you should get to know. This particular e-zine will probably remain ad-free for eternity—which only lends to its publisher's credibility. Also notable at this site is another one of Geoff's ventures, DVD Talk (which also sports a phenomenal e-mail newsletter on the latest DVD steals and deals).

Net Announce

http://www.erspros.com/net-announce/

Their Blurb: "The purpose of Net Announce is to provide a forum for promoting awareness of events, resources, and information relating to the Internet. Appropriate postings include announcements of upcoming events, new Web sites and other Internet resources, and updates about new content at existing resources."

My Notes: It's a good e-bulletin to receive, and a great resource in which to have your e-zine announced.

Netsurfer

http://www.netsurf.com/

Their Blurb: "Each week it brings you short, crisp news bites, notices, and reviews designed to provide an informative and entertaining snapshot of the vast wired world."

My Notes: The oldest e-publication from this site is the Netsurfer Digest (which has been around since 1994). It is delivered through e-mail on a weekly basis in HTML format only. It has two sister e-zines: Netsurfer Science and Netsurfer Books.

NOSPIN Group

http://nospin.com/pc/online.html

My Notes: Here you can sign up for PCBUILD, "designed for discussion about IBM-compatible computer hardware"; PCSOFT, which "covers IBM-compatible computer software and applications, but not the operating system itself"; or COMPUTERLADY, which is "a weekly advice newsletter for beginning computer users, with answers to your questions, weekly tips, and interesting Web sites."

Online Insider

http://www.onlineinsider.com/

My Notes: Robert Seidner presents a good example of how one person can make a difference; he covers the "hottest" Internet topics every couple of weeks (or so). If you have opinions, you might as well share them with the rest of the world— you never know who's going to listen.

Online Publishers Mailing List

http://www.ideastation.com/op.html

Their Blurb: "Online Publishers is a moderated discussion list that covers topics of interest to businesses wishing to create or improve their e-mail newsletter."

Oracle Service Humor Mailing List

http://www.oraclehumor.com/

My Notes: I don't think there was anybody on my university campus who didn't read Oracle Humor mailings (either through subscribing directly or via a friend); it's always good for a laugh. I'm not sure which is older, though: dirt or this list. Longevity on the Internet is often a sign of popularity and high quality—two things Oracle Humor list has going for it.

The Outrage
http://theoutrage.com/

My Notes: I hope that this book isn't upsetting you. But, in the unlikely event that it is, I'd encourage you to vent your anger here (and NOT through the nearest window). It will be less damaging in the long run, and you'll actually get to read what upsets other people, too. The owners also encourage visitors to syndicate Outrage content on their own site.

Parenting Toolbox
http://www.parentingtoolbox.com/

My Notes: This site was built for both the traditional and nontraditional parent. It features the "Parenting Thoughts, Quotes, & Smiles Newsletter" and "FAMILY 2000: Preparing Families for the New Millennium." The e-zine's maintainer also has a parenting book to sell; this is an example of how a dedicated following of subscribers can positively impact product sales.

Passport Wine Club
http://www.topwine.com/

Their Blurb: "Every month, our expert tasting panel samples hundreds of wines from California, France, Italy, Australia, and other premier regions, to select the award-winning wines for your monthly shipment."

My Notes: But (and here's where you'll want to sit up and take notice) they'll send anyone their free wine tips e-mail newsletter. While visitors will be attracted only to the e-zine initially, there's a good chance they'll come back to join the Wine Club if they enjoy what they read.

ResearchBuzz
http://www.coppersky.com/ongir/news/

My Notes: Someone asked me how they could research "stuff" on the Internet. Most people would answer: "Look in the search engines." But, nine times out of ten, you're not going to find what you're looking for by going that route. Tara Calishain, on the other hand, has either already found the "stuff" you need, or will find it for you; she's a research goddess, and her e-mail newsletter proves it.

The Rock

http://www.paintedrock.com/

Their Blurb: "The Rock Mailing List (prock) is a weekly e-mail magazine for writers and readers. Each Sunday, subscribers receive the text version of The Rock. It includes articles on writing, profiles on authors, interviews with editors, and the upcoming events for the week on the Web site, including workshops, author chats, book discussions, and other programs."

Sci Fi Guys

http://www.scifiguys.com/

Their Blurb: "After debating the merits of much of the science fiction world, we went public. We are now a rapidly expanding group of guys and girls who love science fiction, but can keep a sense of humor about it. Join us biweekly for news, insights, and a chuckle about the sci-fi world and the people in it."

My Notes: They will also deliver their missives in one of three formats: plain text, HTML, and/or "AOL (America Online) e-mail format."

The Stones Mailing List

http://www.henge.demon.co.uk/

Their Blurb: "The primary reason for starting this mailing list was for a small group of interested Webmasters and others to be able to chat about issues relating to ancient sites. Membership has grown over the months and we now have a wide range of people with expertise in all kinds of different areas taking part. All are welcome; whatever their angle on ancient sites their input will be appreciated."

Suck

http://www.suck.com/

My Notes: When people talk about e-zines, Suck usually enters the conversation at some point. It's a corporate-driven e-publication, but the content is fresh and original. It's delivered only in HTML format, but I believe most e-mail circulars will be that way in a few years. Don't think that your strategies have to match Suck's; if you can consistently distribute something worth reading, you're halfway home.

Surfing the Net with Kids

http://www.surfnetkids.com/emailedition.htm

Their Blurb: "My weekly syndicated newspaper column ferrets out the best of the online world for kids, families, teachers, and the young-at-heart. Each week I feature five fun, educational Web sites on diverse topics."

My Notes: The e-mail edition is available in both text and HTML formats. This is a classic example of how a syndicated print column can easily make the leap online, creating stronger brand and name awareness.

Television Production Monthly

http://indigoskyeproductions.hypermart.net/

Their Blurb: "A free e-zine about the art of creating television programs. Geared toward the beginning videographer/television producer, you will find articles on both the technical and the managerial side of television production."

Tod Maffin's Future File

http://www.futurefile.com/

Their Blurb: "Stay ahead of the news in our twice-monthly newsletter about emerging trends in business, technology, medicine, physics, and media. Guaranteed easy reading, and 100% spam-free . . . written in punchy and bite-sized chunks."

My Notes: Tod is a veritable tech stud in Canadian circles. The best parts of each issue (in my opinion) are his useless-but-interesting "Todbits."

Toy Train Mailing List

http://www.traincollectors.org/mailing.html

Their Blurb: "This [list] . . . was formed to provide a platform where toy-train enthusiasts can discuss, argue, comment, inquire about, impart knowledge, add to the rumor mill on: relative merits, quality, how to, identification, repair information, operation, current products, and other news bits regarding toy trains."

Tricia's Tips (Newton Manufacturing Company)

http://www.adyourimprint.com/

My Notes: This site will help you create name-branded promotional products (pens, mouse pads, duffel bags, etc.); they would all make great guerrilla marketing tools. A monthly mailing, "Tricia's Tips," also is available; it will give you ideas about how others have promoted their businesses using branded products. Each issue will also let you know of any specials/contests that adyourimprint.com is running.

VetQuest

http://members.aol.com/vetquest/

Their Blurb: "A . . . weekly e-mail magazine of interest to all veterans, active-duty service members, and their families. Army, Navy, Air Force, Coast Guard, and Marines: you've come to the right place for veterans. [Includes information on] benefits, resources, and news that affects you. VetQuest is published by veterans, for veterans."

Weather24

http://www.weather24.com/

Their Blurb: "Find yourself on the Web or watching TV just to get the latest weather forecast? Weather24's free service will send the [short-term] forecast to your e-mail address so you'll always have the latest info."

My Notes: The mailings can be delivered in HTML or text format; it is one of the messages I look forward to receiving when I first check my e-mail in the morning. Weather24 provides listings only for U.S. cities/states at this point but plans on going international eventually.

Woody's Office

http://www.wopr.com/

My Notes: A couple of really excellent newsletters are available here: Woody's Office Watch (WOW) covers anything related to Microsoft Office and is available in text format, and Woody's Windows Watch (WWW) tackles Microsoft Windows stuff in HTML format. Since Woody (and his entourage) are authors and editors, they've always got books to sell.

World Wide Recipes

http://www.wwrecipes.com/

Their Blurb: "Our recipes have been collected over several 'lifetimes' of living overseas, traveling six continents, and loving food. They range from classics that are served in the finest restaurants the world over to things that you may not have heard of. Some are so simple that you will wonder why you didn't think of them yourself, and others are so sophisticated that your family and friends will marvel at your culinary prowess."

My Notes: Each day of the week, you'll get a different component of a regular meal: appetizer, soup, side dish, entrée, etc. Hey—ya gotta eat sometime.

World Wide Web Security

http://www-ns.rutgers.edu/www-security/

Their Blurb: "The www-security list is intended as a forum for encouraging and stimulating the open discussion, design, and development of all aspects of security within the World Wide Web paradigm. Our intent is to promote the development of Internet standards for WWW security, and support the implementation of such standards."

ZENtertainment

http://www.zentertainment.com/

Their Blurb: "Approximately twice each week, ZEN e-mails out the best of this site's news and notice of other features here to . . . fellow entertainment junkies."

My Notes: If it's entertaining, it'll probably reach ZEN: music, television, movies, toys, electronics, print, attractions, food, etc.

Appendix E

E-mail Programs

Hundreds of e-mail applications are available, but you don't need to try them all; find and stick with whatever works best for you.

It's worth noting that some of the best e-mail programs are absolutely free, and may be installed on your computer already. Many people have installed Netscape Communicator on their systems, and its e-mail program Netscape Messenger works just fine for sending, receiving, and managing your e-mail. And most Windows users have Outlook Express available as an e-mail client (which comes with later versions of Windows 95 and all versions of Windows 98). Others may have stepped up to the very robust Microsoft Outlook (which isn't free, but comes with all versions of Microsoft Office). Microsoft e-mail programs can be found at http://www.microsoft.com/ and Netscape e-mail programs may be downloaded from http://www.netscape.com/.

The following list is just a sampling of what else is available out there. Some of these programs are free, others are not. Since the programmers might change their prices and versions without notice, I decided to list only the title, the corresponding Web site, the operating systems it works with, and a few of the most notable features of each product. Most of these applications were *not* specifically designed to help you distribute or manage your e-mail publication; this information is here only to assist you in finding send and receive e-mail software. Note, too, that some packages have more features than others, and no two programs are likely to have the same set of features.

Acorn Email
http://www.pacifier.com/~tfm/
System Requirements: Windows 9x/NT
Features: Multiple profiles (each with its own set of mail folders and Internet settings), built-in text editor, Explorer-like management.

AK-Mail

http://www.akmail.com/

System Requirements: Windows 9x/NT

Features: HTML mail capabilities, sharing of address books over a LAN, enhanced signature system, nested folders.

Arrow

http://www.cco.caltech.edu/~glenn/arrow/

System Requirements: Linux

Features: GUI mail manager for Linux, PGP support, saves even if an X server crash occurs.

Atismail Regular & Light

http://www.atisnet.com/

System Requirements: Windows

Features: IMAP4 support, runs on Windows 3.11, manages multiple mailboxes.

Balsa

http://www.balsa.net/

System Requirements: Linux/GNOME

Features: Designed for the GNOME environment, handles attachments, spell checker enabled.

Becky!

http://www.rimarts.co.jp/becky.htm

System Requirements: Windows 9x/NT

Features: Comes with powerful text e-mail editor, draft and reminder capabilities, clickable URLs.

BeOS E-mail Clients

http://www.be.com/beware/Network.html

System Requirements: BeOS

Features: Any one of these programs listed on this Web page will work in the BeOS environment (downloads include a Pine port).

Calypso

http://www.mcsdallas.com/mcs/calypso/

System Requirements: Windows 9x/NT

Features: Multiuser environment, extensive filtering system, autoresponse, and HTML mail capabilities.

Canine Mail

http://www.ajcs.on.ca/

System Requirements: Windows 9x/NT

Features: Multiple account support, Hotmail account access, requires few system resources.

ConsulNet eReply

http://www.consulnet.com/

System Requirements: Windows 9x/NT

Features: This works like an autoresponder, except that you do all the responding (instead of your mail server).

CyberCreek Mail Professional or Express

http://www.cybercreek.com/

System Requirements: Windows 9x/NT

Features: Built-in pager support, multiple signatures, inline images, advanced searching and filtering.

DTS Mail

http://dtsoftware.simplenet.com/

System Requirements: Windows

Features: RTF and HTML messages, on-the-fly spell checking, thesaurus included.

Elm

http://www.myxa.com/old/elm.html

System Requirements: UNIX

Features: This is an easy-to-use command line mail program; if you have shell access and don't like Pine, ask whether Elm is available.

E-Mail PossaLink

http://www.bravomail.com/

System Requirements: Windows 9x/NT

Features: Advanced compression for multimedia messages, support for digital cameras, works with AOL and MSN.

Email 97

http://www.e-corp.com/

System Requirements: Windows 9x/NT

Features: Six-language translation engine, message compression, customizable interface.

EmailTools

http://www.westcodesoft.com/emailtools/

System Requirements: Macintosh

Features: This was designed to be an add-on for Claris Emailer 2.0 (another Macintosh e-mail program that can be found at http://www.claris.com/).

Eudora Pro and/or Light

http://www.eudora.com/

System Requirements: Macintosh, Windows

Features: One of the world's most popular e-mail clients, advanced search functions, IMAP support.

FoxMail

http://www.aerofox.com/fox/

System Requirements: Windows 9x/NT

Features: Reply flag, HTML message viewer, background sending/receiving.

Ishmail

http://www.ishmail.com/

System Requirements: UNIX

Features: Advanced filing and filtering, handles ASCII and MIME text, external text editor support.

JS Office

http://www.jennisoft.com/

System Requirements: Windows 9x/NT

Features: Recordable tasks and appointments, send and receive faxes, automatically zip attachments with password.

LingoMAIL

http://www.lingomail.com/

System Requirements: Windows 9x/NT

Features: Unified solution for Internet Mail and LAN Mail, supports over 30 languages for the same e-mail message, sophisticated filtering engine.

MailCat

http://www.blackpaw.com/

System Requirements: Windows 9x/NT

Features: HTML mail support, multiple address books, displays inline images, CompuServe support.

Mailbutler

http://www.tashcom.com/

System Requirements: Windows 9x/NT

Features: Distribution list handling, basic address book, automatic URL highlighting.

Mailpuccino

http://members.xoom.com/konget/mailpuccino/

System Requirements: Java Support

Features: Multiple folder hierarchy, mailing-list and alias support, limited attachment support.

Mailsmith

http://web.barebones.com/

System Requirements: Macintosh

Features: Multithreaded processing, "fuzzy" and advanced searching, handles OSA scripting.

Microsoft Internet Mail and News
http://www.microsoft.com/windows/ie/ie3/
System Requirements: Windows
Features: Limit size of downloadable messages, basic folder management, import data from other popular e-mail programs.

ML
http://people.netscape.com/max/ml/
System Requirements: UNIX/X Windows, Motif
Features: IMAP support, configurable MIME support, clickable URLs, scripting for repetitive tasks.

Mutt
http://www.mutt.org/
System Requirements: UNIX
Features: Message threading, customizable (including key bindings), .mailrc-style configuration files.

netMessenger
http://www.netmessenger.com/
System Requirements: Windows 9x/NT
Features: Automatic install and configuration, mail server password change support, IMAP Support.

Paladin Email
http://www.paladincorp.com.au/
System Requirements: Windows 9x/NT
Features: This is pretty much being pushed as an IMAP4 e-mail client; it handles both local and remote storage, PGP encryption, and mailbox quotas.

PC iMail
http://www.prosoftapps.com/
System Requirements: Windows 9x/NT
Features: Explorer-like interface, advanced filtering, robust address book administration.

Pegasus Mail

http://www.pegasus.usa.com/

System Requirements: DOS, Macintosh, Windows
Features: HTML, RTF support, multiple folders, simple distribution list management.

PowerMail

http://www.ctmdev.com/

System Requirements: Macintosh
Features: IMAP4 support, high-speed message archiving and retrieval, multiple language support.

QuickMail

http://www.cesoft.com/

System Requirements: Macintosh, Windows
Features: Message preview, advanced filtering, Finger and LDAP support.

Shark!mail

http://www.lanshark.com/

System Requirements: Windows 9x/NT
Features: Single-client access to multiple mail transport systems, rules wizards, asynchronous multitasking, built-in Web browser (IE).

SmartMail

http://www.netcplus.com/

System Requirements: Windows 9x/NT
Features: Supports multiple users and multiple mailboxes, mailing-list and alias support, built-in support for faxing.

StarNine Mail

http://www.starnine.com/mail/mail.html

System Requirements: Macintosh
Features: Integrated spell checker; drag and drop support; filters for filing, forwarding, and replying to messages.

StartMail

http://gallery.uunet.be/daniel.meynen/dmsoft/

System Requirements: Windows

Features: Message personalization (mail merge), dial-up support, logging options.

TeamWARE Embla

http://www.embla.com/

System Requirements: Windows 9x/NT

Features: IMAP4 support, filtering and automatic-reply functionality, server- and client-based mail folders.

TecaMail

http://www.tecapro.com/tecamail/indexeng.htm

System Requirements: Windows 9x/NT

Features: Spanish and English orthographic correction, message and attachment compression, transmits compressed voice messages.

The Bat!

http://www.ritlabs.com/

System Requirements: Windows

Features: Real-time spell checker, mail ticker for new messages, powerful filtering, data import abilities.

The Mail Explorer

http://www.city-net.com/~mbt/

System Requirements: Windows 9x/NT

Features: Multiple document interface; filtering rules; replies can be sent, spooled, or postponed.

TkMail

http://www.slac.stanford.edu/~raines/tkmail.html

System Requirements: UNIX/X Windows

Features: Listbox interface to messages, reads aliases from either standard .mailrc or Elm aliases.txt, user-friendly options editor.

Winbox

http://www.uv.es/~lopezj/

System Requirements: Windows

Features: Supports IMAP2, IMAP4, POP3, SMTP, NNTP, and MIME protocols.

XFMail

http://burka.netvision.net.il/xfmail/

System Requirements: UNIX

Features: Three-pane view, mail can be sent using sendmail or directly via SMTP gateway, Usenet posting, support for IMAP4 remote folders, supports MH and Elm-style local mailboxes.

E-mail Program Support Sites

(Un)Official Pegasus Mail Support Site:

http://www.bzs.tu-graz.ac.at/software/pegasus/en/

Eudora FAQs & Links:

http://wso.williams.edu/~eudora/

OESetup -- Outlook Express Setup Guide:

http://surf.to/oesetup/

Mailing-List E-mail Commands

This appendix provides a rundown of the most common mailing-list management commands for the four most popular software packages: ListProc, LISTSERV, Lyris, and Majordomo. The easiest way to find out what software a mailing list uses is to ask the moderator or list administrator.

You issue these commands via e-mail to manage your list. Commands should be entered within the message body, and are case-sensitive unless otherwise noted.

These commands (and more) are also available for your reference online. The Mailing List Manager Commands FAQ (version 1.5.7), last updated on October 26, 1997, by James Milles, is an excellent place to start; I used it as a foundation for this appendix. Send a message containing only the line GET MAILSER CMD NETTRAIN to LISTSERV@listserv.acsu.buffalo.edu to receive it. Or visit the Web site http://lawwww.cwru.edu/cwrulaw/faculty/milles/mailser.html.

For more software-specific mailing list commands, visit these sites:

- LISTSERV General User's Guide
  http://www.lsoft.com/manuals/1.8d/user/user.html
- ListProc (CREN) Documentation
  http://list.cren.net/listproc/docs/
- Lyris E-mail Commands
  http://www.lyris.com/help/LyrisEmailCommands.html
- Majordomo Manual
  ftp://ftp.greatcircle.com/pub/majordomo/majordomo.manual.txt

ListProc

Subscribing to a List
```
SUBSCRIBE [listname] [firstname] [lastname]
```

Unsubscribing from a List
UNSUBSCRIBE [listname]

Receiving a List in Digest Format (When Available)
SET [listname] MAIL DIGEST

Canceling Digest Format
SET [listname] MAIL ACK

Suspending List Messages Temporarily
SET [listname] MAIL POSTPONE

Resuming Message Delivery after Suspending
SET [listname] MAIL ACK
SET [listname] MAIL NOACK
SET [listname] MAIL DIGEST

Receiving Copies of Your Own Posts
SET [listname] MAIL ACK

Stopping Receiving Copies of Your Own Posts
SET [listname] MAIL NOACK

Getting a Copy of the Subscriber Database
RECIPIENTS [listname]

Concealing Your Address Completely
SET [listname] CONCEAL YES
SET [listname] CONCEAL NO (to keep your address public)

Finding Out What Other Lists are Sent by the Mail Server
LISTS

Obtaining a List of Archive Files for a Particular List
INDEX [listname]

Retrieving an Archived File
GET [listname] [document]

LISTSERV

Subscribing to a List
```
SUBSCRIBE [listname] [firstname] [lastname]
```

Unsubscribing from a List
```
SIGNOFF [listname]
UNSUBSCRIBE [listname]
```

Receiving a List in Digest Format (When Available)
```
SET [listname] DIGEST
```

Canceling Digest Format
```
SET [listname] MAIL
SET [listname] NODIGEST
```

Suspending List Messages Temporarily
```
SET [listname] NOMAIL
```

Resuming Message Delivery after Suspending
```
SET [listname] MAIL
```

Receiving Copies of Your Own Posts
```
SET [listname] REPRO
SET [listname] ACK (for post verification)
```

Stopping Receiving Copies of Your Own Posts
```
SET [listname] NOREPRO
```

Getting a Copy of the Subscriber Database
```
REVIEW [listname] F=MAIL
REVIEW [listname] BY NAME F=MAIL (to sort by name)
REVIEW [listname] BY COUNTRY F=MAIL (to sort by country)
```

Concealing Your Address Completely
```
SET [listname] CONCEAL
SET [listname] NOCONCEAL (to keep your address public)
```

Finding Out What Other Lists are Sent by the Mail Server
LISTS
LISTS GLOBAL (for every LISTSERV list)
LISTS GLOBAL /[keyword] (for every LISTSERV list containing your keyword(s))

Obtaining a List of Archive Files for a Particular List
INDEX [listname]

Retrieving an Archived File
GET [document] [filetype] [listname] F=MAIL

Lyris

Subscribing to a List
SUBSCRIBE [listname]
SUBSCRIBE [listname] [yourname]
SUBSCRIBE [listname] [yourname] [password]

Unsubscribing from a List
UNSUBSCRIBE [listname]
UNSUBSCRIBE [listname] [e-mail address]
(Other acceptable words include unsub, uns, signoff, leave, remove, and off.)

Receiving a List in Digest Format (When Available)
SET [listname] DIGEST

Canceling Digest Format
SET [listname] MAIL

Suspending List Messages Temporarily
SET [listname] NOMAIL

Resuming Message Delivery after Suspending
SET [listname] MAIL

Receiving Copies of Your Own Posts
SET [listname] repro

Stopping Receiving Copies of Your Own Posts

```
SET [listname] norepro
```

Getting a Copy of the Subscriber Database

```
login [password] review [listname]
```

Concealing Your Address Completely

All addresses are automatically concealed.

Finding Out What Other Lists are Sent by the Mail Server

LISTS

Obtaining a List of Archive Files for a Particular List

```
Get [listname] [first-message-id]-[last-message-id]
```

Retrieving an Archived File

```
GET [listname] [document]
```

Majordomo

Subscribing to a List

```
SUBSCRIBE [listname]
SUBSCRIBE [listname] [e-mail address]
```

Unsubscribing from a List

```
UNSUBSCRIBE [listname]
UNSUBSCRIBE [listname] [e-mail address]
```

Receiving a List in Digest Format (When Available)

```
SUBSCRIBE [listname]-DIGEST
```

Canceling Digest Format

```
UNSUBSCRIBE [listname]-DIGEST
```

Receiving Copies of Your Own Posts

Your posted messages are always received.

Getting a Copy of the Subscriber Database

WHO [listname]

Finding Out What Other Lists are Sent by the Mail Server

LISTS

Obtaining a List of Archive Files for a Particular List

INDEX [listname]

Retrieving an Archived File

GET [listname] [document]

Appendix G

Fifty Great E-publishing Tips

1. Be prepared to work. Don't depend on someone else to do the job for you. Starting something successful on the Internet today is a tough job for anyone. You can't be in it for the short run; building a name and subscriber base will take time.

2. Be sure you bite off only as much as you can chew. Start small, and develop over time. In the beginning, you'll have tons of energy for your e-publication, but that enthusiasm will probably dissipate in less than six months.

3. While you don't need to be a computer expert to manage an e-mail publication, it would be wise if you had some practical experience on the Internet beforehand. Talk to other Internet-savvy friends; they might be willing to help and could offer suggestions.

4. Target your audience. If you like boating, why not make a boating e-publication? If you like pasta, why not make a pasta recipes e-publication? If you like antiques, why not . . . you get the point. Above all: Be as specific as possible. The more precise the topic, the greater the chance of subscriber interest.

5. Write about what you know and what you like. If you don't know a thing about eighteenth-century homemade Amish swimwear, then do us a favor and don't write about it.

6. Even if the topic happens to be the latest craze, you'll find yourself in a daze within a few issues.

7. You can't be in it for the short run. E-mail publications, while novel, aren't a quick moneymaker. You must build a subscriber base and work with other online entities to become a recognized name.

8. Once you've decided you're going to create an e-mail publication, contact your closest friends and let them know. Some of them couldn't care less, but others will support and applaud your efforts.

9. Think of an original name. "Bob's Cooking Tips" doesn't sound as catchy as "Pots & Pans." Steer clear from overused terms such as "Net," "Cyber," "Tech," or "Compu." Don't be afraid to have fun with the name.

10. Try to do something new. People are more apt to pay attention to something that hasn't been done before. Do it first, and people will remember you. Don't copy someone else's idea; you can take and build upon what you see, but if it doesn't scream "original," you might as well not even bother.

11. Remember to have fun with your publication. I realize that might not sound like much of a tip at this point, but hey—if your heart isn't into this, then you're not going to give it all you've got . . . and your subscribers will pick that up immediately.

12. Don't fear competition—welcome it. You'll have a devout following of subscribers before long. It won't matter if similar zines are out there. If yours is good, your subscribers shouldn't leave you.

13. Listen to your subscribers. If 90 percent of them don't like something, knock it off. If a majority of them love something, think about doing more of it. If they're not reading what you're writing, try a new approach. You're not going to get anywhere without loyal and happy subscribers.

14. The average start-up e-mail publication reaches 2,000 people. Don't be depressed if you don't make it to this mark. You can't expect to have a million subscribers at the drop of a pin. Be proud of your accomplishments, and don't let anyone depress you with larger stats or larger subscriber numbers.

15. Don't spam (that is, cross-post to unrelated newsgroups, send unsolicited e-mail messages to someone you don't know, purchase questionable e-mail databases, and so on). Enough people out there are giving legitimate e-mail publications a bad name.

16. Don't purchase e-mail databases from list brokers. Purchasing lists sounds like the easy way out, but it is also an easy way to tarnish your reputation.

17. Advertise your e-mail publication in other e-mail publications. In my experience, it beats banner advertisement. You can be more descriptive with a text ad. Plus, people who subscribe to one e-mail publication are likely to subscribe to another one. An e-mail message is easier to read than a Web page; subscribers read an e-mail publication at their leisure. Once it

is in their Inbox, they don't have to mess with being connected to the Internet anymore.

18. When people ask how many impressions your Web site receives, tell them how many subscribers you have instead, and why they would be more interested in advertising in your e-publication than on your Web site.

19. While it is wise to accompany your e-mail publication with some sort of Web page or site, you should use it only to advertise your e-publication's offerings. People often forget about the sites they visit, but once they're signed on to your e-pub, you've got a guaranteed audience (unless they unsubscribe).

20. Make sure people know that your site advertises an e-mailed publication, not a webzine. Put the subscription form as close to the top on the front page as possible, and draw special attention to it.

21. Contact people who have related resources on the Web. If your e-mail publication is about skateboarding, then find all the skateboarding sites (big or small), and let them know about what you're doing. They could be helpful in spreading the word about your new publication.

22. Advertising can defray costs. In the beginning, you should be able to get by without advertising income, but if you get a domain name (whatever.com), you'll need to find a virtual host to carry your site, and that service costs money. Depending on your topic, you might be able to find some "small spenders" who will be willing to plop down a couple of bucks to get the word out about their product or service.

23. Make a graphical logo for your site (88 pixels wide by 31 pixels high . . . that's the standard size on Web pages). A graphic catches Web surfers' eyes.

24. When you mention a Web site in your e-mail publication, contact someone from that site on the chance he'll want to announce that his site appeared in your e-mail publication.

25. If possible, try to get a small description or personal accolade to accompany ANY link. It gives you more credibility.

26. If subscribers like what they see, they'll tell their friends. There's no better advertisement than word of mouth. If you had to choose between 10 products, and your friend recommended one of them, you'd probably go with that one.

27. Count on your e-mail publication reaching more people than those who are subscribed; many people print e-publications out and pass them

around the office. That isn't a bad thing, either. At least you know that people are talking about what you're doing.

28. Get links to your Web site and e-mail publication on topically related Web sites. If you had a car-related e-publication, you'd want your link on as many car-related pages as possible, for example. Links will drive more subscribers to your mailing list.

29. If people see enough links to you, they'll eventually check you out. Surfers become familiar with a certain name, and they begin to trust it. Some will come to you just because they keep seeing your button or link all over the place. They'll think, "Well, gee . . . if I keep seeing it everywhere, it must be good."

30. Find out where people who subscribe are hearing about your publication. If you're discovering subscriptions coming from a certain site or other e-mail publication, see whether you can do something in conjunction with them.

31. Choose your allies intelligently. You don't want to get a bad name for yourself right out of the starting gate. If you feel that a site's content isn't as good as it could possibly be, you don't have to work with its owners. Everything will reflect back upon your name and publication.

32. If you find a publication that complements yours, inquire about joint promotion opportunities.

33. Be careful about using banners on your site or in your HTML newsletter without researching them first. Some banner advertising schemes sound great, but unless you have a ton of traffic, chances are, you're not going to gain any money by using them. And be sure not to place more than one banner in a row on your site if you want your visitors to see you as a "professional" site. Nothing looks worse than a page with five banners in a row. The page takes forever to load, and the banners don't improve the quality of your Web page or newsletter.

34. Everywhere you go, talk about your publication. Every subscriber counts.

35. Don't be afraid to ask your subscribers to recommend your zine to their friends, family members, co-workers, supervisors, and so on. You don't want to beat them over the head with it, but a constant reminder is effective in getting more "quality" subscribers.

36. Keep the line between advertising and editorial clearly drawn. You'll lose your readers' trust if they can't tell the difference.

37. Don't concentrate too much on promoting your online services offline. You'll get more bang for your buck if you promote and advertise online.

38. It's true that (for the most part) you need to spend money to make money, but you can keep your costs extremely low when e-publishing. Don't employ more people than necessary.

39. Use a simple e-mail program to distribute the e-publication in the beginning. (Refer to Appendix E for a few choices.) Try to find one that will suppress other subscribers' addresses (using a BCC feature). Broadcasting someone's e-mail address to others is very bad manners.

40. You can choose to charge a subscription fee, but I would strongly advise against it. The Internet's climate isn't ready for "pay" e-pubs yet. If you're going to charge for subscriptions, be sure you have a free version available, too. Remember how easy it is for an individual to pass along messages to an infinite number of others. It would be very difficult to keep control over that. If you really want to generate funds, try advertising.

41. Start with a free Web page. Plenty of services online host free Web pages. Or set up one with your current Internet account.

42. Make sure you let your ISP know that you're doing an e-mail publication—that way, if someone whines about you sending junk e-mail, the service provider already knows.

43. If your mailing list is small (5,000 subscribers or fewer), consider using a free mailing-list service. Once you get into the 10,000-subscriber range, consider going to a dedicated list service (which will most likely cost you a few pennies). You're entering the realm of "professional" at that point. Suits and ties are still optional.

44. Treat your subscribers fairly, and don't be afraid to receive and implement feedback. Yes, you'll get negative comments from time to time, but that's going to happen. Not everyone will be happy with your service. The subscribers aren't always right, but they do have valid points and ideas that can only help your readership grow. Give subscribers credit if they offer some content to your publication.

45. Never share your list information (aside from total subscriber count) with anyone else. If your subscribers start appearing on junk e-mail lists after they subscribe to your e-mail publication, who do you think they're going to blame? Besides, there's little money to be made by selling name lists smaller than a million anymore.

46. Give people an easy way to unsubscribe. People's expectations might not match your e-mail publication's content; they'll feel trapped and offended if you don't offer them an easy way out.

47. Answer e-mail personally, and as soon as possible. Answering every message takes time, but people enjoy knowing that you're not a computer. If you keep your replies personal, they'll feel a bond with you and be less apt to drop the subscription.

48. Keep your subscription database clean. When an address bounces, remove it. When a user needs to change his address, make sure it gets done. Certain list software packages work better than others with list management, so not everything needs to be done by hand.

49. Maintain quality control. People won't take you seriously unless you take yourself seriously first. If you want to run with the big boys, find a virtual host with a fast connection, purchase a Web domain, and hire a designer if you can't design your way out of a wet paper bag.

50. Go through each issue with a fine-tooth comb, checking spelling, punctuation, grammar, and so on. If you're a good writer, people will love you. There's nothing better than an excellent writing style that keeps people entertained and informed at the same time.

by freelance writing, 156

by links, reciprocal, 150–151, 152–153

by logos, 151

low cost, high return, 145

lurking, 149

on mailing lists, 149–150

message board marketing, 226

Naked PC, The (TNPC), 226–227

by offline avenues, 155–156

by online avenues, 154–155

by peer endorsements, 146–149

by public relations (PR) contacts, 157–158

recommendation scripts, 147–149

signature lines for, 149–150

subscribers, 145–146

by subscription forms, 157

by syndication, 156, 168, 187

by URLs, 154–155, 156, 157

by Web page, 156–157

Web rings, 151–152

Web site for, 43, 44, 45–46, 156–157

Mary Fifield Associates, 222

mentality of service providers, 140

message board marketing, 226

"me too" virus, 126, 130

microtarget audience, 24

MIME-Version: 1.0, 107

mission statement, 219–220

moderated discussion groups

  benefits and disadvantages, 4–5, 123

  directing discussions, 129–131

  quality control, 127–128, 193

software for, 120

Monitor column for *BYTE Online,* 207

monospaced fonts, 91

moving the list problems, 184

multiple list capability, 136

N

Naked PC, The (TNPC), 217–227

  advertisement swaps, 227

  business plan, 218–219

  contributing editor, 222

  cross marketing, 226–227

  editor-in-chief, 221–222

  as free newsletter, 222–226

  goals, defined, 223

  as group effort, 219, 220–222

  inspiration for, 218–220

  list servers, 226

  marketing, 226–227

  message board marketing, 226

  mission statement, 219–220

  naming of, 224–225

  newsgroup marketing, 226

  promotion, not hype, 223–224

  publishers, 220–221

  referrer logs, 227

  software, 226

  Web site as partner, 225

  writing for other newsletters, 227

name branding, 29–30

"nasty" e-mails, xxiii, 16

net growth rate, 178

netiquette (etiquette), 16–20

networking, 192

THE CDNOW STORY: RAGS TO RICHES ON THE INTERNET

How Twin Brothers in a Basement Built an Internet Success

Early in 1994 twin brothers Jason and Matthew Olim began creating CDnow, an Internet music store. Working in their parent's basement, on a shoe-string budget, they competed against Fortune 500 companies with tens of millions of dollars to spend . . . and won. In 1997 CDnow earned almost three times as much as its nearest rival, and owned one third of the online music business. From first-month revenues of $387 in August of 1994, the company grew to sales of $16.4 million in 1997, and industry analysts predict 1998 revenues of $60 million.

How did two kids barely out of college, with no business or retail experience, build one of the world's largest Internet stores? By focusing on a single purpose—building a better music store. *The CDnow Story* explains how they did it: what they did right and what they did wrong. Jason Olim describes how he and his brother began by creating a store that had no shelves and no stock—customers buy CDs online and the Olims pass the orders on to a distributor. He explains how they brought people to their Web site and compares their strategies with their competitors, explaining why they came out on top.

With Internet commerce growing at a tremendous pace, many companies are floundering in cyberspace. Millions of dollars have been lost on ill-conceived and poorly executed online projects. Unlimited budgets are no guarantee of success, but CDnow has shown that shoe-string operations *can* succeed. Let the Olims, founders of one of the most successful companies in cyberspace, teach you how to compete online.

Twin brothers Jason and Matthew Olim are the founders of CDnow, the world's largest online music store. Peter Kent is the author of 36 computer and business books, including *Poor Richard's Web Site* (also from Top Floor Publishing), and the best selling *Complete Idiot's Guide to the Internet* (Que).

The CDnow Story: Rags to Riches on the Internet is available in bookstores both online and offline, and at http://TopFloor.com/ by Jason Olim, with Matthew Olim and Peter Kent   ISBN: 0-9661032-6-2

MP3 AND THE DIGITAL MUSIC REVOLUTION:

Turn Your PC into a CD-Quality Digital Jukebox!

Hundreds of thousands of computer users around the world are discovering new ways to play and manage music—through their computers. Music is software, and computers are being used to play and manipulate it. Using the new MP3 format, computers can store CD-quality music in 1MB/minute files. Along with the music, the computer files can also store album art, recording-artist bios, notes, and even the songs' lyrics.

With the tools on the included disk, PC users can play music on their computers—if they have good sound cards and speakers, it will sound as good as a CD. They can copy music from their CDs—or tapes and vinyl—and save it on their computers. With a low-cost cable they can connect their computers to their audio systems, integrating the two systems. They can create playlists, selecting tracks from different CDs. Having a party? Create an 8-hour playlist, start playing at the beginning of the party, and the computer will handle the rest.

Digital music is portable, too. Users will learn how to create customized tapes—cassettes and DAT—from their music collection, and even how to cut their own music CDs. And they'll hear about the new MP3 players, products with no moving parts that allow you to carry your music with you wherever you go. This book explains the entire process, from installing the enclosed software to cutting CDs. Readers will learn how to shift their music from one medium to another with ease, and even how to find public domain and "freeware" music on the Internet. Band members will learn how to use the new music formats to promote their bands by releasing music on the Internet.

POOR RICHARD'S INTERNET MARKETING AND PROMOTIONS:

How to Promote Yourself, Your Business, Your Ideas Online

Much of what you've read about marketing on the Internet is wrong: registering a Web site with the search engines *won't* create a flood of orders; banner advertising *doesn't* work for most companies; online malls *do not* push large amounts of traffic to their client Web sites. . . .

What you really need is some geek-free, commonsense advice on marketing and promoting on the Internet, by somebody's who's actually done it! Most books and articles are written by freelance writers assigned to investigate a particular subject. *Poor Richard's Internet Marketing and Promotions* is written by a small-business person who's been successfully marketing online for a decade.

Poor Richard's Internet Marketing and Promotions uses the same down-to-earth style so highly praised in *Poor Richard's Web Site*. You'll learn how to plan an Internet marketing campaign, find your target audience, use giveaways to bring people to your site, integrate an email newsletter into your promotions campaign, buy advertising that works, use real-world PR, and more.

You'll also learn to track results, by seeing who is linking to your site, by hearing who is talking about you, and by measuring visits to your site.

If you are planning to promote an idea, product, or service on the Internet . . . you need *Poor Richard's Internet Marketing and Promotions!*

POOR RICHARD'S WEB SITE:

Geek-Free, Commonsense Advice on Building a Low-Cost Web Site

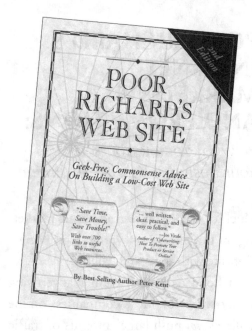

Poor Richard's Web Site is the *only* book that explains the entire process of creating a Web site, from deciding whether you really need a site—and what you can do with it—through picking a place to put the site, creating the site, and bringing people to the site. It is full of commonsense advice that Amazon.com called an "antidote to this swirl of confusion" and "straightforward information." Praised by *BYTE magazine*, *Publisher's Weekly*, and *USA Today*, *Poor Richard's Web Site* can save you thousands of dollars and hundreds of hours.

❝**Poor Richard's Good Advice.** With all great new things comes a proliferation of hucksters and snake-oil salesmen, and the Internet is no exception. The antidote to this swirl of confusion lies in Peter Kent's *Poor Richard's Web Site*. The analogy to Ben Franklin's volume is appropriate: the book is filled with the kind of straightforward information the Founding Father himself would have appreciated."

—Jennifer Buckendorff
amazon.com

❝We highly recommend this book."
—Peter Cook & Scott Manning
Philadelphia Inquirer

❝We highly recommend that you get a copy."
—*Marketing Technology*

❝Very well written."
—*Library Journal*

❝Buy This Book! . . . The lessons of just the first three chapters, alone, saved us thousands of dollars and many hours of work."
—David Garvey
The New England Nonprofit Quarterly

❝I've found a great book that explains it all—*Poor Richard's Web Site*. This is a practical, no-nonsense guide that lucidly covers topics like how to set up a domain with the InterNIC, how to promote your Web site, and how to actually use all those features that hosting services provide."
—David Methvin

Poor Richard's Web Site
is available in bookstores both online and offline, and at http://PoorRichard.com/

Poor Richard's Web Site:
Geek-Free, Commonsense Advice on Building a Low-Cost Web Site
by Peter Kent   ISBN: 0-9661032-8-9

FREE INFORMATION ABOUT SETTING UP A WEB SITE

http://PoorRichard.com/

If you are setting up a Web site, or just thinking about doing so, visit http://PoorRichard.com/, the site associated with *Poor Richard's Web Site: Geek-Free, Commonsense Advice on Building a Low-Cost Web Site.* You'll find free information of all kinds: special reports on various subjects—such as a directory of over 75 shopping-cart programs and services, and a list of places to register e-mail newsletters—links to hundreds of Web sites with services that will help you set up and promote your site, several chapters from the book, and more.

Also, sign up for the free e-mail newsletter, *Poor Richard's Web Site News.* With 12,000 subscribers in over 80 countries, this is one of the most respected newsletters on the subject.

You can read back issues and subscribe to the newsletter at http://PoorRichard.com/newsltr/, or to subscribe by e-mail, send an e-mail message to subpr@PoorRichard.com.

The Main Page: http://PoorRichard.com/

The Newsletter: http://PoorRichard.com/newsltr/

E-mail Subscriptions: send a blank e-mail message to subpr@PoorRichard.com

☞ *(continued from the back cover)* . . .

Poor Richard's E-mail Publishing contains everything you need to know on the mechanics, the marketing, and the morals of electronic publishing. This is really three books in one. The primary section covers rudimentary and advanced e-mail publishing concepts, the secondary section contains personal stories from others in the e-publishing industry, and the final section is the most comprehensive listing of e-mail publishing resources available in print.

You will learn how to set up an HTML newsletter, going beyond the basics to discover what other HTML publishers too often forget. You'll find out how to get a good list service, what questions you should ask your potential service provider, and tips for maintaining your subscriber list. Did you know that it's possible to run an electronic newsletter using your own e-mail program? However, most e-mail programs, such as Microsoft Outlook and Netscape Messenger, don't make this particularly easy. *Poor Richard's E-mail Publishing* will tell you about a couple of shareware programs that are ideal for running small newsletters. Still, if your newsletter grows too big—over one or two thousand subscribers—you'll need to find software or a newsletter server. You'll learn about the *free* services you can use for a small newsletter. But you'll also learn what to do when your list grows too big for one of these free services, that is, how to find an industrial-strength newsletter server capable of handling hundreds of thousands of subscribers. You'll find out *where* to find such services, and how to choose the right one.

But *Poor Richard's E-mail Publishing* explains more than the technology of e-mail publishing; you'll learn all about the business, too. Perhaps you've heard that Internet businesses aren't supposed to make money. But many newsletters are operating very much in the black. E-mail newsletters provide a great way for an independent entrepreneur to make a living. *Poor Richard's E-mail Publishing* explains:

- Some newsletter publishers are making a good living selling advertising in their newsletters
- How to find advertisers
- How to find products to sell in your newsletter, by signing up for affiliate programs
- Using guerrilla promotions to bring in new subscribers
- Promoting your Internet newsletter *off* the newsletter
- Swapping advertisements with other newsletter publishers

After you've mastered the technical aspects of e-mail publishing, you'll need to get subscribers. This isn't "A Field of Dreams." If you build it, they won't necessarily come. So how do you get people to subscribe to your new (or